Cold War Games

SPORT AND SOCIETY

Series Editors
Randy Roberts
Aram Goudsouzian

Founding Editors
Benjamin G. Rader
Randy Roberts

*A list of books in the series appears
at the end of this book.*

Cold War Games

Propaganda, the Olympics, and U.S. Foreign Policy

TOBY C. RIDER

University of Illinois Press

URBANA, CHICAGO, AND SPRINGFIELD

Library of Congress Cataloging-in-Publication Data
Names: Rider, Toby C.
Title: Cold war games : propaganda, the Olympics, and U.S. foreign
    policy / Toby C. Rider.
Description: Urbana : University of Illinois Press, 2016. | Series: Sport
    and society | Includes bibliographical references and index.
Identifiers: LCCN 2015037811 | ISBN 9780252040238 (hardback) |
    ISBN 9780252081699 (paperback) | ISBN 9780252098451 (e-book)
Subjects: LCSH: Olympics—Political aspects—United States—
    History—20th century. | Sports—Political aspects—United
    States—History—20th century. | Sports and state—United States—
    History—20th century. | Sports—Social aspects—United States—
    History—20th century. | Cold War—Social aspects—United States.
    | Propaganda, Anti-communist—United States—History—20th
    century. | National characteristics, American—History—20th
    century. | United States—Foreign relations—Soviet Union. |
    Soviet Union—Foreign relations—United States. | United States—
    Politics and government—1945–1989. | United States—Social
    conditions—1945- | BISAC: HISTORY / United States / 20th
    Century. | SPORTS & RECREATION / Olympics.
Classification: LCC GV721.5 .R54 2016 | DDC 796.48—dc23
    LC record available at http://lccn.loc.gov/2015037811

Contents

Acknowledgments

In the years that were consumed with the writing of this book, I have benefited from the assistance of many people and institutions. Like other historians, I have leant heavily upon the expertise of numerous patient and congenial archivists. My sincere thanks go out to Jim Leyerzapf, Chalsea Millner, Catherine Cain, and Valoise Armstrong at the Dwight D. Eisenhower Library in Abilene; to Randy Sowell at the Harry S. Truman Library in Independence; to Sheila Conway and Deborah Whiteman at the Department of Archives and Special Collections at Santa Clara University; to Pam Marshall at the Amateur Athletic Union of the United States archives in Lake Buena Vista; to Vera Ekechukwu and Geoffrey Stark at the University of Arkansas Libraries Special Collections; to Wayne Wilson at the LA84 Foundation in Los Angeles; to Regula Cardinaux and Nuria Puig at the International Olympic Committee Archives in Lausanne, Switzerland; and to all the excellent and diligent staff at the National Archives in College Park, Maryland, the Hoover Institution at Stanford University, the Baseball Hall of Fame Archives in Cooperstown, the Brotherton Library at the University of Leeds, the Seeley G. Mudd Manuscript Library at Princeton University, the Bentley Historical Library at the University of Michigan, and the International Centre for Olympic Studies at Western University. Finally, it would never have been possible to visit these archives if not for the research grants I was awarded by the International Olympic Committee, the International Society of Olympic Historians, and Penn State Berks.

I owe a debt of gratitude to many others. Willis Regier, Danny Nasset, Tad Ringo, Geof Garvey, and all the staff at the University of Illinois Press have been a delight to work with. Elsewhere, Walter Zimmerman offered expert counseling on sources when I first conceived of the topic. Péter Strausz generously tendered his diacritical expertise. Katalin Kádár Lynn has thoughtfully responded to my endless e-mails and has been a remarkable advocate of my work through thick and thin. Michael and Gwyn Johnson provided generous hospitality during my time in Abilene, not to mention fine company. Carl Ashley supplied accommodation and camaraderie in College Park, Lindsay Krasnoff has been a wellspring of information on research at the National Archives, and Heather Dichter has been kind enough to share not only documents but also her own extensive knowledge of state and private materials on sport and the Cold War. Furthermore, it has been to my great advantage to have sought and been given advice by Scott Lucas, Nicholas Cull, Kevin Witherspoon, Thomas Hunt, Kenneth Osgood, Hugh Wilford, Laura Belmonte, Bob Edelman, John Soares, Mark Dyreson, Peter Beck, Matthew Llewellyn, John Gleaves, Damion Thomas, Anna Mazurkiewicz, Jonathon H. L'Hommedieu, Veronika Durin-Hornyik, Kevin Wamsley, Michael Heine, Don Morrow, Donald Abelson, and many others besides. I must also give my sincere thanks to Gladys and Paul Szápáry, whose father, Count Anthony Szápáry, is a prominent character in this study. From the first moment that I contacted Gladys, she has been enthusiastic about my research. Indeed, both Gladys and her brother, Paul, allowed me to consult their father's personal papers and provided the kindest hospitality imaginable for a graduate student that they had never met.

The fact that the past few years have been as productive and enjoyable as they have been is due in no small measure to Bob and Ashleigh Barney. As my PhD supervisor, Bob has influenced the way I work more than any other scholar. I thank him for his guidance and friendship and the outstanding example he has set in the writing of sport and Olympic history. Bob was always available to talk and offer guidance, whether it was in the classroom, over coffee in his office, during one of Ashleigh's stellar dinner parties, or even while renovating his house and repairing his roof. To put it bluntly, I could not have asked for a better supervisor.

My family on either side of the Atlantic has been a constant source of support and, moreover, valuable distraction. I offer my hearty regards to the Riders and the Kichaks. A special mention must also go to Bob, Bonnie, and Melissa Kichak, who provided the most tremendous lodging and company (and access to a bottomless beer fridge) in Livonia when I researched at the University of Michigan Library or flew out of Detroit for my many research trips. And, last, this book is dedicated to my wife, Shannon Rider. Some say that the writing of history is a solitary occupation. She ensured that it was not the case for me. Her endless support and encouragement is the reason that I managed to complete this work at all. This book is for her, and our three children, Gus, Milly, and Sam.

Abbreviations

AAU	Amateur Athletic Union of the United States
ACEN	Assembly of Captive European Nations
CIA	Central Intelligence Agency
CIAA	Office of the Coordinator of Inter-American Affairs
CPI	Committee on Public Information
FEC	Free Europe Committee (formerly NCFE)
HNC	Hungarian National Council
HNSF	Hungarian National Sports Federation
IAAF	International Amateur Athletic Federation
IIA	International Information Administration
IOC	International Olympic Committee
IOD	International Organizations Division
IRI	Office of Research and Intelligence
NATO	North Atlantic Treaty Organization
NCFE	National Committee for a Free Europe
NOC	National Olympic Committee
NSC	National Security Council
OCB	Operations Coordinating Board
OPC	Office of Policy Coordination
OSS	Office of Strategic Services
OWI	Office of War Information
PPS	Policy Planning Staff
PSB	Psychological Strategy Board
PWB	Psychological Warfare Branch
RFE	Radio Free Europe
SCVYV	Santa Clara Valley Youth Village
UFEES	Union of Free Eastern European Sportsmen

UFHS	Union of Free Hungarian Students
UN	United Nations
USIA	United States Information Agency
USIE	United States International Information and Educational Exchange Program
USIS	United States Information Service
USOC	United States Olympic Committee
USSR	Union of Soviet Socialist Republics
VOA	Voice of America

Introduction

On the evening of 9 June 1955, Republican senator John Marshall Butler addressed an audience at the Friendship International Airport in Baltimore, Maryland. The topic of his speech, he claimed, reached everyone in "contemporary life." He spoke of sport and the Olympic Games: "Are we in the United States—where our record of excellence in the field of amateur sportsmanship is a by-product of our unique system of government—allowing the Soviet Union to pollute the Olympic Games; to use, with diabolic deceit, the spirit of sportsmanship itself as a velvet gloved iron fist to ruthlessly hammer out their Godless propaganda?"[1] Butler wanted to "expose" the threat of Soviet sport, for, he thought, it portrayed Soviet political and ideological strength at a time when such things were of singular importance. The senator did not hold this sincere concern alone. The U.S. public and media had for several years been saying much the same thing.

That the performances of Soviet athletes at the Olympics became a matter of such pointed interest to so many Americans can be attributed to the irreconcilable state of international politics that followed the events of World War II. Although the development and escalation of the Cold War between the United States and the Soviet Union may not have led either country into a direct military confrontation with the other, in some ways it still resembled the hot war that directly preceded it. Just like the monumental struggle to stop Hitler, the United States became embroiled in a total conflict, wherein the aim of defeating the Soviet Union and repelling communism stretched far beyond a massive budget for military spending, the accumulation of nuclear arms, or even diplomatic and economic measures. As the Cold War emerged, U.S. officials quickly realized that it would also largely be fought in the trenches of public opinion. And in order to win what has so frequently been called a "battle for hearts and minds," U.S. policymakers increasingly deployed techniques of persuasion that they referred to as propaganda or psychological warfare.[2] This imperative to shape the opinions of audiences at home and abroad, notes Kenneth Osgood, "infused a wide range" of activities with political and diplomatic connotations. The issue of "psychological significance," he adds, thus reached into a range of cultural avenues and endeavors.[3] Through exhaustive research in newly released archival materials, Osgood and a number of other writers have shown that the U.S. government left few stones unturned in its efforts to promote U.S. ideals and to denigrate those of Soviet-style communism. To take but a few examples, Washington officials overtly and covertly funded the publication of hundreds of books; organized tours of musicians, orchestras, ballet troupes, and poets; arranged cultural congresses and symposia across the world; invested millions of dollars in U.S. artists and abstract expressionism; and secretly created and funded a range of intellectual journals.[4]

It is surprising, then, that while many mainstream historians have looked to engage in a cultural approach to understanding U.S. actions during the Cold War, very few of them have managed to explore one of the nation's most ubiquitous cultural forms of all: sport. Cultural studies of the Cold War abound with treatments of music, dance, literature, academia, and art, while, with rare exceptions, sport is mentioned only fleetingly.[5] There are no reasonable grounds for this neglect. Sport historians, in contrast, have for decades been studying how the Cold War pervaded sport in many ways and by many means. It is now a common assertion, for instance, that global sporting events such as the Olympic Games served as grand public spectacles for Soviet and U.S. athletes to compete against one another in "symbolic combat."[6] In much the same vein, Peter Beck has commented that during the Cold War, sport provided a "high-profile battlefield" whereon "superiority was not an abstraction, but a reality to be demonstrated repeatedly and conspicuously."[7] The relationship between sport and the state has formed a natural strand of this scholarship, revealing how governments in both the East and West utilized their athletes for the generation and promulgation of national prestige. Without question, the mobilization of sport for political objectives in the communist bloc has been studied at length.[8] Historians have long recognized that the Soviet Union used sport as a vehicle to promote communism to the world at large, and that after 1945, the Soviet effort became more deliberate beyond its borders and more comprehensive in scale.[9] It has also been well documented that once the Soviet Union entered the Olympic Movement in 1951, Soviet sports officials prepared athletes for specific events on the Olympic program, as they believed that victory at the festival served as powerful propaganda.

Senator Butler's assessment of Soviet sport, therefore, was not altogether wrong. It is plain, however, that the political implications of what happened in "friendly" sporting contests was not only the concern of officials in the Soviet Union or its East European satellites.[10] The U.S. perspective has proven this to some extent. Studies into U.S. policy toward international sport, and efforts to follow through on it, are steadily expanding. The decision by U.S. president Jimmy Carter to boycott the 1980 Moscow Olympics has justifiably received a great deal of attention, while a sprinkling of works have examined various administrations throughout the Cold War era. Much of the time it is a story of inaction. Sport, it appears, tended to play an "underappreciated" role in the White House's foreign policy.[11] Strangely enough, the closer we get to the outbreak of the Cold War, the very height of superpower "tensions," the less we know about the U.S. government's position on sport or the Olympic Games in the global conflict.[12]

One study on the early Cold War years does stand apart from the others. No scholar has been able to integrate the issue of sport and psychological warfare to the degree achieved by Thomas Domer. It is the only piece of research that overlaps with the present study, in terms of both the time period it covers and the subject it probes. In his 1976 doctoral dissertation, Domer explored the diplomatic and political use of sport in the Eisenhower and Kennedy administrations. He claims that both administrations were deeply aware of the importance of sport in the Cold War and tried to "take every opportunity short of direct and total subsidy to enhance the sports image of the United States." In particular, Domer uncovered groundbreaking information on the Eisenhower administration's plans to target the 1956 Summer Olympics in overt and covert propaganda operations.[13] Yet the plans were more complex than Domer thought them to be. In his defense, many of the documents that reveal the complexity entered the public domain only in the last twenty years, long after Domer completed his research. It is also clear from this new evidence that the Olympics became a Cold War issue before Dwight D. Eisenhower even took office. These ideas began to foment during the presidency of Harry S. Truman (1945–52).[14]

By the early 1950s, many in the U.S. government had already reached the conclusion that Soviet sport represented a growing ideological threat to U.S. interests abroad. Numerous meetings between government officials and widely distributed reports reveal the extent and nature of the fears that resulted. Psychological warfare experts were concerned that Soviet dominance of international sport was an immensely effective form of propaganda, suggesting to millions that "communists are young, vigorous, full of promise for the future while democrats or Americans are effete, decadent, dissipated, and destined for early extinction."[15] The U.S. response to this challenge, however, was bound by the shackles of tradition. In the past, the U.S. Olympic Movement had, in large part, been immune to state interference and was guided by amateur principles, while the U.S. Olympic team had always been funded by private donations rather than federal dollars. Few Americans wanted this to change, including those on Capitol Hill. If America wanted to win an Olympic propaganda war, it had to be done through subtler methods.

These methods form the subject matter of this book. It reveals how the U.S. government used the Olympic Games as a propaganda platform to promote U.S. foreign policy objectives during the early years of the Cold War. Moreover, it argues that government officials became increasingly alarmed by Soviet attempts to exploit the Olympic Movement and met this postwar challenge earlier, and far more aggressively, than scholarly examination has previously acknowledged. The response was not a replication of the state-directed Soviet sports system but instead was often instigated through covert propaganda operations. The impetus for action came primarily through Washington's newly created psychological warfare apparatus, a diverse and often complicated machinery that rapidly expanded under the presidencies of Truman and Eisenhower. In fact, some of the government's most prominent and influential propaganda experts believed that the Olympics, and international sport in general, were formidable vehicles for transmitting ideological messages to audiences on either side of the Iron Curtain. These and other experts also believed that the best way to harness the Olympics would be to follow the same strategy deployed in countless other government propaganda campaigns—the secret use of "words" and "deeds."[16]

During the period under consideration, the problem of *attribution* is a notable feature of many government initiatives in relation to the Olympic Games. Even if a plan or course of action stemmed from official sources, it was often executed by unofficial means. One unofficial channel was private actors working for the government or in compliance with it. Indeed, the cultivation of links between the state and the private sphere is a central aspect of this study and follows the persuasive research of several scholars. Scott Lucas, for instance, argues that just like the Soviet Union, the United States embraced an ideology. It may not have been as clearly defined as Marxism-Leninism, but it existed nonetheless. While the Cold War penetrated nearly all aspects of U.S. society, it was also a cultural conflict in which the United States tried to convince audiences that it had a better way of life. The rallying call of this position and the ideological component that buttressed it was the "U.S. guardianship of 'freedom' and 'democracy.'" The fight was undertaken by Americans in both the public and private sectors. Lucas asserts that the Cold War was not solely waged by high-level diplomats and army generals, but also by "covert operators," and with the cooperation of private groups. This last point is crucial. The establishment of a "state–private network" provided the necessary façade to prove that "freedom" was not just an empty claim, and that the U.S. public thought and acted independently in its mutual disdain for communism. Though the state–private network was funded primarily through the Central Intelligence Agency (CIA), it gave the impression of independence, a matter consistently compared with the "restrictive" and "undemocratic" society of the Soviet Union.[17]

By 1950, this network had begun to stretch toward the Olympic Games. Fearing communist influence in the Olympic Movement and the way in which this influence could be used to promote Soviet foreign policy, U.S. officials started to look upon the Olympics in a completely new light. No longer was it just a sporting event that could be dismissed from national strategy. Because of the nature of the Cold War, it now demanded attention. For the remainder of the decade, U.S. propaganda experts debated and strategized over how they, and not just the Soviets, could harness the games for Cold War advantage. The years between 1950 and 1960 thus mark a decisive period in U.S. sport history. In order to meet the challenge of the Soviet sports offensive, the U.S. government took an unprecedented interest in the global power of the Olympic Games and, in so doing, made sport a matter of political significance to a degree that it had never done before.

As well as chronicling the evolution of government concerns about the Olympics in the context of the emerging Cold War, this book also demonstrates that U.S. efforts to exploit the global power of the Olympic Games followed three main themes. First, it explores how the United States attempted to manipulate and gain leverage within the Olympic Movement on various occasions, and largely without being detected. Unlike the Jimmy Carter administration in 1980, government strategists in the 1950s correctly assessed the peculiar terrain of Olympic affairs. The leaders of the International Olympic Committee (IOC), an organization guided by staunchly conservative sporting ideals, believed that the Olympic Movement should be sustained and perpetuated through private individuals and groups. Diplomats and governments, they held, meant politics, and politics only corrupted sport. Although working with state bureaucracies was often unavoidable, particularly when it came to holding and funding Olympic festivals, the IOC still preferred that such instances be kept to a minimum. As many Americans had contributed to the development of these ideas and practices, the same general philosophy infused the Olympic establishment in the United States. Accepting these limitations, the U.S. government sought to access the Olympic Movement by secretly working with and through private entities, thus hiding its involvement. Throughout the 1950s, the United States broke the shackles of tradition and forged cooperative relationships with various individuals and groups in the U.S. Olympic establishment, including the United States Olympic Committee and the Amateur Athletic Union of the United States. Yet the extent of state–private cooperation far exceeded these boundaries. Various other private actors, ranging from Pan American Airways to *Sports Illustrated* magazine, were embroiled in the government's network and voluntarily joined the fight against the communist enemy. Possibly none of these private entities, however, was as deeply motivated as the multiple Eastern European émigré groups clandestinely funded through the CIA. These refugee organizations, including the National Committee for a Free Europe and the Hungarian National Sports Federation, were able to communicate with the IOC and push an anticommunist agenda without Olympic officials ever suspecting official U.S. involvement. In the 1950s, the IOC was continuously engaged in a total war, but at times its members did not even suspect it.

The second theme of this book focuses on how the U.S. government exploited the Olympic Games through the hosting cities, for both summer and winter games, from 1952 to 1960. This tactic, of course, was nothing new. Ever since the modern Olympic Movement was formed more than a century ago, the games of each Olympiad have provided a powerful and compelling conduit to shape and sculpt public opinion. From the very start, sporting patriots and the media have equated the performance of athletes at the Olympics with the strength and prestige of the nations they represent. As the festival has grown into a global and commercial mega-event, Olympic organizing committees have also continually used the event as a forum to project favorable images of the hosting city and country. Dating back to Athens in 1896, Olympic cities have endeavored to put on a good show for those who listened to or read about the events, or for those who attended and watched.[18] For a short time, Olympic cities become a magnet of sorts by attracting the eyes of the world. Recognizing this phenomenon, U.S. planners viewed Olympic cities as ideal forums to reach and mold the opinions of a massive populace at home and abroad. They used Olympic venues to distribute propaganda materials, to show pro-U.S. movies, to organize exhibitions, to make contact with Soviet bloc tourists, and to help Eastern European athletes to defect. Government officials accepted that little could be done to influence the symbolic battle of the sporting competitions, but prestige could be won or lost in many other ways in and around Olympic cities.

Third, this book highlights how U.S. propaganda experts attempted to utilize the medium of the Olympic message for political gain. In a war of words, Olympism, or the philosophical underpinning of the Olympic Movement, was extremely well suited to influencing public opinion. The founder of the modern games, Baron Pierre de Coubertin, wrote voluminously about the Olympic message of peaceful "internationalism,"[19] but his ruminations are replete with digressions and contradictions. Regardless of one's ideological or political beliefs, it is easy enough to read Coubertin's work and find something that can be adapted or bent to suit it. And so it proved in the Cold War. The Soviet Union, for example, claimed that the peaceful internationalism of Olympism could be fruitfully compared with the guiding principles of communism.[20] Americans, on the other hand, argued that the Olympics represented and promoted the purest form of liberal democracy.[21] In U.S. propaganda released before, during, and after each Olympic festival in the 1950s, it is clear to see that much of this material deliberately attempted to connect the ideological foundations of the U.S. political and athletic culture to the mythical and mysterious values of Olympism. Therefore, U.S. propaganda presented a carefully constructed image of U.S. participation at each Olympic festival, an image that depicted the athletes as paragons of the U.S. "way of life," thriving on the benefits and opportunities afforded by a democratic society. The United States charged, furthermore, that U.S. athletes partook in the Olympic Games with the correct spirit of competition, while communist participants were merely political agents. Although Coubertin may have revived the games to promote his own version of peace, the Olympic medium provided the two superpowers with a potent tool to influence global audiences.

As this study is primarily concerned with the application of psychological warfare and propaganda, it is necessary to expand on these terms and what the U.S. government meant by them. To complicate matters, these and other terms are employed interchangeably throughout classified documents. One might find terms such as "political warfare," "psychological strategy," or even, in the public sphere, the less dramatic euphemism, "information."[22] That considered, a general government definition of psychological warfare is the "planned use by a nation of propaganda and activities other than combat which communicate ideas and information intended to influence the opinions, attitudes, emotions, and behavior of foreign groups in ways that will support the achievement of national aims." As an instrument of psychological warfare, propaganda refers to "any organized effort or movement to disseminate information or a particular doctrine by means of news, special arguments or appeals designed to influence the thoughts and actions of any given group."[23] Psychological warfare experts also tend to distinguish three categories of propaganda. They classify "white" propaganda as official and clearly produced by the U.S. government. "Black" propaganda is information that is secret and subversive, such as faking a communist document to undermine or humiliate a communist regime. The "gray" variety, on the other hand, struck a balance between the white and the black; it appeared to come from a nonofficial or indigenous source, thus making it more acceptable to the intended target than an official statement.[24] The U.S. government's Olympic propaganda often fluctuated between the white and the gray.

Although the main task of this inquiry is to understand how and why the United States targeted the Olympic Games, this is not to say that during this period other sporting events were deliberately avoided by psychological warfare experts; to say so would be erroneous. In the time period under consideration, however, the Olympics were certainly the largest athletic festival in existence, claimed considerable international attention, and represented the most prestigious single event in which the athletic teams of the two superpowers competed. When the U.S. government officials worried about the problem of Soviet sport, in general they worried about it in the context of the Olympic Games. Moreover, this book does not argue that the United States had an overarching Olympic strategy. While there is evidence of widespread interest in the Olympic Movement across government departments and in the state–private network, there was no operative leadership in the process, certainly not from the president, in any case. There was, nevertheless, a general consensus on what Soviet sport represented and how best to counter it. Indeed, many of the different meetings between private groups, government officials, and departments often shared distinct similarities. But to claim that a coordinated and centrally organized approach was in effect is to overstate the case. If an Olympic Cold War strategy existed in any sense, it was as part of a broader cultural program.

Finally, this book offers a perspective that starts with the United States and branches out from there, focusing on the planning, distribution, and themes that guided Olympic propaganda rather than how it was received, or what effect it had. I do not claim that this is an exhaustive account of U.S. operations at the Olympics; it is doubtful whether such a study is possible. As G. M. Trevelyan recognized long ago, "On the shore where Time casts up its stray wreckage we gather corks and broken planks, whence much indeed may be argued and more guessed; but what the great ship was that has gone down into the deep, that we shall never see."[25] There are, I would guess, more documents to be declassified and other secret projects to be uncovered. Only time will tell whether or when this "stray wreckage" is brought from the darkness of the depths to the light of the surface. In any case, for too long sport has been neglected in the tale of the U.S. cultural Cold War. By investigating the U.S. government's interest in the Olympics it is possible to further grasp the total nature of the superpower conflict and the U.S. commitment to winning it. It also, by the same token, reveals a great deal about the Olympic Movement and its complicated role in international politics and affairs.

1 The Cold War, Propaganda, and the State–Private Network

By the time Dwight D. Eisenhower left office in 1961, the United States had developed a far-reaching capability to produce and disseminate propaganda across the globe, not to mention the resources and inclination to launch audacious covert operations. The United States did not, however, enter the Cold War with this machinery in place. These methods had been widely deployed during World War II, but the "usual American procedure of improvident disarmament" largely removed psychological warfare from the scene after the confrontation had ended. "The situation stood thus stagnant," assessed a later government report, "until eventually the realization dawned that here was a weapon which could be used in this twilight war zone in which we found ourselves living."[1] But the reemergence of the U.S. psychological warfare apparatus was not simple, nor was it clear-cut. Those U.S. officials who advocated a resurgence of propaganda to combat communist incursions endured strong criticism from inside and outside government circles. Only in a time of war had the White House created such a structure, and the Cold War was not a conflict of the traditional kind. In spite of these challenges, the machinery for psychological warfare was designed, built, and refined under the presidency of Harry S. Truman and eagerly molded by his successor, Dwight Eisenhower. That both administrations decided to pour time and energy into propaganda also reveals much about the history of the twentieth century. In fact, the United States and many other nations developed mechanisms for shaping public opinion only in response to the peculiarities of what Eric Hobsbawm has called, an "age of extremes."[2]

The U.S. Experience with Propaganda
and Psychological Warfare to 1945

Although mankind has engaged in propaganda since ancient times, during the twentieth century it came to the fore as a persuasive technique. The explosion of communications and transportation technology, linking disparate and remote peoples from the four corners of the earth, made it increasingly feasible to spread information and far easier for people to consume it. Higher levels of literacy, moreover, meant that the opinions and attitudes of a global population could be fashioned and influenced by various media of communication, be it the written word, radio, or film. International politics also was transformed. Diplomacy ceased to be a private matter deliberated only by high-level officials behind closed doors; it was propelled into the public domain, where it could be debated and judged by those who read or wrote about it. As a result of these developments, public opinion had to be considered more than ever in the formulation of foreign policy. This fact became abundantly clear in an age that witnessed the phenomenon of total war. The "wars of the twentieth century," notes Hobsbawm, occurred "on a vaster scale than anything previously experienced." They were more demanding to those who fought in them and, furthermore, to those who stayed at home. Not only were citizens required to help make the endless products that sustain a war effort, but national leaders needed them to emotionally support the cause. For that reason, the warring governments used propaganda to mobilize civilians, soldiers, and allies or as a means to demoralize the enemy.[3]

To some degree, propaganda has always played a role in the conduct of U.S. foreign policy. Nevertheless, the U.S. entry into World War I in 1917 soon led to the establishment of the country's first official propaganda agency. A week after declaring war on Germany, the U.S. president, Woodrow Wilson, created the Committee on Public Information (CPI) and selected a journalist named George Creel to run it. "Under the pressure of tremendous necessities," Creel explained, "an organization grew that not only reached deep into every American community, but that carried to every corner of the civilized globe the full message of America's idealism, unselfishness, and indomitable purpose." After all, he argued, the "approval of the world" would lead to a "steady flow of inspiration to the trenches." The CPI provided domestic and foreign audiences with movies, literature, periodicals, booklets, and carefully selected articles to defend the U.S. entry into the war and to promote all aspects of U.S. life and culture. Private groups and citizens also rallied to assist the objectives of Creel's committee. Patriotic volunteers, known as the "Four Minute Men," delivered short speeches across the country to rouse support for the war, while numerous other private initiatives plowed a similar furrow during this time of national emergency. The CPI was primarily focused on domestic public opinion, but Creel was confident of the impact abroad and claimed that a "world that was either inimical, contemptuous, or indifferent" to the United States "was changed into a world of friends and well-wishers." Even if Creel was proud of what he and his committee had achieved, it did not lead to a permanent governmental information agency. Crucially, as it turned out, Congress was far less supportive of a peacetime information program and, at the war's end, shut the CPI down.[4]

Yet Creel's attempts to project U.S. "ideals" and culture to foreign lands was an undertaking that complicated and compromised the U.S. government's traditional boundaries of public diplomacy. In general, Americans preferred that "cultural proselytizing" be left to private entities, and not to the state. Reifying these ideas, several philanthropic foundations, such as the Carnegie Endowment for International Peace and the Institute of International Education, encouraged cultural and educational exchanges between the United States and foreign countries under the banner of "nongovernmental internationalism." The founder of the latter group, Stephen Duggen, spoke effusively about "a unity among men which transcends differences in the forms of government." But "to know it and understand it," he said in 1934, people "must be brought together." Although the work of Duggen and other private organizations satisfied the U.S. public's preference for keeping state interference to a minimum in cultural relations, the U.S. government did not completely decline to organize or administer some foreign exchanges. In 1908, for instance, Washington set aside funds for Chinese citizens to receive education in the United States through the Boxer Indemnity Scheme.[5]

The emergence of totalitarian regimes, particularly in Nazi Germany and the Soviet Union, provided Americans with more ammunition to have doubts about the prospect of the state overseeing culture and information. At the same time, however, the rise of the Third Reich also created an imposing reason for Washington to reconsider its need for a propaganda program, as Adolf Hitler's agents sought to sow seeds of "disunity" in the Western Hemisphere through radio, subsidized press agencies, movies, cultural centers, athletic clubs, and German businesses.[6] By this point, though, the Franklin D. Roosevelt administration was already beginning to reconsider the nation's political isolation and wanted to start redressing the imbalance in Latin America. Cultural exchanges with Latin American countries would thus counter fascist and Axis power encroachments and complement the administration's new "Good Neighbor Policy." In 1938, Roosevelt created the Division of Cultural Affairs to organize these exchanges and to prove that

Americans were truly good neighbors and not just an exploitative capitalistic force. With a nod to tradition, these cultural relations were organized and financed in tandem with private groups, as the government declined to take full control of cultural matters, or to even acknowledge that it was partaking in propaganda in the first place. Regardless, cultural affairs were starting to bleed into foreign policy.[7]

U.S. activities in Latin America escalated with the outbreak of World War II and began to drastically erode the government's distancing of itself from cultural relations. In 1940, Roosevelt established a new propaganda agency called the Office of the Coordinator of Inter-American Affairs (CIAA). Led by Nelson A. Rockefeller, the CIAA aimed to use "Governmental and private facilities in such fields as arts and sciences, education and travel, the radio, press, and cinema" to "further national defense and strengthen the bonds between the nations of the Western Hemisphere."[8] This strategy of defending the U.S. image and combating Nazi propaganda involved a number of "cultural tactics" facilitated by state and private actors. A Music Committee, for instance, was charged with sending the nation's "best and most representative" music and musicians to Latin America "to bolster American cultural prestige and to refute the widely held belief that the United States was a culturally and musically impoverished country." Other committees worked in areas such as film, art, and sport. With a budget that rose to $60 million in 1943, notes Frank Ninkovich, the CIAA's program "far exceeded" the output of the Division of Cultural Affairs and the "limited initiatives of the philanthropic pioneers."[9]

Such was the fervor that Nazi propaganda had stirred in the United States that Roosevelt came under increasing pressure—from determined private groups and citizens as well as from those in his administration—to form a special state agency for information activities. In 1941, the president acted upon these calls and created the Coordinator of Information (COI) to sculpt public opinion overseas. Although this agency, under the command of William J. Donovan, supplied audiences with "honest" information about the United States through its Foreign Information Service division, it also gathered intelligence and pursued clandestine operations. The balance between overt and covert strategies soon resulted in schisms within the COI and, in time, the agency's downfall. On the one hand, Donovan wanted to "beat the Germans at their own game" by utilizing subversive tactics while, on the other hand, a strong faction within the Foreign Information Service wanted to avoid such immoral" methods and simply follow a "strategy of truth" that remained faithful to democratic principles. These fundamental differences could not be overcome and pressed Roosevelt to make some essential adjustments.[10]

The president did just that in 1942 by consolidating the Foreign Information Service into the newly established Office of War Information (OWI) and moving Donovan's operations into the Office of Strategic Services (OSS). This decision split the U.S. information program along overt (OWI) and covert (OSS) lines. Roosevelt handed the leadership of the OWI to Elmer Davis, a highly educated and nationally well-liked CBS radio broadcaster, who eventually oversaw a sprawling agency with 10,000 employees worldwide. The OWI was formed to explain the U.S. participation in the war to audiences at home and abroad by widely disseminating material such as pictures, leaflets, magazines, films, and cartoons. United States Information Service (USIS) posts in dozens of countries received reams of government material that was designed to present the Allied war aims in a favorable light. Perhaps the most powerful tool at the OWI's disposal was the newly formed government radio network, the Voice of America (VOA). Broadcasting only to foreign audiences, by mid-1944, the VOA was transmitting twenty-four hours a day in forty languages. It confidently stated in its first broadcast, "The news may be good. The news may be bad. But we shall tell you the truth."[11]

From the early stages of the war, the U.S. military had also started to branch out into activities that were broadly termed "psychological warfare." For William J. Donovan, the head of the OSS, psychological warfare "consisted of all means, physical as well as moral, which could be used to break the will of the enemy." Donovan had eagerly studied the art of psychological warfare in the lead up to World War II and felt that he could replicate Nazi methods in a way that could complement Allied military operations. Many of the individuals who filled the OSS were as unorthodox as the organization's leader. In addition to military personnel, Donovan recruited a host of men from the U.S. northeastern elite, many of whom had been educated at the Ivy League schools, were Republicans, and had very little time for Roosevelt or Democratic New Deal policies. Nonetheless, they wanted to contribute to the downfall of Hitler and performed covert assignments such as sabotage, espionage, guerrilla warfare, intelligence, and counterintelligence. One infamous OSS branch focused on "morale operations," or "black" propaganda, by disseminating false information to "incite and spread dissension, confusion and disorder within enemy countries."[12]

As the war progressed, the United States gradually established psychological warfare divisions in the major theaters of battle. In 1942, for instance, General Dwight D. Eisenhower created a Psychological Warfare Branch

(PWB) to assist in the Allied invasion of North Africa. The venture included representatives from the OWI, OSS, the U.S. Army, and the British Political Warfare Executive. Under the authority of General Robert McClure and a publisher named Charles Douglas Jackson, the PWB aimed to facilitate the mass surrender and demoralization of the Axis powers. Although these joint operations were often riddled with internal disputes between civilian and army personnel, the working relationship became more harmonious over time. Indeed, Army leaders eventually developed an appreciation for propaganda as an aid to conventional warfare. Others needed less convincing. When the PWB's activities expanded in Italy, Jackson wrote enthusiastically about the organization's efforts. "We really have quite a show over here now," he commented in 1943. Jackson applauded the PWB's ability to "print and distribute between seven and ten million leaflets a week;" and he praised the branch's mobile radio units, the "communications channels," and the close cooperation with the British. Overall, Jackson judged the spectrum of work as "pretty terrific." Eisenhower was also convinced that propaganda had a vital role in battle and later established a huge Psychological Warfare Division of the Supreme Headquarters Allied Expeditionary Force to prepare the way for the D-Day landings in 1944. "Without doubt," Eisenhower concluded, "psychological warfare has proved its right to a place of dignity in our military arsenal."[13]

Remobilizing Propaganda for the Cold War

At the end of the war, though, the U.S. propaganda apparatus was almost totally dismantled and dissolved. Nevertheless, Roosevelt's successor, Harry S. Truman, still held that the "nature of present-day foreign relations" made "informational activities abroad . . . an integral part of the conduct of our foreign affairs." For that reason, he wanted to ensure that "other peoples receive a full and fair picture of American life and of the aims and policies of the United States Government." Rather than abolishing propaganda, as had been the fate of the CPI after World War I, Truman placed the overseas functions of the OWI and CIAA in the State Department under the aegis of William Benton, the assistant secretary of state for public affairs.[14] For Benton and those who championed the information program, a period of struggle followed. Many in Congress, especially Republicans, had criticized the manner in which propaganda had been used to project America during the war, and their views only hardened in the postwar climate. Some critics charged that the information program was just a mouthpiece for the Democrats, fiscal conservatives charged that propaganda was a "capricious extravagance," and there were even scandals about spies having infiltrated the VOA's staff. Amid this crisis, the government's budget for information and cultural affairs was almost halved from $45 million in 1946 to $25.4 million in 1947. "Modest is perhaps too flattering a word to describe our information activities abroad," Benton complained in one public address.[15]

The emergence of the Cold War gradually changed the congressional aversion to propaganda. The United States and the Soviet Union may have fought together to defeat Germany, but securing agreement on the postwar world proved to be impossible for the two superpowers. While Truman and his advisers may have wanted to "forge an international environment conducive to the American way of life," the path to achieving this goal was obstructed by the parallel objectives of the Soviet premier, Joseph Stalin.[16] Indeed, by the time of Germany's capitulation, the Soviet Union had lost more than 20 million of its population, its infrastructure was bludgeoned, its economy was in ruins, and a large part of its surviving population was either starving or in dire poverty. Stalin was desperate to avoid another catastrophic invasion like the one inflicted by Hitler, and the Red Army's advances in 1944 and 1945 gave him a preponderant position of strength along the Soviet Union's European border, a crucial security buffer. Although Stalin's precise intentions for Eastern Europe remain open to debate, he did encourage communist elements to seek their own "national roads" to communism and initially "share political power with other 'patriotic' socialist and democratic parties" in the region. The Soviet Union, argues Norman Naimark, "followed flexible policies in establishing its influence" in Eastern Europe, often adjusting to the particular conditions or geopolitical importance of each country in the Soviet security zone. In the case of Yugoslavia, a strong communist movement had already been established and required only moderate Soviet military support. In Poland and Romania, however, the Soviet Union enforced its will and military presence to facilitate communist takeovers.[17] At any rate, the prospect of further communist expansion appeared to cast a long and menacing shadow over Washington. "Unless Russia is faced with an iron fist and strong language another war is in the making," Truman stated ominously.[18]

The relationship between the Soviet Union and the United States soon lurched toward an unrecoverable slide. In 1947, Truman asked Congress to provide financial and military aid to Greece and Turkey in order to prevent both countries from being engulfed by totalitarianism. "At the present moment in world history," Truman told Congress, "nearly every nation must choose between alternative ways of life. The choice is too often not a free one."[19] Although the president never mentioned the Soviet Union, the implication was clear. The administration soon followed the Truman Doctrine by devising a further dramatic plan, this time to provide financial assistance to the devastated countries of Europe. Government officials did not think that the Soviet Union was ready for war, but that Moscow could use psychological warfare to gain a foothold across Europe by exploiting the dire economic conditions. With this in mind, George C. Marshall, the secretary of state, called for billions of U.S. dollars to fund a European Recovery Program (the Marshall Plan) that would provide a support to the global economy and also foster "the emergence of political and social conditions in which free institutions can exist." The United States included Eastern Europe and the Soviet Union in the strategy but accepted that Stalin would probably not allow the countries in his sphere of influence to be lured into financial cooperation with the United States. As expected, the Soviet leader prevented the "people's democracies" from partaking in the initiative and responded by forming the Communist Information Bureau (Cominform), an organization designed to ensure that the communist parties of Europe fell in line with the Soviet example.[20]

The Marshall Plan itself was a grand act of psychological warfare that earned the U.S. goodwill on the European continent and exposed Stalin's own priorities. But the machinery for psychological warfare was already being slowly reassembled while the Truman Doctrine and the Marshall Plan were capturing worldwide attention. Although Truman had liquidated the OSS in 1945, the demands for accurate and useful intelligence on the policies of foreign governments became ever more vital with the advent of the Cold War. In January 1946, a presidential directive attempted to solve this problem by creating a Central Intelligence Group from the embers of the OSS.[21] Then, a year later, the National Security Act (1947)—a great restructuring of the U.S. government—amended the intelligence apparatus once again. Part of the act established a National Security Council (NSC) to coordinate policy formulation and transformed the Central Intelligence Group into the Central Intelligence Agency (CIA). The CIA was formed to coordinate, correlate, and evaluate intelligence information. It did not, however, have a clear charter for psychological warfare, but rather a vague stipulation that it should "perform such other functions and duties related to intelligence affecting the national security."[22]

The conditions in Europe necessitated some clarity on the matter. The Truman administration was particularly alarmed by Communist Party momentum in Italy and France. NSC paper 1/1 recommended that the United States should "actively combat communist propaganda in Italy by an effective information program and by all other practical means."[23] Psychological, political, and military aid would be provided, but questions arose about who would execute the plan. Much like the arrangement in World War II, the responsibilities were divided. The council subsequently approved NSC 4, which stipulated that all overt "information activities" were the responsibility of the State Department, while a secret annex, NSC 4-A, placed "covert psychological operations" in the CIA under the Special Procedures Group. On the day this directive was approved (22 December 1947), a CIA team left for Italy under the command of former OSS officer James Jesus Angleton. The United States spent an estimated sum between $10 and $20 million on sabotaging the Italian election, which included "covert aid to democratic anti-communist parties." When one of those parties, the Christian Democrats, triumphed in the April election, U.S. covert operators reveled in their ability to use psychological warfare to dam the advance of communism.[24]

Yet this was only a prelude. The world situation still appeared fragile. To the east, China looked ripe for a communist revolution. In February 1948, a communist coup succeeded in Czechoslovakia. Soon after, the Soviet Union organized a blockade of western supplies to West Berlin, a tactic employed to halt the formation of a separate West German state. It caused the reverse. The United States sped up preparations for a West German state and organized a prodigious airlift of supplies to West Berlin. Moreover, the blockade ushered in a further division between east and west. The United States and a group of allies subsequently signed the North Atlantic Treaty, promising to come to each other's aid in the event that any were attacked.

In this delicate state of international relations, many in Washington were of the opinion that a more concerted and coordinated covert function was required to grasp the Cold War initiative.[25] One U.S. policy expert who shared that outlook was George Kennan, the director of the State Department's Policy Planning Staff (PPS). In May 1948, Kennan and his staff produced a paper titled "The Inauguration of Organized Political Warfare." The paper was crucial to the future organization of U.S. covert operations and explained, "In broadest definition, political warfare is the employment of all means at a nation's command, short of war, to achieve its national objectives. Such operations are both overt and covert. They range from such overt actions as political alliances, economic measures (as ERP), and 'white' propaganda to such covert operations as clandestine support of 'friendly' foreign elements, 'black' psychological warfare and even encouragement of underground resistance in hostile states."[26]

The Kennan-inspired paper led to National Security Council 10/2, a directive that created a top secret government agency to administer covert operations. Established on 1 September 1948, this covert mechanism was initially called the Office of Special Projects, but it was soon renamed the

Office of Policy Coordination (OPC). Its operations "were to be so planned and executed that any U.S. Government responsibility for them would not be evident to unauthorized persons." If, however, the government ties were uncovered, the White House would "be able to disclaim plausibly any responsibility for them." Veiled by a shroud of plausible deniability, the OPC undertook propaganda, economic warfare, sabotage, demolition, subversion, guerrilla warfare, and supported anticommunist movements. The leadership of the Office of Policy Coordination was handed to Frank Wisner, a former OSS officer, who quickly found himself at the helm of a remarkably well-funded endeavor. By 1952, the OPC had 2,812 agents on its payroll and a further 3,142 personnel under contract overseas, and its budget expanded from $4.7 million at the outset to $82 million three years later. At the end of 1952, the OPC had access to a further $200 million in counterpart funds. Kennan made sure that control of this agency would fall to the State Department and not the CIA, chiefly because he had little respect for the incumbent director of central intelligence, Admiral Roscoe Hillenkoetter. Still, the OPC was hidden within the CIA and, in 1952, fully absorbed by the agency.[27]

In June 1948, U.S. morale was given a boost when Yugoslavia, under the leadership of Josip Broz Tito, broke away from Soviet hegemony. The PPS reacted by recommending an aggressive policy of putting the "greatest possible strain on the structure of relationships by which Soviet domination of [Eastern Europe] is maintained." This aim was reinforced and fortified by NSC 20/4, which called for ambitious plans to reduce "the power and influence of the USSR to limits which no longer constitute a threat to the peace, national independence and stability of the world family of nations."[28] And ambitious plans resulted from this aggressive rallying cry. British and U.S. covert operators, funded mostly by the OPC, collaborated in several attempts to start a civil war in Albania and other satellite countries. Intelligence officers trained guerrilla units of Eastern European émigrés who were then secretly dropped behind enemy lines, whereupon they were expected to instigate unrest and revolution. Some operations were devised without scruples, even using Romanian fascists who had committed atrocities during the war. Most of these missions ended in complete failure. Soviet agents infiltrated the top-secret British and U.S. preparations, so that when the unfortunate refugees landed in enemy territory they were caught and punished by way of imprisonment or execution.[29] Regardless of how these plans unraveled, the addition of NSC 20/4 provides persuasive evidence that the U.S. government was committed to a policy far more aggressive than its public pronouncements of "containing" communism. The goal of "liberating" Eastern Europe from

Soviet power is more often associated with the presidency of Eisenhower, but it is clear that from 1948 the Truman administration was attempting much the same thing.[30]

With the Cold War battle lines drawn, the beleaguered U.S. information program began to resuscitate. In a minor way, the government had already made some progress in the field of cultural relations with the passing of the Fulbright Act in 1946. Only later did this piece of legislation, originally enacted with an eye on promoting "liberal internationalism" in the wake of World War II through educational exchanges, become an "instrument" of the Cold War.[31] In NSC 4, the National Security Council had maintained that the Fulbright Act and other overt programs should be strengthened to "counteract" the "effects of anti-U.S. propaganda."[32] Persisting with his own personal crusade, William Benton linked the need for a stronger information program to the Truman Doctrine and argued that the task of telling the world about U.S. policy should not be left solely to the private sphere. He demanded that Soviet propaganda be countered by a stronger government-directed campaign. Aided by the hardening of the U.S. position toward the Soviet Union, Benton further strengthened his hand by helping to organize a trip to Europe for representatives and senators to investigate the information program's effectiveness. Spearheaded by Senator Alexander Smith (R–NJ) and Congressman Karl Mundt (R–SD), the group returned with numerous concerns about the negative image Europeans held of U.S. society and its people. "Worried about losing the war of ideas to a sophisticated Communist propaganda apparatus," Congress passed the U.S. Information and Educational Exchange Act in January 1948. The Smith-Mundt Act, as the legislation was otherwise known, finally secured a permanent status for the overseas information program. It advocated the use of print, film, radio, exchange programs, and exhibitions to "promote the better understanding of the United States among the peoples of the world and to strengthen cooperative international relations." Appropriations for the information program doubled in its first full year as the United States embarked on a revitalized propaganda attack on communism.[33]

The program grew as the Cold War developed. Soviet propaganda became more virulent, accusing the United States of behaving like an imperialist aggressor, while styling communism as a great arbiter of peace. "The Communist effort to misrepresent and discredit the aims and nature of American life, and the aims and nature of American foreign policy, has primarily a great strategic value in the furtherance of Communist World objectives," charged the secretary of state, Dean Acheson. "This Communist campaign," he said, "jeopardizes the security of the United States and is a threat to the security of the free world." The communist coup in Czechoslovakia, the Berlin blockade, Soviet testing of an atomic bomb, and the fall of China to communism guaranteed that fewer were opposed to strengthening the U.S. ability to respond with an enlarged propaganda strategy.[34]

One of the key government men to coordinate the new onslaught was Edward Barrett, who became the assistant secretary of state for Public Affairs in 1950. Having directed the OWI's overseas branch in World War II, in between stints as the editor of *Newsweek* magazine, Barrett seemed like a sound choice to run the information program. A devout believer in the power of propaganda, Barrett demanded an "all-out effort to penetrate the Iron Curtain with our ideas" and to counter Soviet "lies" about the United States. The offensive plan he called for was eventually labeled the Campaign of Truth. Truman gave it his full support. "We must make ourselves known as we really are—not as Communist propaganda pictures us," the president announced in April 1950. "We must pool our efforts with those of the other free peoples in a sustained, intensified program to promote the cause of freedom against the propaganda of slavery. We must make ourselves heard round the world in a great campaign of truth." The outbreak of the Korean War convinced members of Congress to take action. A supplemental appropriation of nearly $80 million bolstered operations in radio, press and publications, film, exchanges of persons, and other cultural activities.[35]

The Campaign of Truth appeared shortly after the completion of the now famous U.S. policy document NSC 68. During spring 1950, Paul Nitze, Kennan's replacement as head of the PPS, studied the new problem of Soviet atomic capability. The result of his and his team's analysis was NSC 68, a document that restated previous aims to break up Soviet control in Eastern Europe through economic assistance, military aid, covert operations, and psychological warfare. The unique aspect of NSC 68, however, was that it called for a massive escalation in these plans, most notably in military spending. Oddly, few believed that the Soviet Union would start a nuclear war. As the historian Melvin Leffler has noted, building military and atomic superiority was a way for the United States to simply appear to be more powerful in order to secure global preeminence. "Perplexed" by the actions of the Soviet Union, reasons Leffler, U.S. officials reproduced their own "nightmare." "If U.S. diplomacy were not active and vigilant, if U.S. aid were not forthcoming, and if U.S. determination were not evident to friends and foes alike, the industrial workshops of Europe and Asia and their attendant markets and raw materials could gravitate out of the U.S. orbit. The United States could become isolated in a hostile world."[36]

The Campaign of Truth may have provided the impetus for a plethora of propaganda operations, but it also created a problem of organization and coordination. Work in the field was undertaken by the State Department, the Economic Cooperation Administration (promoting the Marshall Plan in Europe), the CIA, and the OPC. Yet there was, at this stage, no single body to ensure that all these departments were singing from the same hymn sheet. In 1951, Truman tried to alleviate the confusion by approving the formation of the Psychological Strategy Board, which included among its members the director of the CIA, the undersecretary of state, and the deputy secretary of defense. As an independent entity, "the PSB was authorized to plan psychological operations on the strategic level of the NSC, to coordinate implementation of . . . psychological strategy by the operating agencies, and to evaluate the results of the entire psychological effort in its fulfillment of national policy." The greatest obstacle to the PSB's effectiveness came from the State Department, which refused to acknowledge that the PSB should be involved in, or responsible for, making policy.[37]

The PSB had been initiated to pull together the disparate strands of psychological operations but coordination remained an issue, as did overall strategy. The Truman administration had instigated a huge resurgence of psychological warfare in the years after World War II, yet the Soviet Union was still strong in Europe, even after the death of Stalin in 1953. The information program was in constant "flux" despite the Smith-Mundt Act, changing names on four occasions from the Office of International Information and Cultural Affairs, to the Office of International Information and Educational Exchange, then the U.S. International Information and Educational Exchange Program, and finally, in 1952, the U.S. International Information Administration. Many argued, moreover, that a truly effective program could be achieved only with an independent information agency outside the State Department.[38] For others, there were even bigger questions to answer. In May 1952, several participants in a top secret meeting at Princeton University expressed deep concerns over the government's handling of political warfare and how far it would go to liberate Eastern Europe. Charles Douglas Jackson, a leading propaganda expert, noted with some frustration that psychological warfare had "possibly created a frown" on Stalin's "brow," but that more needed to be done.[39]

For historian Kenneth Osgood, an additional constraint to the implementation of the U.S. propaganda program was that Truman himself "evinced little interest in or understanding of psychological warfare." But the "next American president," Osgood asserts, "would make psychological strategy a key element of his election campaign and a priority of his administration."[40] A World War II hero, Eisenhower took office on a Republican platform of liberating Europe from Stalin's hold. Part of his "New Look" policy to achieve this required—indeed demanded—the tactical use of propaganda. His intentions were of no real surprise. Eisenhower had openly admitted that propaganda had been a useful device in military operations during World War II and spoke of the importance of psychological warfare in his election campaign. "We must realize that as a nation," he said, "everything we say, everything we do, and everything we fail to say or do will have its impact in other lands. It will affect the minds and wills of men and women there." When Eisenhower took office in 1953, he signaled his commitment to the "p-factor" by creating a new position within his administration to specialize in it. The first man he chose to serve as his special assistant for psychological warfare was Charles Douglas Jackson.[41]

Jackson served for just one year in this new role, but his relevance to the history of the U.S. psychological warfare program is far deeper than his brief tenure might signal. From World War II into the early Cold War years, Jackson was one of the most influential U.S. purveyors of psychological warfare. Like numerous other publicists and advertisers the government hired to assist in propaganda operations, he was plucked out of the private sector. Jackson graduated from Princeton in 1924, and his early career path was spent ascending through the ranks of Time Incorporated. He became a vice president of the company and acted as the publisher of *Fortune* and *Life* magazines. Jackson was heavily involved with the administration of propaganda and psychological warfare in World War II, at which time he worked for the Office of War Information in North Africa and served in General Eisenhower's commands in the Mediterranean and Europe. Jackson's expertise made his services a commodity of great value during the Cold War, and he gave his services willingly. Before taking his position under Eisenhower, Jackson served on the Truman administration's PSB, regularly advised the government on Cold War planning, and was instrumental in the creation of the CIA-funded Radio Free Europe. Without question, Eisenhower prized Jackson's creativity, imagination, and ideas. For his part, Jackson fully appreciated Eisenhower's enthusiasm for the "art" of psychological warfare and gushed that the president judged it to be "just about the only way to win World War III without having to fight it."[42]

In keeping with Eisenhower's perspective on the value of propaganda, the information program came under intense scrutiny in 1953 when five investigations simultaneously looked into the subject, two of which were initiated by the president. One of the most important of these studies was the President's Committee on International Information Activities or, as it became known, the Jackson Committee, named after William H. Jackson, who chaired it. The inquiry began in January 1953, and the committee completed its final report six months later, in June. In order to challenge the Soviet Union's considerable propaganda capabilities, the Jackson Committee called for a more centralized propaganda program, with leadership from the president. The report urged that propaganda should not be separated from official policy but work in harmony with it. There was also to be a change in tone. It was recommended that the strident propaganda that marked the Campaign of Truth should be replaced by a more measured, positive, and honest approach through "straight news." The Jackson Committee also advised that official propaganda should be reduced. It reasoned that too much material bore the label of the U.S. government and that audiences were "particularly quick to take offense at advice and exhortation received from abroad." The committee advised that "unattributed" or "gray" propaganda would have a greater impact overseas. Far from discounting an aggressive approach, the committee suggested that this could be achieved through "private" means—such as Radio Free Europe—so that the government could get its message across without taking responsibility. In contrast to other investigations, the Jackson Committee also recommended that the information program should remain in the State Department, but Eisenhower rejected the proposal. Instead, he created an independent United States Information Agency (1953) and appointed Theodore Streibert, a former dean of the Harvard Business School and a radio executive, as its first director. "This new structure," writes Shawn Parry-Giles, "placed the USIA at the helm of America's propaganda operations, where it defined and coordinated the themes of the new propaganda offensive against the Soviet Union."[43]

The Jackson Committee was also responsible for the dissolution of the PSB, Truman's answer to his own administration's approach to overcoming the Soviet Union. The PSB only lasted from 1951 to 1953 and failed because of one key issue: its foreign policy objectives impinged on the work of the State Department. The solution to the schism between the State Department and the PSB was to replace the latter with the Operations Coordinating Board (OCB) in September 1953. The OCB's purpose: "get the psychological factor into all operations." In order to free the OCB from bureaucratic difficulties, it was placed in the NSC and formed as an interagency group to follow through on NSC policies. The first executive officer of the OCB listed its objectives as "(a) assuring coordinated implementation of national security policies approved by the President, (b) allocating agency responsibilities, (c) anticipating emerging problems, (d) developing agreed-upon plans of operations, and (e) reporting to the NSC on actions taken." The OCB operated through a system of working groups, each assigned to a particular issue of psychological importance to the United States. A working group, once established, gathered information on the actions of all government departments involved with a

specific issue and formulated an action plan that coordinated an interdepartmental effort. Once a plan was finalized, and agreed upon by the OCB
directors, each department carried out its part of the strategy. The process
was very much like a military operation. Some working groups dealt with
concerns in a particular region, others with sensitive issues such as nuclear
testing. Although the OCB considered public opinion at home as important;
the "climate of opinion" abroad provided the key target audience.[44]

The State–Private Network

In its final report, the Jackson Committee placed an emphasis on the use
of private groups to fight the Cold War. This, of course, was not an entirely
new strategy. In previous decades, from the CPI through to the OWI, the
U.S. government had formed cooperative links with private individuals and
organizations in the realm of public diplomacy. The Cold War continued
the tradition. "The brunt of the battle may be borne by the government, but
like modern war," the acting assistant secretary for Public Affairs, Harold H.
Howland, noted in 1948, "this is a total effort in which we are all equally engaged, whether in a commanding or supporting role." The Smith-Mundt Act,
for instance, demanded that some government propaganda should be sub-
contracted out to private media outlets, educational and cultural exchanges
were often administered in concert with private organizations, and Truman
and Eisenhower frequently appointed men such as Barrett and Jackson from
the commercial field to advise on or direct the nation's information strategy.
The state–private cooperation was not always overt. When U.S. covert operators manipulated the 1948 Italian elections, the CIA clandestinely financed
noncommunist parties and VOA broadcasts to Italy included anticommunist
appeals from prominent Italian-Americans. The Campaign of Truth, moreover, expanded the level of state–private interactions even more deeply.[45]

Once again, the United States was responding, in many ways, to Soviet
tactics. In this case, covert operators were reacting to the host of Soviet
front organizations that, they determined, "spoke out in favor of peace and
solidarity in order to prepare the unwary for subtle indoctrination into the
Communist Ideology." Officials feared that innocent people were being duped
by Soviet groups such as the World Peace Council, the World Federation
of Democratic Youth, the World Federation of Scientific Workers, and the
International Union of Students. "As instruments of psychological warfare,"
argued U.S. policymakers, "their announced aims were so estimable that it
was difficult to devise a defense except in kind."[46] Crucially, George Kennan
and the PPS staff had reached this conclusion in their planning paper, "The

Inauguration of Organized Political Warfare:" "What is proposed here is an operation in the traditional American form: organized public support of resistance to tyranny in foreign countries. Throughout our history, private American citizens have banded together to champion the cause of freedom for people suffering under oppression. Our proposal is that this tradition be revived specifically to further American national interests in the present crisis."[47]

As part of Kennan's broader strategy of political warfare, the U.S. government quickly embarked on an unprecedented peacetime effort to work with and through private businesses, groups, and organizations to support U.S. foreign policy objectives. Washington would thus try to draw upon U.S. voluntary traditions and direct them at the people of the "free world" and the Soviet bloc. This ensured, argues Scott Lucas, that every "sector of U.S. society—business, labor, journalists, youth, women, African Americans, athletes—was to play a part in a total Cold War." Although this "state–private network" had an overt dimension, U.S. officials understood that the general public, both at home and abroad, was wary of official government propaganda. The main thrust of the network was therefore developed covertly to shield state involvement and orchestrated by Frank Wisner's newly created Office of Policy Coordination.[48] The CIA eventually consolidated these operations into its International Organizations Division (IOD). Tom Braden, who led the IOD in its early years, later wrote: "By 1953 we were operating or influencing international organizations in every field where communist fronts had previously seized ground, and in some where they had not even begun to operate."[49]

In general, the government developed the network in two ways. It either formed associations with "preexisting" private groups or created its own new front organizations.[50] An example of the latter was based on the idea of "liberation committees" outlined in Kennan's proposal for political warfare; it was named the National Committee for a Free Europe (NCFE). The NCFE's origins, long obscured, are now known. Because reliable intelligence and information that the United States could gather from the Soviet bloc was distinctly lacking, the PPS suggested the possibility of utilizing refugees who fled the Soviet Union or one of its satellites. There were politicians, cabinet members, writers, and academics, all of whom could be harnessed to breach the Iron Curtain. Kennan and Wisner thought it an area that could indeed reap crucial rewards and, with support from the U.S. intelligence community, the OPC started to prepare the formation of the new émigré group, find it office space in New York (in the Empire State Building), and, of course, funding. The level of OPC monies given to the NCFE for the first year reached

$69,000, but as the NCFE's operations expanded, the amount rose above $16 million in 1952.[51]

The NCFE was incorporated on 11 May 1949, and Joseph Grew, the former undersecretary of state and chair of the new committee, later announced to the media, "We will aid these [exiled] leaders to continue their stand against communism, anticipating the day when the Iron Curtain will fall and Eastern Europe will be ripe for democratic remaking."[52] The NCFE operated as an ostensibly private group, run by eminent U.S. citizens that represented the will of the U.S. people to denounce communism. Notable members included Dwight D. Eisenhower, Henry Luce of Time, Inc., and Dewitt Wallace, the owner of *Reader's Digest*. Nevertheless, the membership of the organization also contained people steeped in government intelligence work. For instance, the group's first president, Dewitt C. Poole, headed the OSS Foreign Nationalities Branch in World War II, and Allen Dulles, OSS director for Europe, and later director of the CIA, chaired the Executive Committee. As the background of these men tends to suggest, the NCFE was far from philanthropic and was designed to work in step with U.S. foreign policy. Secrecy was essential. Under the guise of a private organization, the government officials who controlled the NCFE could operate without the restrictions and accountability that often marred the effectiveness of overt programs.[53]

When the Truman administration enlarged its propaganda offensive in the Campaign of Truth, Barrett and Wisner concurred that the NCFE "would have to speed up its program considerably if it [was] to be of real usefulness in the near future."[54] Radio Free Europe (RFE) rapidly became the main cannon in the organization's armory. Described as a "tough slugging weapon of propaganda that would counter-attack the loud voice of the Kremlin,"[55] an RFE policy handbook explained it would "contribute to the liberation of the nations imprisoned behind the Iron Curtain by sustaining their morale and stimulating in them a spirit of non-cooperation with the Soviet-dominated regimes by which they are, for the time being, ruled."[56] This unique and vastly complicated logistical initiative started out with a fairly feeble 7.5-kilowatt transmitter, named Barbara, based in Germany. The first broadcast on 4 July 1950 was brief, but it merely started the process. In 1951, the NCFE built headquarters for the radio in Munich and soon purchased powerful transmitters to blast the airwaves of Eastern Europe with propaganda. The programming of RFE replicated what might be found in any commercial radio network, with news and educational and cultural programs filling the schedule. But unlike the VOA, RFE did not have the restrictions of an official government organ. The head of radio operations commented that RFE was "unhampered by the niceties of intercourse. We enter this fight with bare fists." Within two years of work, RFE broadcast to six Iron Curtain countries in seven languages.[57]

Still, financial credibility for such a large project was required as cover. The group had to appear to be self-sustaining, even if it was not. To do so, the NCFE created its own fundraising organization, the Crusade for Freedom. Chaired by World War II hero General Lucius Clay, the crusade raised money for RFE, served to heighten the public profile of the NCFE's work, and tried to provoke a national reaction in favor of defeating communism in Europe. Abbott Washburn, a former OSS officer who worked for General Mills in Minneapolis, was drafted to help lead the project. He and an associate selected the Freedom Bell, inspired by the Liberty Bell, as the symbol for the campaign. A firm in England cast the giant ten-ton bell, and it arrived in New York in September 1950. It was the centerpiece of a parade on Broadway and later toured the country for a month aboard the Freedom Train. Those who witnessed the huge metal device were asked to sign Freedom Scrolls, and some 100,000 people obliged. Once the tour was completed, the bell was conveyed to its final resting place in West Berlin, where around 400,000 Germans gathered in the Schoenenberger Platz to watch its installation in the tower of city hall. The crusade, eventually incorporated, established offices in sixteen U.S. cities and garnered a wealth of publicity in newspapers and television. It used celebrities to promote the parades, including sports stars such as Jesse Owens and Luke Appling of the Chicago White Sox, and even conveyed its message behind the Iron Curtain by way of balloons designed to drop millions of leaflets across the continent. Despite all the fanfare, the crusade contributed only $3.5 million to the NCFE in its first two years, not nearly enough to sustain the work of RFE on its own.[58]

In addition to these publicity tactics, the NCFE committed itself to supporting dozens of émigré projects. On the intellectual front, it ran the Mid-European Studies Center filled with "trained research analysts" from disciplines such as history, sociology, economics, and literature. The center published books, pamphlets, and articles on topics such as "The Romanian Oil Industry," "Institutional Changes in the Post-War Economy of Poland," and "Forced Labor in the People's Democracies." Other intellectual initiatives included the East European Inquiry, the Mid-European Law Project, the East European Accessions List, and the Free Europe University in Exile, located in Strasbourg, France. One of the ways in which the NCFE may have "most touched the lives of the greatest number of refugees from behind the Iron Curtain" was through its sponsorship of national councils, bodies filled with exiled politicians from several Eastern European countries.[59] Further projects also spoke to diverse segments of the exile and "imprisoned" community, with money finding its way to groups such as the Assembly of Captive European Nations, the International Peasant Union, the Hungarian Student and Youth Service, the International Center of Free Trade Unionists in Exile, the Federation of Former Hungarian Political Prisoners, the Christian Democratic Union of Central Europe, and the Hungarian Boy Scouts. For the NCFE, the "importance of these exile organizations" lay in their "symbolic representation of their countrymen's aspirations for freedom and independence."[60]

Freedom and independence, then, was the ultimate goal. In a communication with Jackson that chastised Soviet propaganda, Washburn wrote, "Their purpose is to convince the prisoner peoples that it is hopeless to resist. They want to create a vacuum of despair. Into this vacuum we must shine a new light of hope—a new vista of a very different future." Washburn continued: "The American ideal has within it the dynamism to undermine the Soviet empire . . . provided we can get it across and show that we mean it. Our success in this job may well determine whether we can, indeed, win World War III without fighting it."[61] Washburn's letter reveals the depth of faith that some government officials had in psychological warfare. The activities of the NCFE are also demonstrative of the shift in the U.S. government's commitment to propaganda as the Cold War unfolded. For only a few short years after World War II, the White House had largely dismantled its machinery for psychological warfare. By 1948, the mechanism was in swift rehabilitation and, through overt and covert means, it would help to mobilize U.S. culture and U.S. cultural representatives to wage the Cold War. Sports could not be insulated from this total war; the Olympics could not be excluded from such a battle. Indeed, by the time the Cold War had started on its long course, the Olympic Games had become the largest and most prestigious international athletic festival in the world. That made it, in turn, a perfect target for psychological exploitation.

2 The United States, the Soviet Union, and the Olympic Games

In May 1951, the membership of the International Olympic Committee (IOC) gathered in Vienna, Austria, for the organization's Forty-Sixth General Session. Leopold Figl, the Austrian federal chancellor, opened the meeting and welcomed those before him to the city and to the country. "I believe that hardly any other institution is as well suited to bring [people] together as the Olympic Games, and to teach the many different nations how to respect and to understand one another," Figl proclaimed. "Understanding and mutual respect are the preconditions for a proper, and above all for a peaceful, approach towards those that live beyond one's own frontiers." The audience, no doubt, would have nodded in approval when hearing these words. Yet over the coming days, the IOC would debate and vote upon a range of issues that might have seemed more appropriate for discussion in the United Nations, let alone in an assembly of sporting advocates and administrators. One of the most pressing matters on the agenda was a recognition request from the recently formed national Olympic committee of the Soviet Union. By this point, there was never much doubt that the IOC's membership would welcome the Soviets with open arms, at least publicly and officially. As long as the "reds" respected and followed the rules of the Olympic Charter, then they, like any other nation, would be granted the right to partake in what Figl called a "noble manifestation of peace."[1] So it proved. In 1952, Soviet athletes marched into an Olympic stadium for the first time at the Helsinki summer games.

Many observers in the Western world hoped that the participation of Stalin's athletes in the Olympics would lessen the tensions of the Cold War and introduce the Soviet Union to ideas on fair play and good sportsmanship. In the months leading up to Helsinki, however, others could see darker issues at stake. The influential sports columnist Arthur Daley argued in the *New York Times* that the Soviets were only heading to Finland to promote communist propaganda. "This isn't just another sports-loving nation joining fellow sportsmen," asserted Daley. "This is the Soviet Union where the Kremlin controls muscles just as it controls thoughts."[2] Despite Daley's flair for the dramatic, there was a great deal of substance to his point. Ultimately Stalin made the decision to send a Soviet team to Helsinki, and he did so only because he thought the Soviet Union could win the most medals.[3] In addition, Daley and the countless Americans who shared his perspective feared that communism was corrupting the spirit and nature of sport itself, as personified in the Olympic Movement. But if there is anything we know about modern international sport, it is that it is a cultural practice fraught with contradictions and double standards. The international sporting system, within which the Olympics reside, emerged in the nineteenth and twentieth centuries as a force of peace and goodwill. It also grew in strength and global popularity because it was built to accommodate national rivalries. The Soviet Union may have brought politics into the Olympic Movement, but they were not the first to do so, nor would they be the last.

The Olympic Games and Their Politics

The British historian Eric Hobsbawm has noted that during the thirty or so years that preceded the outbreak of World War I, Europeans "enthusiastically" mass-produced, or "invented," traditions. One "of the most significant of the new social practices" in this era, writes Hobsbawm, was the "institutionalization of most sports on a national and even international scale."[4] At a time, therefore, when international sport was gradually coming to life, a French aristocrat named Baron Pierre de Coubertin invited a host of social elites to the Sorbonne in Paris for an international congress that would forever alter the global sporting community.[5] Held in June 1894, the Sorbonne congress witnessed the revival of an ancient athletic festival that had largely been in abeyance for more than fifteen hundred years. By the time that this small assembly of wealthy and influential individuals had eaten the last of the food, consumed a sizable amount of champagne, applauded the lavish entertainment, and concluded their deliberations, they had voted to establish the modern Olympic Games and formed the International Olympic Committee to administer the fledging movement. Two years later, the first of Coubertin's games were watched by thousands of excited spectators in Athens, Greece.

A range of historical events brought the baron to this climactic moment. Born in 1863, Pierre de Coubertin was still a child when France was defeated by Prussia in the war of 1870–71. He, like so many of his countrymen, was devastated by the French capitulation. In his adult years, Coubertin pressed the French government to initiate a national program of physical education that would restore France's military strength and fortify a nobility "imprisoned in the ruins of a dead past."[6] The type of physical education he preferred was very specific. Rather than recommending a form of gymnastics so prevalent in several European countries, Coubertin was inspired by the organized sports that were played in the public schools of England and the colleges of America. The baron became a disciple of the cult of athleticism. "His romanticized version of Anglo-American organized, competitive athletics," comments John Lucas, "was rivalled only by his youthful conviction that these nations were the greatest powers in the world, due, in large measure, to a tradition of pervasive, virile, honorable and exhilarating games-playing."[7] But Coubertin's hopes of reenergizing the physical condition of France's population through competitive sports would be dashed when French authorities failed to share his enthusiasm.

He turned instead to a new project. Although Coubertin's ideas on the value of physical education were shaped by a number of social thinkers, his philosophy was, nonetheless, deeply influenced by an English physician named William Penny Brookes. This philanthropic doctor spent much of his life trying to raise the mental and physical competency of the local people in his hometown of Much Wenlock, in Shropshire. Aside from educational initiatives, Brookes also established Olympian games, an athletic festival for locals that included some of the events and pageantry from the ancient Olympic program. In the course of time, he and Coubertin exchanged several letters, until Brookes eventually invited his friend to visit England. Coubertin accepted the offer and watched a special installment of the Wenlock Olympian games before the doctor filled his ears with the history of the ancient festival and previous attempts to rekindle the Olympics in Greece. Before this meeting, there is no evidence to suggest that Coubertin desired to revive the Olympic Games. Yet the baron took the idea, claimed it for his own, and from there took a path that led to the 1894 congress in Paris. For the next thirty years, he would direct and govern the Olympic Movement as an administrator, as the IOC president, and as the intellectual architect of Olympism.[8]

The young festival grew slowly and not without setbacks. Indeed, the larger the games became, the larger were its complications. In many ways, Coubertin was to blame for the troubles. A foundational principle of Olympism was his belief in the merits of peaceful internationalism. "Wars break out," wrote the baron, "because nations misunderstand each other. We shall not have peace until the prejudices which now separate the different races shall have been outlived. To attain this end, what better means than to bring the youth of all countries periodically together for amicable trials of muscular strength and agility?"[9] Like many other adherents of nineteenth-century liberalism, Coubertin believed that nationality was "the indispensable core of individual identity."[10] Sport, he held, could and should be a lightning rod for the exaltation of national identity. "One may be filled with desire to see the colors of one's club or college triumph in a national meeting," he wrote in 1896, "but how much stronger is the feeling when the colors of one's country are at stake!"[11] The structure and organization of the Olympic Movement therefore reflected Coubertin's preoccupation with promoting internationalism through national rivalry. Almost from the very start, athletes were required to compete at the games for a nation and had to be members of a national Olympic committee. Olympic stadiums of the time were festooned, and still are, with national flags and patriotic symbolism.[12] This fundamental aspect of the games has made them inherently political. For while the games may well contribute to mutual understanding and even peace, they also serve as a barometer to measure one nation against another.

This became more evident with each passing festival. In 1908, for instance, the athletic rivalry between Great Britain and the United States descended into full-blown animosity. The British organizers in London forgot to erect the U.S. flag in the stadium, an act deprecated by U.S. Olympic officials, and the relationship between the two nations became increasingly fractious after a series of controversial events both on and off the track. Perturbed by the ill will generated between the two countries, the U.S. president, Theodore Roosevelt, grumbled, "I do not believe in these international matches . . . Where the feeling is so intense it is almost impossible that there should not be misunderstandings."[13] Others shared this view. The premium placed on achieving athletic superiority at the games, combined with the ever growing political incidents that had accompanied the festival since its inception, left some to even wonder whether the Olympics were "doomed." When more controversy tainted the 1924 games in Paris, a correspondent for *The Times* of London contended that the movement's aim of binding the "youth of all nations in a brotherhood so close and loving that it would form a bulwark against the outbreak of all international animosities" was surely an impossibility. "There has for a long time been profound and widespread misgiving," judged the writer, "whether the Games had not in practice served to inflame animosities rather than to allay them."[14]

A little more than a decade later, the politicization of the Olympics seemed to reach new heights when Hitler's Germany hosted the 1936 summer games in Berlin. The IOC had awarded the festival to the city before Hitler ascended into power, and the organization's members wondered how or whether the German leader would support the staging of the games. For Hitler, the games were in fact quite timely. A few days before he withdrew Germany from the League of Nations, Hitler acknowledged that the country was in a "very bad and difficult situation internationally." The games, he believed, provided a perfect opportunity to "show the world what the new Germany can do culturally." Although what scholars now refer to as the "Nazi Olympics" were an organizational and logistical triumph, it prompted critics to further question the integrity of the IOC for allowing a festival to occur in a country where, among other things, the rights of Jewish citizens were systemically removed.[15] One historian was moved to comment that the 1936 games "were an obscuring layer of shimmering froth on a noxious wave of destiny."[16]

The U.S. Olympic Experience

That the Olympics quickly emerged as a powerful medium to promote the state and political ideology naturally lent the festival to the propaganda battles of the Cold War. Here was a stage where deeds could be trumpeted and manipulated for psychological significance. Without a doubt, the games provided a global arena for athletes from the east and west to compete head to head in a symbolic war. But there was more to it than this. The manner of participation also was significant. The rules for entry had to be both followed and revered. But *the* most critical regulation of all was that athletes had to be pure and legitimate amateurs. In this sense, the IOC ensured that the movement buttressed the prevailing athletic doctrine preached in much of Europe and also in America.

Invented by upper-middle-class Victorians in the second half of the nineteenth century, amateurism became an immensely powerful sporting ideology that guided not only "*who* could play but also *how* they played." The ideal amateur "stood modest in victory, gracious in defeat, honorable, courageous, not fanatical or too partisan, and avoided elaborate training or specialization." Just as important, the amateur also played for the "love of the game" and not, under any circumstances, for financial rewards.[17] This last aspect of the amateur code became the most controversial, as it turned into a mechanism to bar the working classes from competing in certain sporting events or from membership in particular exclusive clubs. According to these arbitrary regulations, a "gentleman" was regarded as an "amateur" and a "professional" as a member of the "working class." In time, the rule received amendments that stipulated that no athlete who derived profit from sport either directly or indirectly could retain amateur status. Many sports, such as soccer and rugby league, simply ignored the snobbery and became fully professional. Other sports, such as track and field, sailed against the currents of commercialization and zealously enforced the amateur ideal. At any rate, as the concept of amateurism began to spread and drop roots in various countries, the rule itself became subject to multiple interpretations that depended on when and where it was applied. Coubertin was actually ambivalent on the question of amateurism, even though he adored the philosophy of British-style Victorian sport. But the pragmatist in him accepted that in order to make the movement work, he needed the support of the amateur clique that dominated international sport. By taking the amateur rule and making it part of the Olympic structure, the baron and his colleagues guaranteed nearly a century of relentless furor over what amateurism meant and who was following the letter or even the spirit of the rule.[18]

In few other countries was amateurism so forcefully promoted and protected as in the United States. U.S. sporting traditions had gradually crystallized throughout the nineteenth century as the nation evolved into an industrialized and urbanized state. Although Americans, unlike the majority of people around the world, did not take to the organized team sports developed in England, they did adopt and glorify the amateur ideal. Just as in England, however, amateurism did not guide the organization of all U.S. sports—baseball, for instance, was amateur only for a short time before the sheer popularity and commercial potential of the "national pastime" took it almost inevitably toward professionalism. Rather, Americans poured their passion for the amateur code into two main areas of their physical culture: collegiate athletics and track and field. In terms of the latter, "apostles of amateurism" moved to consolidate their control over the various track and field disciplines when, in 1888, the New York Athletic Club and eight other clubs formed the Amateur Athletic Union (AAU) of the United States. The organization grew into an inexorable force by diligently regulating which athletes could compete at its sanctioned events and barring for life those who elected not to adhere to its amateur rule. By the end of the century, the AAU's national championship was regarded as the national championship of America. Indeed, the sheer influence of the organization, and the prevalence of track and field events at the Olympics, ensured that it would also become a central cog in the administration of the U.S. Olympic effort.[19]

In spite of the waxing power of the AAU over amateur athletics, U.S. participants at the first three modern Olympic Games journeyed to the host cities as individuals, funded by wealthy patrons or clubs. The temporary American Olympic Committee (AOC) was formed for each of these early festivals, but not until 1906 did it start to select a national team or raise money for it. The committee, filled largely by the wealthy bureaucrats of the AAU, operated without a constitution or by-laws and was, at best, "loosely structured." It also steadily became incapable of organizing the ever-growing U.S. Olympic presence. By the 1920s, the task of assembling and funding the U.S. Olympic team had become a sizeable logistical operation, all of which considerably overwhelmed what amounted to a special committee. The AOC's disastrous transportation arrangements for the 1920 games in Antwerp, which included the athletes crossing the Atlantic in a rat-infested ship, put the need for reform firmly under the public spotlight. In 1921, the AOC Committee on Reorganization devised and discussed plans for a single permanent Olympic structure that, in the same year, resulted in the creation of the American Olympic Association (AOA).[20]

These bureaucratic changes were demonstrative of the budding U.S. obsession with the Olympic Games. After all, Coubertin's creation provided the most pronounced avenue for Americans to compete in international competition against foreign representatives. The uniquely U.S. pastimes of baseball and football were, for one reason or another, unable to gain a foothold in foreign markets flooded by British sports and games. Outside the United States, a child was far more likely to kick a soccer ball than to try to hit a homerun. At the Olympics, by contrast, Americans could jump, throw, or run against athletes from around the planet. The Olympic format also helped to feed and shape U.S. national identity. Almost immediately, the U.S. media began to suggest that the success of Uncle Sam's athletes was synonymous with the nation's strength and prestige. U.S. sports officials trumpeted a similar theme. In the process of evaluating the achievements of the United States at the 1912 Stockholm games, the AOC president, James Sullivan, explained that "the Americans went on a mission." "This mission," Sullivan opined, "was to create a good feeling; to show the type of man this great country of ours produces; to bring to them the type of sportsman that comes from this glorious nation of ours, and to show the world that we play the game fairly."[21] Clarence Bush, the publicity director of the AOA, and a keen essayist, also wrote several short articles on the subject. In his "Americanism in the Olympic Games," Bush mused over why America's democracy had triumphed at the Olympic Games "over rivals from aristocratic, monarchist and despotic nations." The answer, he declared, "is found in our competitive way of life, surviving from pioneer days, giving all an equal chance but handsomely rewarding the fittest in all realms of activity."[22]

In other respects, too, U.S. athletic missionaries began to leave their mark on the development of international sport and the Olympic Movement. The powerful group of media and business moguls who organized the 1932 Los

Angeles summer games, writes Barbara Keys, managed to transform "the Olympics from a relatively marginal and elitist event into an entertainment extravaganza with wide popular appeal." By staging a festival inspired by U.S. consumerist culture, Los Angeles introduced the Olympics to new levels of commercialization, publicity, and celebrity glamour. Refusing to be stifled by the Depression, the organizers created, promoted, and sold a massive spectacle with state-of-the-art communications technology and marketing techniques. Foreign and domestic companies used the venue as a platform to sell their products and to raise the status of their brands, while Hollywood celebrities mingled with crowds throughout the city. Signifying the lasting legacy of Los Angeles as a blueprint for future festivals, officials charged with orchestrating the 1936 games in Berlin looked on and eagerly took notes. Yet the impact of the United States on the global community of sport far exceeded event management. During the 1920s, and particularly the 1930s, U.S. sports officials facilitated thousands of overseas tours for athletes, coaches, trainers, and managers. These exchanges, notes Keys, "disseminated information and techniques, as well as ideas, attitudes, and perceptions that shaped foreign views of the United States and Americans' attitudes about their place in the world." AAU officials believed that sport could forge a climate of international harmony, that it was democracy in action. It was their responsibility, furthermore, to send this message far and wide.[23]

While U.S. athletes were fueling and sculpting national pride at the early Olympic festivals, U.S. political leaders were championing the connection between physical activity and national virility. Theodore Roosevelt, a famous advocate of the "strenuous life," praised the moral qualities that could be learned from competitive athletics. In 1907, he told an audience of Harvard students, "In any republic, courage is a prime necessity for the average citizen if he is to be a good citizen; and he needs physical courage no less than moral courage, the courage that dares as well as the courage that endures, the courage that will fight valiantly alike against the foes of the soul and the foes of the body."[24] Be that as it may, U.S. Olympic officials also derived a great deal of pride from the private traditions of their work. Their pride was indicative of the historical development of sport in the United States. During the early nineteenth century, Alexis de Tocqueville famously noted the huge "production of voluntary associations" in the United States, and his observation certainly applied to the nation's sporting establishment. Like so many other clubs, teams, and organizations that were formed during the rise of U.S. sporting culture, both the AAU and the AOA were strictly private endeavors; they did not answer to the U.S. government and handled their own affairs in what often amounted to splendid isolation.[25] "National subsidies as granted in other countries have never been favoured here," remarked a U.S. Olympic official in 1932, "and it has always been felt that the sport loving public of the United States would willingly defray the cost of sending their teams to the Games."[26] The public, it seems, never seriously disputed this state of affairs and neither, for that matter, did the government.

This division between U.S. Olympic authorities and the state closely tracked an important element of the IOC's general operational structure. The IOC is, for the most part, a self-electing club that constantly strives to maintain its independence from any government. Coubertin once announced that "the very fact that this committee is self-recruiting makes it immune to all political interference, and it is not swayed by intense nationalism nor influenced by corporative interests." Always keenly aware of potential challengers to this autonomy, he was deeply suspicious of the "selfish and gigantic figure of the state." Even though Coubertin's assessment of the IOC's "immunity" from diplomats and politicians was somewhat exaggerated, the organization has managed to move at its own pace for much of its existence. The same ideas apply, of course, for national Olympic committees. For a national committee to gain recognition from the IOC, it had to be able to demonstrate that it was independent from its national government.[27] But like so many other IOC regulations, this rule was bent and often broken by Olympic authorities in many countries and was completely ignored by fascist or communist regimes.

During the Cold War, the U.S. government and U.S. sports officials proudly pointed to the political independence of the U.S. Olympic Movement and repeatedly weighed it against the example of the Soviet Union. It was not an unreasonable observation. Unlike several European countries, the U.S. government pursued a generally isolationist policy toward international sport and the Olympics prior to the Cold War.[28] There were, however, some instances that illustrate how the state and private spheres were not entirely separate before the battle for hearts and minds significantly eroded the national tradition. Although some scholars have noted that fascist and communist states were the first to mobilize sport for diplomatic ends, Mark Dyreson has argued that the United States indulged in a similar exercise during the 1920s and 1930s. Reacting to requests from U.S. sports businesses that were looking for global markets to exploit, the U.S. Department of Commerce called upon Foreign Service posts to gather information on the demand for certain sports and sporting products overseas. Dyreson contends that through these diplomatic channels Washington became a "willing partner in opening . . . new markets by promoting American Olympic teams as international advertisements for American ways of life."[29]

Yet state involvement was more an exception than the general rule. The U.S. government's ambivalence to officially sponsored sporting diplomacy before the Cold War mirrored its ambivalence to cultural diplomacy in general.

Culture was an area in which private groups were to take the reins. When a cascade of U.S. athletes toured throughout the world in the 1930s, it was the AAU, not the State Department, that organized the endeavors. Government officials expressed support for these tours and their role in contributing to "international accord," but nothing more. A rare deviation from this policy occurred, though, when the Franklin D. Roosevelt administration began to engage in cultural diplomacy in Latin America to counteract Nazi propaganda in the Western Hemisphere. This program, under the Office of the Coordinator of Inter-American Affairs (CIAA), housed a small sports section directed by the U.S. Olympic official Asa S. Bushnell. The CIAA organized several projects in this field, such as a tour of Latin America by the U.S. Lawn Tennis Team and a multievent trip to the United States of a South American swimming team. Speaking on the activities of his office, Bushnell explained, "Sports lovers of all countries speak the same language. Their friendly rivalries bring normal development of mutual understanding and mutual liking which cannot be as fully attained in any other way." The work of the sports section ended when the United States entered the war, but Bushnell's sentiments on the role of sport in foreign diplomacy were later echoed by U.S. propaganda experts in the Cold War years.[30]

The division between state and private realms of society also generally held sway in U.S. Olympic matters, although this traditional arrangement was put on pause during the AOC's preparations for the 1920 games in Antwerp. The AOC had been limping along in its temporary status since 1896, before a series of misfortunes further complicated the committee's work. Several key administrators, Sullivan the chief among them, passed away or resigned between 1914 and 1919 and left the organization in some disarray. The carnage of World War I—which had also caused the cancelation of the 1916 games—ceased in 1918 and left the AOC precious little time to raise funds for the trip to Belgium. The AOC president, Gustavus Town Kirby, appealed to the U.S. government for financial assistance. He had good cause for optimism. The U.S. president, Woodrow Wilson, was an honorary president of the AOC, the U.S. military had representatives on the committee, and many members of the armed forces competed on the U.S. Olympic team. When Congress subsequently debated the issue, the heavy baggage of tradition was set to one side in order to accommodate the extraordinary circumstances of the AOC's request. The U.S. team was given use of the U.S. Navy's *Princess Matoika*, a ship that had just returned from Europe filled with the bodies of dead soldiers. The government had provided unprecedented aid to the AOC, but when the athletes on the U.S. team returned home from Belgium, they directed a torrent of abuse at the organization for the appalling conditions

aboard the vessel. "If I had it to do over again, I would do many things dif-
ferently," Kirby admitted.[31]

But this case aside, the U.S. Olympic team was funded by voluntary donations and coordinated by enthusiasts in the private sphere. Even the 1936
Olympics, one of the most controversial in history, failed to draw an intervention from Washington. A string of reports sent to the State Department by
George S. Messersmith, the consul-general in Berlin, gave the White House
full warning of the Nazi's activities in relation to the games. Messersmith
wrote that "as the Jews under the Nuremburg Laws are not first class German citizens, there is no longer any doubt that all persons with any strain of
Jewish blood, no matter how attenuated, will not be permitted to compete for
Germany." He implored the White House to inform the U.S. Olympic Committee of these German transgressions, but the State Department declined.
When the U.S. public and sports officials debated furiously whether to send
a team to Berlin, the Roosevelt administration remained aloof from the dilemma. The secretary of state, Cordell Hull, captured the prevailing attitude
in the White House when he stated that the issue did not "fall within the
competence of any agency of this government but it is a matter exclusively
for determination by the private organizations directly concerned." [32]

No American believed in these Olympic ideals more, or defended them
with greater zeal, than Avery Brundage. Throughout his life, Brundage gradually emerged as a towering figure in international sport. Born in 1887 and
raised in Chicago, he graduated from the University of Illinois with a degree
in civil engineering and later became a self-made multimillionaire, mostly
through investments in real estate and construction. A fine sportsmen in
high school and college, Brundage later became a member of the Chicago
Athletic Association, where he diligently trained for the "all-round" competition, another name for the decathlon. Such was his ability that he qualified
for the 1912 U.S. Olympic team, quit his job, and embarked on the voyage to
Stockholm. As his biographer notes, it was possibly this sacrifice that drove
Brundage to expect a similar effort from others when it came to enforcing
the amateur rule. In an odd turn of events, Brundage failed to finish the decathlon, electing to withdraw after having fallen far behind in total points. He
regretted the decision for the rest of his life, but the Olympic experience filled
him with joy and admiration: "My conversion, along with many others, to
Coubertin's religion, the Olympic Movement, was complete." After Brundage
returned from Stockholm, he won the all-round athletic championship of
the United States on three occasions (1914, 1916, 1918) and developed into a
first-rate handball player. The next phase of his sporting career brought him
world renown as an administrator. He served as the president of the AAU

from 1928 to 1935 (except for 1933) and led the AOA from 1928 until 1953. In 1945, he became vice president of the IOC and, in 1952, he was elected the organization's president. He presided over the IOC until 1972. One of his last, and most famous, acts in this leadership role was to announce that the "Games must go on" after the catastrophic terrorist attack at the 1972 Munich Olympics.[33]

Considering the time period that spanned Brundage's involvement with the Olympics, it seems incredible that he could not fully accept that it was a political event. On occasion, however, he conceded the contradictions. Brundage liked to tell the story of when he complimented the president of Venezuela on the absence of politics at the Bolivar games, whereupon the Venezuelan responded, "Ah, but that is the best politics."[34] Still, anyone who reads the correspondence of Brundage cannot but notice his relentless repetition of the Olympic credo that sport and politics should not mix. In just the same way, he could not repeat enough that all those who competed at the games should be amateurs. Coubertin was never as boisterous about amateurism as Brundage. Few in history were. In protesting these two pillars of Olympic conduct—politics and amateurism—Brundage would seldom recoil or stand aside from battle, justifying his decisions by quoting the rules as written in the Olympic Charter.[35] His personality was suited to the task. A brusque, obstinate, and pedantic individual, his tenure as IOC president attracted worldwide criticism. To some he was anachronistic. To others he was a devout believer in the Olympic Games and was responsible for holding the movement together during some of its most trying years.[36]

The Soviet Olympic Experience

By the close of the nineteenth century, many of the modern sports developed in Great Britain had spread across much of Europe and also penetrated into Russia. Like the United States, Russia had one representative in the inaugural IOC, and a small team of Russian athletes competed in the London games in 1908. In 1911, Russian IOC members contributed to the formation of the country's national Olympic committee and arranged for a large contingent of well over a hundred athletes to attend the 1912 games in Stockholm. Russian newspapers, which had covered the earliest Olympic festivals, followed the events in Sweden with even greater interest, but journalists were disappointed to report that the team's considerable size was not matched by its achievements. A meager haul of medals prompted the government to apply more organization to sports, a considerable task when taking into account the vast size of the country. Yet the fruits of this limited exercise were not reaped by the tsars. World War I eliminated the 1916 Olympics, and the Russian Revolution subsequently removed the monarchy from its despotic rule only a year later. As a result of the latter event, the country was transformed into a communist state within the Soviet Union. The Soviets thus inherited a weak sporting infrastructure, although the amendments made prior to the revolution at least ensured that the feeble administration was centralized.[37]

The Soviet Union moved further away from, rather than closer to, the burgeoning world of international sport. Competitions like the Olympic Games, led by European and American social and economic elites, did not suit the doctrine preached in the Kremlin, nor did the IOC appear to be a welcoming home. Some scholars of the Olympic Games have been inclined to look upon the IOC's relationship with communism and see only the workings of an organization that put up impenetrable walls against Marxism. Carolyn Marvin, for instance, has claimed that "Avery Brundage's Olympic movement was eternally mobilized against Communism."[38] At any rate, after the Russian Revolution, it was initially the choice of the Soviet Union to avoid the Olympic Games and all other "bourgeois" sports competitions. Sport would serve a new role in Soviet society, distinct from the capitalistic concoction experienced in much of the West. This presented a doctrinal challenge. Although Marx was given to predicting the process of the communist revolution, he was not so keen on producing a blueprint for its realization. As the philosopher Peter Singer notes, though Marx was confident in dealing with the past and his present, he could not predict "the form to be taken by the new society to be built by the free human beings of the new era."[39] This process was made none the easier when Marx's pen fell silent; and sport was a case in point. So little did Marx write on physical activity that it is futile to lay undue weight on his scattered quotes that do exist on the matter. Similarly, Lenin's writings were far from voluminous on the subject. But, as James Riordan suggests, when contemplating the thought of Marx and Lenin on sport, it is the "implications of their teaching that are generally referred to."[40]

In the 1920s, Soviet sport was characterized by a proletarian physical culture that was diverse in form and in theory. Soviet physical educators and state organizations—be it trade unions, the army, the Komsomol, and so on—all accepted that physical culture was vital to the population's health, military preparation, economic productivity, education, and ideological and political understanding, but they pursued these aims in a variety of ways. Some educators promoted "labour gymnastics, corrective exercises, games, pageants and excursions," while others saw the benefits of some sports. Rallying against the forces of capitalism, Soviet authorities at least agreed on the need to eschew the individualism, competition, and record-breaking elements of Western sport.[41] Yet even this rough consensus was flawed. The national sport of soccer, for instance, was rife with professionalism, commercial motivations, a win-at-all-costs mentality, and "crooked business deals." It was not uncommon, moreover, for players to hack and kick one another or for fans to fight and riot.[42]

The Soviet Union engaged in international competition to a very limited degree, mainly through its participation in and manipulation of worker's sport, a socialist movement that rejected the ideology of Western sports competitions such as the Olympic Games.[43] But the rise of Hitler's Germany, with its pronounced hostility to communism, pushed Stalin to introduce a Popular Front against the Nazis by reaching out for support from capitalist countries. In 1934, the Soviet Union joined the League of Nations. Domestically, on the other hand, the Soviet Union was also moving toward more "conservative social and cultural policies" and a push to match or even exceed the industrial output of "bourgeois" nations. As well, like so many other countries, the Soviets came to view international sport as a strategic device in propaganda and diplomacy. Soon mass forms of noncompetitive physical culture were replaced by the slogan "catch up to and overtake bourgeois records in sport." To administer the movement, the organization of sport became increasingly centralized with a greater emphasis on training methods and tactics. Drawn into the "imagined community" of globalized sport, the Soviet Union shifted away from its isolation and began to seek contacts and exchanges with capitalist countries. This process started when a delegation of Soviet athletes competed in a series of events in Czechoslovakia, which included a highly publicized soccer match between Spartak Moscow and Židenice Brno.[44]

The only thing that stopped the Soviet Union from becoming a full member of the international sporting community was its absence from international sports federations. In general, many federations were reluctant to accept them. When pressed on the issue in 1934, the IOC president, Count Henri de Baillet-Latour, unreservedly opposed welcoming the "reds." At the same time, Soviet attitudes toward the games had hardly been friendly, with the communist media regularly labeling the Olympics a "bourgeois invention striving to plunge the world into new wars."[45] And war did soon arrive, but for other reasons. Hitler's quest for Lebensraum had yielded the dictator most of Europe. Not satisfied with his conquests, though, Hitler also sent an immense invading force into Soviet territory. When the Soviets managed to repel the invasion, only after suffering monumental losses, it took a new position in international affairs and expanded its sphere of influence. In the postwar years, the demonstration of athletic prowess became a powerful tool of communist propaganda in the changed international conditions. A government decree published in 1945 spoke of the need to "stimulate greater sports proficiency" and to "award monetary prizes for outstanding sports results." Western observers looked on in great surprise as the Soviet Union began to join international sports federations. When federation officials raised the matter of the amateur rule, Soviet authorities reversed the resolution on monetary rewards, but this was only a sop.[46] The state-controlled Soviet sport system was not changed because Western sports federations asked for it. The determination to win was now policy. A Communist Party resolution from 1948 declared that government sports committees were "to spread sport to every corner of the land, to raise the level of skill and, on that basis, to help Soviet athletes win world supremacy in major sports in the immediate future."[47]

The Cold War and the Olympic Games

By 1945, it was clear that the Soviet Union had decided to reverse its policy on competing in Western sports organizations, not only intending for Soviet athletes to perform in international events, but also intending to dominate them. When the IOC reconvened after World War II, it could not avoid the issue. The Olympic mission of peaceful internationalism demanded that if the Soviet Union asked for recognition, then the IOC should give it. The preeminence of the Olympics as an international sports event was also at stake. As the IOC president, Sweden's J. Sigfrid Edström, duly acknowledged, not to accept the Soviet Union into the IOC would leave "the athletic world divided in two big sections—East and West."[48] Edström's comment still did not make the decision easy. The very design and administration of the Soviet sports system, when placed side by side with the requirements of the Olympic Charter, could not have been more different. Primarily, the charter called for a national Olympic committee to be independent of government control—and, thus, free from political influence—and financially self-sufficient, while the athletes that the committee represents must be purely amateur. Reports on the professionalism of Soviet athletes left Brundage "lukewarm" about inviting the Soviet Union into the movement, while Edström knew full well that "Of course everything in Russia is governed by the state."[49] To include the Soviet Union meant that many members of the IOC had to rethink long-held perceptions about what sport represented as an ideal, and whether that ideal should be open to interpretation. Edström put this question to his fellow IOC members: "From the Western point of view we must question ourselves if the Russian athletes can be considered as amateurs. We must face the fact that many of them are professionals. We have thus a different idea of sport in Eastern Europe and in the West. The question is how shall we proceed in the future."[50]

Both Brundage and Edström wrestled with personal politics on the issue of communist sport. As a conservative Republican and self-made millionaire, Brundage undoubtedly preferred capitalism to Marxism.[51] Edström's thoughts on communism dovetailed with those of his colleague. An aristocrat by birth, he was trained as a civil engineer and became president of the Swedish General Electric Company in 1903. Sport was Edström's obsession. He competed in the 100-meter race at the first Olympics in Athens, later founded the International Amateur Athletic Federation (IAAF), and led the organizing committee for the 1912 Olympics in Stockholm. When the IOC president, Count Henri de Baillet-Latour, died in 1942, Edström served as acting president for four years until, in 1946, he was elected president. Politically, Edström has been described as "arch conservative" and right-wing. Like Brundage, he displayed strains of anti-Semitism.[52] There was no ambiguity, however, when he spoke of communism. In a private letter written to friends and relatives in 1950, he summed up his feelings about postwar Europe. He recalled a conversation with the English ambassador in Stockholm before the hostilities, in which Edström asked the gentleman why "England made a contract with Russia to fight Hitler," since Stalin was a "thief, bank robber and murderer." Edström complained that after the war the Soviet Union had gained control in Eastern Europe only by "treachery and force": "Why do the Allied Powers not wake up? Do they not see the danger? It is horrible!"[53] While these opinions frequently bubbled to the surface, they did not rule the decisions Edström made as president of the IOC; nor were Brundage's prejudices about communism allowed to dictate whether the Soviet Union could gain recognition. The rules of the Olympic Charter had to be overlooked, and they were. This predicament never sat easily with either man and remained a constant aggravation to Brundage throughout his leadership. But as Allen Guttmann has argued, "Despite the fact that Edström, Brundage . . . and all the other influential members of the IOC were vehemently anti-Communist, their public commitment to the universalistic ideal of Olympism was stronger than their private hostility toward communism."[54]

When communist regimes were established in postwar Eastern Europe, the sporting culture in the region was readjusted to mirror that of the Soviet Union. Again, the IOC knew it. "It is impossible, therefore, to find an NOC [national Olympic committee] in any Communist country that is free and not under complete state control," lamented Brundage in 1950.[55] Despite this state of affairs, the problem of recognition was not quite so difficult for several of the countries in the Soviet bloc. Many already had a national committee in good standing from before the war, and their membership would not change. But the Soviet Union had never been a member of the Olympic Movement. The first step in the process of recognition was membership in the various international sports federations that cooperated with the IOC. In his capacity as president of the IAAF, Edström offered an olive branch to Soviet sports officials in 1945, a gesture that received no immediate response. When the Soviets finally reacted to the overtures, they presented a set of three demands: Russian should be made an official IAAF language, a Soviet representative must be elected to the IAAF Executive Committee, and fascist Spain should be jettisoned from the organization. These bold requests were tartly refused. When the Soviet conditions were withdrawn, the IAAF accepted the application.[56]

Likewise, in 1947 the IOC chancellor, Otto Mayer, twice encouraged the chairman of the Soviet Sports Committee, Nikolai Romanov, to form a national Olympic committee and join the Olympic Movement in time for the 1948 festivals. Again, there was silence. Romanov did not simply ignore the letters from the IOC out of rudeness. He could not act without the permission of his political superiors, and the evidence indicates that they themselves were undecided. Not everyone believed in the need to enter the Olympics, and Stalin apparently indicated that a team should be sent only if victory could be guaranteed. Before Romanov's superiors fully digested his assurances on Soviet athletic prospects, a purge of pro-Western elements in Soviet society kept proposals to compete in a "capitalist" sports festival firmly out of the question. Not until 1951 did preparations to enter the Olympics become a priority in Moscow. The 1948 games in London came and passed without the involvement of the Soviet Union. The British government had tried repeatedly to get a Soviet team in London, with one idealistic Olympic official arguing that it would be "a starting point for new thinking about international relations among the peoples of the world." Nevertheless, the British efforts were in vain. Only Soviet government officials made their way to England, and did so only to observe.[57]

When the Soviets attempted the same three-demand maneuver with their application to the IOC, they were again forced to reconsider the doomed strategy. Eventually, a cable from Moscow confirmed that Soviet officials accepted the IOC statutes and would apply for official recognition at the IOC's Vienna session in 1951. The Soviets made no demands in the communication and put Konstantin Andrianov forward as the Soviet candidate for membership in the IOC.[58] Brundage observed that the behavior of the Soviet representatives in Vienna was "quite correct." Although there had been a good deal of opposition to the recognition request, Brundage noted, "Others felt that if Russian youth became acquainted with the Olympic Code of fair play and good sportsmanship, benefits might accrue, not only to the participants, but also to the rest of the world." On the other hand, Brundage feared that if the "application for recognition was denied, it was apparent that there would be a noisy Communist outburst against the committee which would be charged with violating its own regulations against introducing politics in sport."[59] In the end, the IOC voted almost unanimously for Soviet recognition. Andrianov became the first Soviet IOC member and was followed, a year later, by Aleksei Romanov. From thereon in, they and other Soviet delegates would unofficially lead the Eastern European members in the process of decision making in the committee. Even after the vote in Vienna, however, the communist perspective in the IOC was carefully monitored, even quietly loathed, by some Western members. When Hungary asked for an additional representative in the IOC, Edström feared that further Iron Curtain countries would initiate the same proposal, adding to what was already a "disagreeable minority in our Olympic Committee."[60]

The Vienna session, one of the decisive meetings in the history of the modern games, marked the full penetration of the Cold War into the Olympic Movement. Another critical episode soon followed. Although the Soviets declined to send a team to the 1952 winter games in Oslo, only a few months later, at the summer games in Helsinki, Soviet athletes competed in the Olympics for the first time ever. The two superpowers, already committed to an ideological confrontation, would now get to vie for supremacy on the Olympic stage. All eyes quickly turned to the medal table as the media tallied the scores in one event after another. This fervent interest in victory and defeat became a growing concern for Brundage. "The Olympic Games are a contest between individuals, there is no point scoring and no nation 'wins' them," he griped to a colleague. If the Olympics "are allowed to develop . . . into a battle between countries trying to demonstrate the superiority of their political systems, it will only be a short step until hired gladiators are being used."[61] But as much as he may have wanted to, he still could not hide from the reality of the situation. "We are handicapped in stopping this talk about point scoring since we emphasize nationalism with our victory ceremony, the athletes' parade, etc.," he conceded.[62] The Cold War could not be elbowed out of the games simply because Brundage demanded it; the structure of the movement was, in fact, ideally suited to channeling Cold War antagonisms.

For this reason, the amateur question came under increasing scrutiny as athletes in the East and West sought the upper hand in the Cold War athletic rivalry. The amateur problem had been in and around the Olympics for decades, though it gained cachet during the 1950s as many, especially in the United States, looked for an additional reason to moan about communism. It was true that sport in the Soviet bloc was directed by the state, and true that athletes were given financial subsidies—some more than others. When people picked up on this predicament, they cried foul play because they thought, quite correctly, that the practice broke amateur rules. It was a favorite argument, but a broken one. The practice of state funding had been in existence long before the Cold War, and countries that would commonly be called democratic partook in it. Even more conspicuous, as Brundage well knew, was general professionalism. When he questioned and harried Soviet authorities about the financial rewards or amateur status of their athletes, he did not deny, in fact he chastised, the suspicious activities of sportsmen in the United States and other Western countries. The IOC attempted to curb these infractions and control how national committees were administered, but the results were not perfect, nor would they ever be. Professionalism could not be stopped. Mayer admitted as much to Andrianov: "Unfortunately we are living in a time where materialism is ruling the World and I don't think that I am much wrong if I say that 90% (if not all) top athletes participating in the Games have received money at one time or at another."[63]

Eventually Brundage began to accept that nothing could be done to change the communist practice of state subsidies for athletics. And the Soviet bloc countries even became more accepting of him. In 1954, the IOC president journeyed to the Soviet Union and marveled at the remarkable scale of the nation's athletic structure and described a monumental sport parade in Moscow as "undoubtedly the greatest gymnastic display I have ever seen."[64] In a lighter moment with Mayer, Brundage commented, "In the thirties I was called a Nazi for talking about the German system; recently I have been talking so much about the Russians that they will probably call me a communist before they get through, although this has not happened yet."[65] Some, indeed, exaggerated. When critics in the United States accused Brundage of being "brain-washed in Russia," he retorted, "I have heard scores of stories about Russian violations, but so far not one has been accompanied by the necessary evidence for action. Rumors and gossip, yes, but documentary evidence, none."[66] As one Olympic historian has asserted, Brundage became a far more astute diplomat upon assuming the IOC presidency.[67]

Yet Brundage still understood the precarious nature of his position. "In a world engaged in a titanic struggle between different political systems," he remarked at an IOC session in 1955, "it is not a simple matter to keep aloof."[68] Indeed, for the duration of the Cold War, the IOC would be faced with one political incident after another. Brundage and his colleagues debated what to do with a divided Germany, the two Chinas, and the two Koreas; they watched but did not act when revolutions flared in Eastern Europe; they struggled with boycotts, protests, and voting blocs; they fretted over rival festivals and the emerging third world; they worried about excessive nationalism and poor sportsmanship; they downplayed and disputed the significance of the medal count; they continued to fight and lose their war against amateurism; and they refused to allow terrorist attacks or mass murder to compromise or interrupt their beloved festival of peace. In many ways, though, all these troubles helped to further feed and sustain the Olympic spectacle, just as they had done from the very start. Cold War rivalries and politics captured worldwide attention, expanded the brand, and created a product that was perfect for television and, therefore, commercial exploitation.[69]

"Some misguided persons seem to think that Olympic sport can be made a political tool," said Brundage on one occasion. "This is as erroneous as anything can be. The minute political activities are permitted in Olympic affairs the Games are finished."[70] In reality, the reverse was true.

3   A Campaign of Truth

In late 1945, the Young Men's Christian Association of Chicago sent a communication to the U.S. State Department on the subject of arranging volleyball contests between Soviet and U.S. teams. The proposal, earnest in appearance, certainly garnered a warm reception from the U.S. embassy in Moscow. The U.S. ambassador, W. Averell Harriman, fully endorsed the idea and praised the concept of sporting competition between the two superpowers as a means to enhance "understanding." In an enthusiastic report, he recalled how the tour of the Soviet soccer team, Dynamo Moscow, through England, Scotland, and Wales in October had been viewed by the British Foreign Office as a "valuable" diplomatic exercise. Harriman accepted that in the Soviet Union, sports were "organized officially and controlled by the government" and that international contests were viewed "primarily from the standpoint of national prestige." But overall, he was inclined to think that sporting ties might help to remedy mutual ignorance by opening a window into the culture of both countries.[1] George Kennan, working under Harriman at the time, pressed the State Department to give the proposal "full support."[2]

Harriman, in fact, had been calling for more cultural interchange between the United States and the Soviet Union for some time. When he alluded, moreover, to the positive aspects of the Dynamo Moscow tour of Great Britain, he drew a conclusion that many agreed with, especially in the British press. Yet not everyone reacted the same way. George Orwell, for one, commented on the tour in an article for the London-based *Tribune*, and famously wrote that modern international sport was the equivalent of "war minus the shooting."[3] Within U.S. government circles, too, conversations on Soviet sport were increasingly defined by Cold War rhetoric, the red threat, and communist expansion with each passing year. Cold War politics therefore shaped the sporting relations between the two superpowers and took precedence over calls for friendly athletic contacts. In 1950, a typical analysis from the U.S. Embassy in Moscow stated that the "main purpose" of Soviet participants in "any tournament was to win" and that victories were then "propagandized" as an indication of the "superiority of either socialist man, the Soviet state, or both."[4]

The entrance of the Soviet Union into the Olympic Movement added another dimension to this problem. Realizing that the Soviet Union would use the games as a further means to promote anti-U.S. propaganda, information experts in the U.S. government prepared plans of their own. These plans were inspired and driven by the Truman administration's Campaign of Truth, a worldwide psychological initiative to scotch the lies issuing from the Kremlin. As a result, U.S. participation at both Olympic festivals in 1952 was carefully manipulated by Washington officials. Information officers devised plans to showcase the friendliness and sportsmanship of the U.S. Olympic team and encouraged private businesses to make the hosting cities a showground for U.S. enterprise and culture. In tandem with these efforts, U.S. propaganda depicted communist sport in a highly negative manner by alleging that athletes in the Soviet bloc were prisoners of a garrison state and that Soviet authorities were tainting the Olympic spirit. In order to create and implement a propaganda strategy for the winter and summer games of 1952, the U.S. information program also facilitated cooperation with both the United States Olympic Committee (USOC)[5] and the Amateur Athletic Union of the United States (AAU). This intervention challenged a long-held tradition, as the U.S. government began to work in concert with the private sphere in sport-related propaganda to new and uncharted levels under the mounting demands of the Cold War.

The Campaign of Truth, the Soviet Sports Offensive, and the Olympic Games

Although the Smith–Mundt Act (1948) was a landmark piece of legislation in the history of U.S. propaganda, it did not end the conversation on the size or effectiveness of the information program. As it turned out, the Czechoslovakian coup, the communist victory in China, the Berlin blockade, and the Soviet detonation of an atomic bomb led government officials to debate the issue even more intently. In the wake of the act, the National Security

Council continued to highlight the fact that the Soviet Union was exploiting "weakness and instability in other states" through "techniques of infiltration and propaganda." Building upon and reaffirming these assertions, the U.S. government's wide-ranging assessment of Cold War policy, NSC 68, emphasized that at the "ideological or psychological level, in the struggle for men's minds, the conflict is world-wide."[6] In particular, policymakers were deeply troubled by what they referred to as Stalin's "peace offensive," a Soviet propaganda strategy that accused the United States of behaving like a belligerent imperialist and, in the same breath, claimed that communism was a force of global harmony and goodwill.[7] Alarmed by the immense scale of the Soviet ploy, in December 1949 a State Department report proposed that "Moscow considers the 'peace offensive' as potentially the most effective means of rallying non-communist foreign support."[8]

In February 1950, Edward W. Barrett was appointed assistant secretary of state for Public Affairs and took charge of the information program in the midst of the Soviet Union's waxing propaganda blitz. Having worked for the Office of War Information, and having seen the impact of propaganda and psychological warfare operations in Europe, he thought the value of such activities was often greatly underestimated. If the United States did not project its own image abroad, then the task might be done for them. And if this task was performed by the Soviet Union, then the outcome could be disastrous.[9] Pressed into action by the recommendations of Barrett and concerned voices in Congress, President Harry Truman launched the Campaign of Truth to confront Stalin's hate America and peace initiative. He addressed the American Society of Newspaper Editors on 20 April 1950 and proclaimed, "The cause of freedom is being challenged throughout the world today by the forces of imperialistic communism. This is a struggle, above all else, for the minds of men." While communist propaganda "portrays the Soviet Union as the world's foremost advocate of peace" it "reviles the United States as a nation of 'warmongers' and 'imperialists.'" But, stated Truman, the "false" and "crude" lies of the Soviet Union could be "overcome by the truth—plain, simple, unvarnished truth."[10]

Administration officials stood before Congress and backed the president. The secretary of state, Dean Acheson, told a subcommittee of the Senate Committee on Foreign Relations that "Communist efforts to foster falsehood about the United States" were preventing a "unified resistance against" Soviet aims. "We must, therefore, make unmistakable the truth about the United States and the other free nations. . . . We must make plain the difference between Communist pretensions and Communist performance."[11] Barrett fired off his own salvo on the issue. "I, for one, am confident," he explained, "that if we hit with the truth hard enough, long enough, and on a sufficient scale—and that means no less than a world-wide scale—we can make the Communist propaganda start backfiring not only outside the Iron Curtain but inside it as well."[12] The invasion of South Korea by the communist North confirmed that nothing could be left to chance. Congress appropriated nearly $80 million to supplement the existing propaganda budget.[13]

Though still the target of congressional criticism and public derision, the Truman administration's information apparatus rapidly expanded. In the lean year of 1948, for instance, the program had only 2,500 staff members. By 1952, the number had risen to 12,000. The rest of the program also ballooned. The government's radio network, the Voice of America, was broadcasting in forty-six languages to one hundred countries and had an estimated global audience that stood at approximately 300 million. More than one hundred and forty U.S. Information Centers in more than seventy countries distributed magazines, books, and newspapers to reams of visitors. The State Department produced in excess of 60 million publications for use overseas, sent daily material to ten thousand foreign newspapers, and claimed that it reached a million people a day through movies translated into more than thirty languages. Reciprocal exchanges flourished, with thousands of scientists, scholars, students, artists, labor leaders, and farmers traveling from or to the United States. Top secret psychological warfare strategies also received an additional stimulus, with the Central Intelligence Agency continuing its covert efforts to "roll back" communism in Eastern Europe. As a result of the sheer diversity of propaganda operations under the jurisdiction of various government departments, Truman created a Psychological Strategy Board to coordinate the U.S. crusade against communism.[14]

Soon the Olympics were swept up in this rising tide. But even earlier, the State Department had been paying far closer attention to what it saw as the reorientation of Soviet sports diplomacy in the postwar years. Government officials noted that although the Kremlin had largely distanced itself from the world of "bourgeois" sporting interactions before 1945, Soviet policy changed when the Soviet Union assumed its new position in the Cold War international order. Rather than representing an area of Western culture that could be criticized and virulently denounced, the Kremlin now viewed sports as a significant platform to promote communist ideology to a global audience through athletic performance and cultural exchanges. More still, U.S. diplomats in Eastern Europe compiled multiple reports on the manner in which sport was being used to solidify Soviet power and influence behind the Iron Curtain. A detailed analysis by the U.S. Embassy in Warsaw, for example, informed the State Department that a centralized state apparatus had been established "to draw closer into the framework of communist ideological control the various athletic and physical culture activities throughout Poland."[15] Upon observing "The Week of Physical Culture" in Sofia, the U.S. legation in Bulgaria reached a similar conclusion, remarking that "all is done really at the order of an outside authority—i.e., Moscow."[16]

There was, though, one major gap in the Soviet sports offensive. Although Soviet athletes and teams were entering competitions in various sports, they did not participate at the first Cold War Olympic Games in London (1948); nor, for that matter, had they taken the necessary steps to join the Olympic Movement. Only in 1951, it appears, was the Kremlin ready to form a national Olympic committee that followed (at least ostensibly) the International Olympic Committee's (IOC's) rules. In April of the same year, the IOC members voted almost unanimously, but not without reservation, to recognize the Soviet Union. With that, the Soviet Union was able, in theory, to send its athletes to the winter games in Oslo and the summer games in Helsinki. In the end, they waited to make their full debut in the Finnish capital.[17] The State Department was well aware of this pivotal moment in Olympic history. "It will be interesting to see," Barrett declared, "how the Kremlin handles its propaganda at the Olympic Games in Helsinki next summer, an event they are entering in force for the first time!"[18]

It was probably a rhetorical question, but it would be answered soon enough in a string of reports from U.S. diplomats in Moscow. John McSweeney, the embassy counselor, compiled one of the earliest of these revealing documents. He reasoned that the Soviet Union's decision to enter the Olympic Movement "was not prompted exclusively by the Soviet desire to pit its athletes against those of the West." Of "equal importance," he continued, "is Soviet recognition of the Games as an opportunity to again apply its talent for twisting international gatherings into vehicles for Soviet propaganda."[19] McSweeney and other embassy officials noted that as the Olympics fast approached, the Soviet media's coverage was increasingly tied to the peace offensive and the anti-U.S. campaign. Among an assortment of attacks on U.S. sporting culture, the communist press claimed that African American athletes were barred from swimming for the United States because they would "defile the water," and that the U.S. Olympic team was an extension of the military.[20] Even before Soviet participation at the Olympics was confirmed, an exasperated official at the Helsinki embassy groaned that a Finnish communist newspaper was using the games to promote Soviet peace propaganda.[21]

Meanwhile, the prospect of a Soviet team marching into the stadium at the 1952 summer games stirred a great deal of interest in the U.S. public and media. "Until recently the Kremlin and its doings made few if any appearances on American sports pages," remarked *New York Times* columnist Harry Schwartz. "That situation has been changed now that the Soviet Union is in training for the 1952 Olympic Games in Helsinki. Today sports writers and fans who follow them are scrambling to find out about a host of Ivans, Vladimirs and Natashas who will wear Stalin's colors in the competition this summer."[22] For some, the situation was ominous. Many worried that the games would be tarnished and manipulated by communist propaganda.[23] These reservations were indicative of the political atmosphere in the early Cold War United States, in which Soviet sport embodied yet another reason to fear the policies and question the intentions of Joseph Stalin. Indeed, at a time when the U.S. hounded the Soviet Union for producing a system that embargoed the rights of its people, the U.S. government and its public launched an assault on individual rights of their own. Films that appeared to have a communist theme were censored; undesirable books were taken from library shelves. By 1951, membership in the American Communist Party dwindled to a mere 32,000. This extreme reaction to the enemy within was perhaps best personified in the often maniacal actions of Senator Joseph McCarthy, who thought nothing less than that a communist conspiracy had captured the U.S. government.[24] Little wonder that at a time when all things Marxist were viewed with suspicion, distrust, and even venom, any product of the communist system would, in turn, be condemned. There was little left untouched in the battle for hearts and minds, sport included.

State–Private Initiatives

In the latter half of 1951, information experts reached the conclusion that the Soviet Union was going to accelerate its propaganda for the Olympics and that something had to be done to counter it. Still unsure, however, whether the Soviets would send a team to Oslo, the U.S. State Department planned to focus on both the summer and winter games.[25] A major component of the government's Olympic strategy mirrored a trusted tactic of the Campaign of Truth by harnessing, as Truman put it, the "imagination and energies of private individuals and groups throughout the country."[26] Barrett therefore delegated much of the strategic and logistical work to Richard B. Walsh, an employee in the information program's Office of Private Enterprise and Cooperation, a small group with responsibility for using the private sphere to promote the aims of the government.[27] By this stage, in fact, the United States had already started to form overt and covert links with private actors in an attempt to forge a united front against communist expansion. Simply put, U.S. policymakers determined that foreign and domestic audiences would be far more responsive to the message of U.S. propaganda if it appeared that the message had not come from official government sources. Moreover, the vast majority of U.S. citizens, inspired by a deep anticommunism, were also eager to support the government's global commitment to defend the "free world."[28] Feeding upon this political consensus, the Office of Private Enterprise and Cooperation contacted U.S. charities, organizations, and businesses to contribute to the mission of the information program, helped publishers to donate books and magazines for use overseas, sought aid from U.S. firms to provide items for government exhibitions, and advised private groups on how to develop international projects. Barrett certainly appreciated the work in this area. He felt that each project on its own might not be decisive, but "taken together, they played an important role in the Campaign of Truth."[29]

It is not surprising, then, that Walsh and his colleagues immediately looked to exploit U.S. participation in the Olympics by rousing support from private channels. He investigated the possibility of securing space in downtown Helsinki so that the "finest possible exhibits with a sports theme" could be put on show and wanted every U.S. "company doing business in Helsinki . . . to arrange . . . displays depicting their growth under the American system of private enterprise." Walsh proposed that General Electric and IBM should showcase their technology and other firms should be encouraged to cooperate. Walsh reported that the National Baseball Museum in Cooperstown, New York, had "expressed interest in sending a special baseball exhibit to Helsinki" and that the Radio Corporation of America considered taking a closed circuit television unit to both Olympic cities.[30] Pan American Airways agreed to track down window display space in Helsinki for U.S. commercial exhibits, and the Steuben Glass Corporation designed a wassail bowl worth $1000 for the U.S. Olympic Committee to donate to the city of Oslo as "an expression of appreciation from America."[31] Walsh tried to convince U.S. networks to capture the television rights for Oslo and Helsinki and urged that airlines and steamship companies be asked to promote the trip to Finland. In the case of the latter, Walsh helped the Finnish Olympic Committee to convince the Trans-Atlantic Shipping Conference to charter a ship from New York to Helsinki carrying more than a thousand Finnish-Americans and students to the games.[32] With special low rates secured, the State Department viewed the voyage as a perfect opportunity for "promoting the objectives of the International Information Program by creating a better understanding between U.S. and Finnish citizens."[33]

A great deal of Walsh's evolving plans for the Olympic festivals of 1952 also required close collaboration with the USOC and the AAU.[34] The first group organized and administered the U.S. Olympic team and the second was the national sanctioning body for athletic eligibility. Although separate in nomenclature, the executive boards of the USOC and the AAU were filled with many of the same men. As a whole, these doyens of U.S. sport shared a profound belief that the country's athletic culture was representative of the national spirit and that sport could, in keeping with Olympic principles, contribute to mutual understanding around the world. The Cold War and the Soviet sports system thus presented a massive challenge to these hardened internationalists who worshipped at the altar of amateurism. They would continue to insist that politics should not contaminate sports, but they too would become active participants in a total war by forging extraordinary ties with Washington. Just as important, these leaders of the U.S. Olympic establishment entered into this relationship willingly. Perhaps, too, the government had not asked for more than they wanted to give. Walsh had not told them that the State Department wanted control of their affairs, nor was it ever discussed. The AAU and USOC were to act with their usual autonomy. To be sure, U.S. sports officials had entered the Cold War, but they did so largely on their own terms. Only their ideals were, in many ways, compromised.[35]

In 1950, the State Department had, in fact, reached out to the USOC president (and IOC vice president), Avery Brundage, for a different purpose. On this occasion, the U.S. was hoping that the IOC would accept West Germany's application for full membership in the Olympic Movement, thus following the Allied prerogative of reintegrating a democratized Germany into the international arena.[36] This case aside, the likelihood of Soviet participation at the 1952 Olympic festivals soon led to deeper links between the U.S. government and U.S. sports officials throughout the final months of 1951. This process started slowly at first, but the real turning point came during a meeting between James Webb, the U.S. undersecretary of state, and the U.S. IOC member, J. Brooks B. Parker. Parker, who already had longstanding ties to the U.S. government, informed Webb about the Soviet application for recognition at the 1951 IOC session in Vienna, and the two men met to discuss Olympic affairs a few months later in August. According to a third person in the room, it was during this meeting that Parker intimated that the USOC was willing to "abandon its long standing policy of operating without reference to or consultation with" Washington.[37] From this moment on, the level of communication and cooperation between U.S. sports officials and the Truman administration began to move far beyond the confines of tradition. As a signal of this change, Webb assigned two government agents to provide policy guidance for the USOC and to act as general liaisons with the State Department. Although Parker died from a heart attack a few months later, he had helped to lay the groundwork for more expansive state–private initiatives.[38]

Barrett confirmed his own growing interest in the Olympics in a letter to Brundage. He explained his confidence that the U.S. team would "represent the fair play and sportsmanship which is deeply rooted in our heritage" at the forthcoming Olympic festivals in Oslo and Helsinki and wrote that a successful U.S. performance in the two events "will have a pronounced effect on peoples all over the world. It is an absolute necessity therefore that the United States is represented by the strongest possible team."[39] At a minimum, the USOC needed $850,000 to cover the costs of participation in Oslo and to send more than four hundred athletes to Finland. Yet the thought of tapping federal funds to raise this amount was simply too much for many U.S. citizens to bear. "Sports lovers," railed one journalist, "want nothing from the Government." The writer intoned that state dollars would lead to bureaucratic interference, all of which would be unacceptable and incompatible with the nation's Olympic traditions.[40] Others lined up to agree. "Unlike other countries, including Russia, which will send teams subsidized by the Government, the United States group is financed wholly on a 'democratic basis,' and is completely dependent upon public support," the *New York Times* declared.[41]

The general U.S. commitment to amateurism did not mean that the USOC would decline to ask for any assistance from the government. Just as he had done in 1947, Brundage again reached out to the White House and appealed to President Truman for a declaration of support to rally public donations. Truman produced a letter of endorsement on each occasion, but his letter in 1951 was far more provocative. "The Olympic competition this coming year is especially significant for many reasons," wrote the president. "Certain countries which have not participated for many years will be represented, others will take part for the first time. . . . This competition is not just another event. It requires the finest American athletes we can send, it requires the fullest support Americans can give. The eyes of the world will be upon us."[42] A year later, Truman, urged on by Congress, designated the seven-day period after 18 May as "Olympic Week." Brundage, in turn, asked newspaper publishers to contribute advertising space for Olympic Week and warned of the propaganda value that Stalin would gain if the United States could not send its strongest team to Helsinki.[43] Indeed, the USOC's fundraising drive was infused with the prevailing anticommunism of the early 1950s and clearly framed in Cold War terms. A "Russian victory would provide Communists with a powerful propaganda weapon to support its claims about the softness and decay inherent in a democracy such as ours," cautioned one advertisement commissioned by the organization. "We can't win with half a team!"[44]

Even if direct federal subsidies for the U.S. team did not occur, state and private cooperation did start to transform in other respects, as the State Department reached into the affairs of the U.S. Olympic establishment more than it ever had before. Walsh made sure of the arrangement by flying to the 1951 AAU convention at Daytona Beach, Florida. By his own account, he received a "pledge of close cooperation" from U.S. sports officials and claimed to have formed a "smooth working arrangement" for Olympic projects.[45] On the final day of the conference, Walsh outlined the government's position in an emphatic address. He explained that during the previous three years, the Soviet Union had continually tried to discredit the United States, and these lies were being countered with government efforts to tell the truth. He added, however, that the Soviets had reverted to "something new" in their propaganda. The evidence supplied by U.S. embassies verified that the Kremlin had "mounted a gigantic cultural offensive" with the intent to "prove the Soviet line of supremacy in the arts as well as on the athletic field." Walsh noted that the Soviets traditionally remained detached from competition "outside their orbit," but now they appeared to be "preparing to display their self-acclaimed supremacy in the field of sports beyond the borders of their domination." Walsh charged that "we do not have to swallow the lie that the Soviet athlete is superior because he is a product of the Soviet regime." He commended the work of the AAU and asked that they continue it. "You have in your hands the finest tools for building the kind of understanding that one day will bring genuine peace," he said. "Our athletes are our finest ambassadors."[46]

Regardless of Walsh's remarks on the diplomatic significance of U.S. sportsmen and sportswomen, the government had generally not displayed an interest in utilizing athletes for political gain.[47] Once again, the Cold War inspired a drift from this position as the State Department sought to organize exhibition tours for U.S. athletes before and after the winter and summer games. Information experts recommended sending competitors to countries where they could do the "most good," and the State Department emphasized that invitations were to be extended through nongovernmental organizations—i.e., the AAU—because public knowledge of government association with the plan was not "desirable."[48] The idea was greeted with enthusiasm by several embassies. An official in Paris thought it timely. He explained that there was a constant demand for U.S. teams in his homeland and that the "publicity value of American sports in France cannot be exaggerated, especially in reaching [a] large popular audience, . . . particularly young workers."[49] The AAU and the USOC administered and funded the tours for athletes already committed to representing the national squad at the games, and Walsh praised both organizations for the goodwill that the exhibitions generated. He was particularly pleased with the performance of U.S. figure skaters, who, having graced the ice in front of a capacity crowd at Oslo's Jordal Arena, were given a standing ovation and "presented with gifts of Norwegian silver by local and national government officials."[50]

Concerned about the general conduct of U.S. athletes at the Olympic cities and how it would reflect upon the United States, on several occasions government officials also briefed Brundage and members of the USOC on the "basic political problems which Olympic athletes may expect to meet while abroad," and the dangers of communist propaganda. Taking things from one extreme to another, information officers even quibbled over whether the athletes should be allowed to shake hands with Soviet competitors. It was later decided that they could. After these consultations, the USOC reassured Department of State officials that athletes under their supervision would be warned about political issues, and Brundage duly sounded the alarm about the possibility of "anti-American demonstrations" in a meeting with the team.[51] Moreover, he and colleagues provided numerous interviews for Voice of America broadcasts, wrote articles for the information program publications, and traveled with two U.S. propaganda experts to Helsinki.[52]

Telling the "Truth" about U.S. Sport

Aside from state–private projects that were well underway, the summer and winter festivals also provided the State Department with an ideal background to tell the "truth" about the United States through its communications network. There was some precedent to taking advantage of such a vehicle. During the late 1940s, the information program had used sport as a way to project the United States in its overseas output through various stories on the national sporting culture. The program also allotted some space for stories and radio broadcasts of the 1948 London Olympics, but nothing very extensive or detailed. The Soviet entrance into the Olympic Movement, however, dramatically altered the program's tactics. Recognizing the political potential of the forthcoming Olympic year, and also recognizing that U.S. overseas information posts had "consistently asked for greater emphasis on sports subjects," the State Department called for an increase in sports coverage to counter the predicted communist propaganda offensive.[53]

This information strategy entailed, for the most part, the perpetuation of a U.S. tradition. For decades before the outbreak of the Cold War, U.S. citizens had argued that the lofty ideals of the Olympic Movement were synonymous with U.S. democracy. For many, the U.S. athletic domination at the Olympics since 1896, and the fair play displayed by U.S. sportsmen and sportswomen, was truly faithful to Pierre de Coubertin's original vision. These ideals, mainly expressed by private groups and individuals, were increasingly trumpeted by the U.S. information program in the early Cold War years. The games would again serve as a vehicle to define freedom and democracy, just as they always had done. As one policy expert put it in November 1951, all aspects of U.S. participation at the Olympics should "project a positive and favorable picture of American life . . . and support US foreign policy objectives."[54] To press this agenda, the State Department created an Olympic news service, dispatched propaganda experts and photographers to Oslo and Helsinki, planned for radio exposure in a range of languages on either side of the Iron Curtain, and produced pamphlets and leaflets for distribution "with or without attribution" at the Olympic cities.[55]

The information program's commitment to sport-related propaganda quickly affected the content of the *U.S.A. Life Air Bulletin* (later renamed *USIS Feature*), a weekly publication sent to U.S. information posts worldwide full of stories on subjects such as U.S. politics, economics, labor, science, technology, education, and culture. Through this and other outlets, notes Laura Belmonte, "U.S. policymakers propagated a carefully constructed narrative of progress, freedom, and happiness" in the United States. "They not only 'imagined' an American 'community,'" Belmonte adds, "but also presented their vision to the world in hopes of persuading foreign peoples to reject communism and adopt democratic capitalism."[56] Sport, which information experts praised for its capacity to reach the "general public very effectively," came to play an important part of this U.S. narrative.[57] Indeed, the number of sports articles carried by the *Bulletin* rose considerably in late 1951, and by 1952 it contained a regular column titled "Sports World." Many of these stories directly confronted communist propaganda about life in the United States by informing overseas audiences about how U.S. citizens enjoyed many sports, games, and outdoor pursuits; how they shared a passion for fair play and good sportsmanship; and how the United States was a willing participant in a global sporting community. *Bulletin*s included copy on the international growth of baseball and basketball, U.S. teams touring abroad, foreign teams competing or training in the United States, charity golf tournaments, black athletes, female prodigies, and the popularity of sports such as water polo and soccer within U.S. borders. In sum, sport offered propaganda planners with a broad canvas to construct images of the United States in a language in which people around the world were already fluent. And while this narrative perforated the rich blend of vignettes on the U.S. "sporting republic," the majority of the stories that coincided with the Campaign of Truth were shaped to harness the medium of the Olympic Movement.[58]

Shaped under the guidance of State Department strategists, propaganda materials relentlessly conveyed the peaceful nature of the Olympic Games, its role in bringing people together in friendly nonpolitical athletic contests, and the dedication of U.S. citizens to upholding this amicable mission.[59] In "Sports World," for instance, writer Carl Shepard outlined the organizational structure of the IOC and the peaceful underpinning of Olympic principles. The games "offer proof that nations of divergent interests, languages, and political philosophies can share in setting up accepted rules and practices and abide by the decisions of a single governing body," reasoned Shepard.[60] Reinforcing this point, articles regularly quoted U.S. athletes and sports officials praising the ability of competitors from various countries and revealed how many foreign athletes trained at U.S. colleges and utilized U.S. facilities and technical expertise. Members of the U.S. Olympic squad, noted the *Bulletin*, were already friends with dozens of athletes from other countries and looked forward to seeing them again in Finland.[61]

Yet if it was vital to convey that the U.S. team revered the "traditional Olympic spirit," it was perhaps just as important to stress that it adhered to all the IOC's regulations, especially those that related to amateurism.[62] In order to articulate this message, the State Department asked Brundage to write a short piece on the subject, and he struck all the right notes in a self-indulgent essay packed with philosophical justifications for the amateur rule and praise for the amateur standing of the United States. "The most important things in life are not measured in money. The Olympic Movement is the cult of the amateur who participates for the love of the game and for the joy and pleasure he gets in competition," he sermonized. "The U.S. Olympic Committee adheres to this code and conducts itself accordingly."[63] Further *Bulletin* stories repeated the theme over and again. A profile of the U.S. Olympic ski team, for instance, carefully explained that all members of the squad earned their "livelihoods" in a "variety" of ways. The team had a "carpenter, bookkeeper, laboratory technician, lumberjack, building contractor, college students, and a naval officer," but no professionals.[64] Of equal importance, too, was the political independence that supposedly resulted from following the Olympic amateur code. Propaganda officials were keen to highlight the fact that athletics in the United States was free from politics, while pointing out, on the other hand, that Olympic teams in many countries received government appropriations. *Bulletin* stories emphasized, therefore, that the U.S. Olympic effort was financed by "internationally-minded citizens," as opposed to the state.[65] Amateurism was thus adapted by propagandists to promote individual liberty and freedom, as opposed to the form of totalitarianism that prevailed in the Soviet bloc.

Other themes also were prominent. Eager to show that U.S. citizens were not ruthlessly exploited by capitalism or tools of war, features depicted the U.S. Olympians as ordinary hard-working people with a variety of hopes, interests, hobbies, and goals, who practiced religion and played musical instruments.[66] While these stories refuted Soviet claims that the United States was a land without culture by highlighting how U.S. athletes possessed a range of creative talents, other profiles helped to counter Soviet accusations about social inequality and racism in the United States. The U.S. team was being selected, read a quote in one piece, "in fair and open competition, without regard to race, color, creed or social status."[67] An article on the "great negro hurdler," Harrison Dillard, explained how he graduated from Baldwin-Wallace College and was "a member of the Ohio State Boxing Commission and on the public relations staff of the Cleveland Indians baseball club."[68] These and other stories told of progress and change in U.S. society without necessarily denying the obvious reality of civil-rights discrimination and unrest. In addition to the race question, propagandists also tackled communist claims that U.S. women were "lazy, promiscuous, and vapid" with a similarly selective approach. Although women made up only a small percentage of the U.S. Olympic squad, U.S. propaganda described U.S. female athletes as motivated and productive members of society who worked or attended college.[69]

There was, however, another side to this general output that followed a central aspect of the overall truth campaign. U.S. propaganda, Barrett underscored, had to expose Soviet intentions. "I think we will have to decide," he contemplated, "whether we want to use the presence of the Russians as an opportunity to beat them over the head, or whether we want to preach sweet reasonableness in the Olympic atmosphere."[70] They tried to do both. Channeling the pronounced anticommunist rhetoric of the Campaign of Truth, U.S. propaganda experts attacked the aims and structure of physical culture in the Soviet bloc. They argued that sport under totalitarianism was not about free choice, peace, amateurism, or global harmony. Rather, U.S. propaganda portrayed sport in the communist bloc in much the same way as it portrayed life under communism in general. The Soviet Union was sullying the ideals of the Olympic Movement, Soviet representatives in the IOC were merely engaged in political maneuvers, while Iron Curtain athletes were tools at the hands of a dictatorship, charged with waging ideological warfare and undermining the democracies of the West. In a story on the traditional Olympic torch relay, "a symbol of peace" for the "Free World," a USIS Feature informed readers that "the chain of foot runners linking the participating nations was regarded as a bond of strength and friendship between them. In recent times, however, the Iron Curtain has weakened this chain." It lamented the refusal of communist countries to allow the torch relay to cross their lands in 1948 or 1952 and suggested that a clue to these actions could be found in the latest edition of the "Small Soviet Encyclopedia," which described physical culture as the "systematic and all around perfecting of the human body in the interest of labor and defense."[71]

In many ways, the information program also depicted communist athletes as victims. Propaganda experts at the Olympic cities, for instance, produced a series of stories that scrutinized the tight security that accompanied the competitors from the satellite countries. In one vignette, U.S. propagandists revealed that the Polish Olympic team was flanked by state security agents during a trip to a local movie theater and that the captives were followed to the toilets.[72] The defection of hundreds of athletes from the Soviet bloc in the late 1940s and early 1950s, including some at the Olympics, supplied further material for propagandists to challenge and contest the legitimacy of communist rule in Eastern Europe. Walsh assessed that the exiles were a potential pressure point for the Soviet Union and recommended that the information program should be prepared for the "maximum exploitation" of this particular weakness. At the winter games, the Voice of America employed the Hungarian speed skater, Kornél Pajor, to do commentaries in his native language and supplemented the commentaries by arranging for the medal-winning Hungarian figure-skating pair, László and Marianna Nagy, to make a statement about U.S. friendship with the people of Hungary. Aside from this, the collective endeavors of exiled athletes to participate at the games as individuals or as a stateless team emerged as a prime opportunity to undermine the claims of the communist regimes about the superiority of life behind the Iron Curtain. Although the IOC eventually blocked these endeavors, propaganda experts were keen to transmit the story of the exiles, the reason they fled their countries, and the sympathetic efforts of Brundage to raise the issue of refugees in IOC meetings.[73]

The war of persuasion, fought as it was through a range of methods, also spilled onto the streets of Helsinki, as the superpowers sought to influence the opinions of locals and tourists at the Olympic city. As the State Department expected, the Soviet Union was trying to take advantage of the Olympic spectacle by connecting the atmosphere of the games to its anti-U.S. campaign. The Soviets organized an affordable camp directed at youths, provided crowds with free entertainment and communist movies, arranged political rallies, and continued to claim that communist sport contributed to the "struggle" for "peace in the whole world" through media outlets.[74] Apprehensive that

Soviet propaganda was making considerable inroads in the lead-up to the summer games, the U.S. government prepared a counteroffensive by renting the largest moving picture theater in downtown Helsinki for the screening of free information program films for the duration of the games.[75] The idea turned into a resounding success. From the moment the operation began, the public response was excellent and remained so throughout. The theater, which held 850 people, was full on all but one occasion, and officials estimated that some 31,000 people enjoyed watching films such as the "Auto Worker in Detroit" and "Junior Chamber of Commerce." Elsewhere, U.S. productions played daily in the Olympic Village (for men) and the College of Nursing (for women). In a separate facility, the Soviet bloc teams watched films produced in the Soviet Union.[76]

While all these activities transpired in and around Oslo and Helsinki, further political issues swirled around the games, revealing the deep and resonant impact of the Cold War on the Olympic Movement. The IOC, already perplexed by the blatant state sponsorship of sport by its communist member nations, also struggled to come to terms with the reconfigured landscape of international affairs and, most notably, the problems posed by the division of Germany and the communist revolution in China. As it turned out, the IOC voted, with its usual inconsistency, to recognize one Germany, in the form of a joint team, and two Chinas, one for the defeated Nationalists who fled to Taiwan and the other for the mainland communists. East German sports authorities duly boycotted the events, as did the Nationalist Chinese.[77] Yet the most compelling storyline from the Olympic year was the competition between the U.S. and Soviet athletes in Helsinki. For a time, at least, it looked like the Soviets might claim an overall victory before the United States, with a surge of medals in the final few days of competition, grasped the initiative. "Once again the United States is the champion nation in the Olympic Games," a writer declared triumphantly in the *New York Times*.[78] Soviet sports officials used an alternative mathematical formulation to obviate this, reworking the value of gold, silver, and bronze medals, but whichever method they used, they could not truthfully alter the final standings. Notwithstanding, Soviet officials claimed for the next fifty years that their athletes had triumphed in Helsinki.[79]

All the U.S. propaganda initiatives that surrounded the 1952 Olympics, as seminal as they were, must also be put into some perspective. Not all the information program's plans were successful. A few officials argued that the government's output was unpopular with overseas audiences, that it had not been conveyed in a timely manner, or, in some cases, that it had not been conveyed at all.[80] Some information experts even questioned the psychological potential of the Olympics, much to the derision of those who thought that sports could be an "effective propaganda vehicle."[81] Aside from these issues, the Voice of America, for instance, battled for months to secure official accreditation to cover the summer games. The rules for broadcasting at Helsinki stated that stations could be accredited only if they operated in the country in which they were based and broadcast directly to that country's people. The organizers argued that VOA failed to meet these requirements because it did "not broadcast to the American public in the English language."[82] In another incident, the proposal for a telecast out of Helsinki by the Radio Corporation of America (RCA) simply could not be arranged. After a great deal of planning and research, a representative of RCA demanded that if the company were to produce a free telecast of the games to the surrounding area, then NBC should be granted the North American television rights at no cost. The Helsinki organizing committee did not take the bait and the deal collapsed.[83]

What is more, U.S. efforts to harness the Olympics for Cold War advantage were dwarfed by the Soviet Union's government directed information nexus and state-subsidized athletic system. And once the games had ended, Soviet propaganda did not cease. A communist political rally, staged before thousands of spectators on the day of the closing ceremony, caused a stir in the IOC. In particular, a Czechoslovakian athlete, Emil Zátopek, had spoken effusively about the peaceful nature of the games, and questioned why the United States could not lay down its arms in Korea for the duration of the festival. When Brundage was made aware of the rally, he reacted with his usual sense of disappointment and anger that politics were able to tarnish the athletic spectacle. In order to prevent any other such occurrence in the future, he drafted a circular letter to warn other national Olympic committees that the "prestige of the Olympic movement will be rapidly lowered . . . if they are used as an occasion for political propaganda."[84] Brundage's ire had been stirred by the coverage of the incident in U.S. newspapers. The *San Francisco Chronicle* carried an editorial on Zátopek's speech that condemned the runner for flattering what it called the "ruthless" Soviet regime. The article charged that "the Olympic Games of 1952 have been misused by the Russians as never before since they were revived by Pierre de Coubertin in 1896—and we are not excepting the 1936 Berlin Games from which Reichsfuehrer Hitler and his be-swastikaed Nazis drew considerable international advantage."[85]

The Ambassador to Helsinki, John M. Cabot, produced his own assessment of the summer Olympics. Cabot thought the games were a triumph for Finland as a feat of organization, and he hoped that they might "do much to dispel the all too prevalent impression that Finland is a Soviet satellite." There had been little controversy, and even the communist press printed generally fair reports, which the ambassador found "surprisingly objective." Cabot observed that relations between Soviet and U.S. athletes had also been completely amicable. In the case of the Soviets, Cabot thought that initially their friendly posture toward the U.S. athletes might have been to "further the Russian 'peace' campaign," but acknowledged that "nothing of this nature developed." Even so, his suspicions returned. "The Russians undoubtedly derived some propaganda advantages from their behavior," he reported. "The conduct of the Russian athletes seems in many instances to have done something to counterbalance the impression left by outrageous Russian acts in other fields." The friendly rivalry displayed in Helsinki led some to wonder, wrote Cabot, whether "it should be possible for the United States and Soviet Russia to have better political relations than now exist." Cabot would not go that far: "Much as we should like to subscribe to this idea, we doubt that it has validity."[86] Even though, as Cabot acknowledged, the games were a peaceful spectacle and that he could recall no unwelcome incidents between U.S. and Soviet athletes, the political underpinnings of Soviet sport could not be ignored. By then, indeed, perceptions of the masquerade of Soviet athletics had settled in the United States. The Olympic Games had entered a new era. So, too, did the U.S government's use of sport.

4 The Union of Free Eastern European Sportsmen

When one of countless letters crossed Avery Brundage's office desk in Chicago early in 1950, Brundage opened it and surveyed the contents. The communication, innocuous at face value, was from a Count Anthony Szápáry. In the missive, the count politely informed Brundage of a group he directed, the Hungarian National Sports Federation (HNSF), and explained that the organization sought to aid Hungarian athletes who had fled from behind the Iron Curtain and now lived on free soil. The political agenda was not hidden. "Our Federation is in the service of anti-communist propaganda and our main purpose is to gain the free, democratic world for the fight against communism," Szápáry openly admitted.[1] The letter had arrived at a well-chosen desk. At the time he received the correspondence, Brundage was possibly the most powerful man in the U.S. sporting administration—president of the United States Olympic Committee and vice president of the International Olympic Committee—and a potentially important ally. One more fact adds to the significance of the letter. Szápáry also told Brundage that the HNSF was at the service of the National Committee for a Free Europe, but the count did not mention that this organization was secretly funded and directed by the highest authorities of the U.S. government's intelligence establishment.

Brundage would have read Szápáry's missive at about the same time as the U.S. State Department was reaching a consensus about communist sport. Reports on the athletic culture behind the Iron Curtain, sent to Washington from U.S. diplomats in the Soviet bloc, had fueled the indignant speech delivered by Richard B. Walsh before the Amateur Athletic Union (AAU) of the United States in 1951. It was the department's first detailed public statement on this particular issue. But Walsh and his colleagues had later found a weakness, to which the Soviet Union was acutely sensitive, and upon which counterpropaganda might be based. For although athletes from Eastern Europe could be symbols of communist supremacy, they could just quite as easily be symbols of its frailty. While covering the Oslo and Helsinki games, the information program had used stories of defecting athletes to reveal a negative side of life behind the Iron Curtain that they most wanted U.S. citizens and the free world to see. After all, no propagandist could say it better than someone who had lived under communist rule. This, indeed, was the theory behind the National Committee for a Free Europe (NCFE) and the very thing that Szápáry's organization provided—athletes from Eastern Europe who had fled to the West with incriminating stories of communism and communist sport.

Keeping refugees in the public eye was therefore a high priority. For this reason, the HNSF and the NCFE constantly lobbied the International Olympic Committee (IOC) to change its rules on the admission of stateless athletes. As it stood, the Olympic Charter dictated that without a country to represent, no one could compete at an Olympic festival. Yet the leaders of the NCFE and HNSF considered the prospect of a refugee athlete competing against the government of their communist homeland, or even under the flag of a capitalist country, as marvelous propaganda that would seriously damage a communist regime's prestige.[2] In order to achieve this outcome, representatives of both groups initiated a campaign to alter the IOC charter, a campaign that continued beyond the 1950s. The first main thrust in this strategy started in 1950 and eventually resulted in the NCFE and HNSF creating another front group, the Union of Free Eastern European Sportsmen. This collection of state–private organizations would, by necessity, embroil Brundage, the IOC, the AAU, and the United States Olympic Committee (USOC) in their plan. Any description of this part of the strategy, though, requires a caveat. The U.S. Central Intelligence Agency (CIA) used an expression for the people who had full knowledge of secret operations. These people were described as "witting."[3] There are numerous instances where the AAU and the USOC intentionally complied and cooperated with the U.S. government on sport-related propaganda activities in the 1950s, but there are also cases when they did so unknowingly. There is no firm evidence that members of the U.S. sporting establishment, or the IOC for that matter, had any knowledge of the CIA connection to the HNSF. It was thus only due to the clandestine nature of the HNSF and the NCFE that their requests were given serious consideration by the IOC in the first place. An official demand from the U.S. government could not have been so effective.

Sport, Propaganda, and the National Committee for a Free Europe

In a general sense, then, the NCFE's overriding objective was the liberation of Eastern Europe and the "eventual restoration of these peoples and their resources to the free world."[4] In order to accomplish this purpose the organization poured millions of secretly channeled CIA dollars into a diverse range of émigré based propaganda activities. The NCFE's intrepid strategy was best epitomized in the philosophy of C. D. Jackson, a career publicist and the group's president from 1951 to 1952. For him, the best way to undermine Soviet control in its satellite countries was to "move with boldness and intelligence, and above all, unorthodox, imaginative thinking."[5] Consequently, sport was just one of many areas that refugees could exploit, and an avenue that Jackson fully endorsed. Almost immediately after the NCFE was formed, its employees used sport as a means to rouse liberating tendencies in Eastern Europe through radio and print propaganda, and by sponsoring émigré sports organizations.

Radio Free Europe (RFE) was by far the largest ongoing operation in the NCFE's considerable and varied psychological warfare portfolio. High-ranking U.S. intelligence officers believed that RFE could not only help to "hinder . . . the cultural, political and economic integration of the satellite states with the Soviet Union," but also, ultimately, prevent it. As the head of the Office of Policy Coordination, Frank Wisner, wrote on one occasion, RFE would bring "hope to our friends and confusion to our enemies."[6] With its first broadcast in 1950, the station functioned as a free forum in which Eastern European émigrés could speak to their own peoples and "seek to persuade their listeners of the monstrous all-devouring ambitions of Soviet imperialism, the cruelty and unworkability of communist institutions, and the proven advantages of the democratic way of life."[7] Although RFE started out as a fairly modest project, it soon mushroomed in size and scope. Within a few years it was broadcasting across Eastern Europe through multiple transmitters and had a staff of more than 2,000 people, three quarters of whom were not U.S. nationals.[8]

Sport quickly emerged as an expedient way for RFE to reach a broad audience in several of the Eastern European regimes. The radio's broadcasting policy expounded on the need to cover the achievements of refugee athletes, highlight the poor sportsmanship of Soviet competitors, and celebrate the amateur status of athletes in the free world and the "democratic character of the organizations in which they received their training."[9] As with other standard material prepared for RFE, sport stories were formulated with propaganda in mind, capitalizing on episodes that programmers estimated might be disruptive behind the Iron Curtain. More straightforward reporting was also important. Sports enthusiasts often care for simply the outcome of a contest rather than any melee that surrounded it. For example, a proposal for Czechoslovakian programming suggested a show named "sports around the world," which included news about Czech and Slovak sportsmen in exile and also reported on up-to-date results for soccer or track and field.[10] In the late 1950s, audience analysis conducted by RFE called for more sport coverage than the radio actually provided. A report on Polish programming ranked sport programs "among the most desired,"[11] and another study, commissioned by RFE and undertaken by Zbigniew Brzezinski of Harvard University, reached a similar conclusion. "Poland, as many modern mass societies, is almost in a state of frenzy over sports, and I think more frequent and fuller sports programs could attract even a wider audience," Brzezinski contended.[12]

One of the benefits that endeared RFE to many people in Eastern Europe was the speed of its reporting on current affairs. It often took communist stations a great deal of time to not only produce a story, but also get it approved for air by senior government officials. RFE did not have such restrictions. Of course, news had to pass through the gaze of an editor, or a translator, but all that could be completed at a pace that left its communist counterparts far behind. Accounts from refugees confirmed this fact. When four Hungarian exiles were interviewed by RFE staff to gauge the effectiveness of the station's content, the question of sport arose in the discussion. One of the refugees replied that he greatly enjoyed sport and that "the listeners at home [in Hungary] especially appreciate it that you [RFE] always broadcast the sports events earlier than Budapest. This has especially become obvious since the Olympic games."[13] In fact, broadcasting the games was an early struggle for RFE. For the same reasons that afflicted the Voice of America, it faced difficulties getting accreditation from the organizers in Helsinki and Oslo. Creativity and determination often overcame red tape. In Oslo, for instance, the broadcast was made from a hotel room.[14]

In addition to using sport as a propaganda tool on the airwaves, it could also be found in the NCFE's printed magazine, *News from behind the Iron Curtain*. Produced by the committee's Research and Publications Service division, *News from behind the Iron Curtain* supplied information to readers about communism in action. By the end of 1952, its circulation reached ten thousand and the NCFE distributed the publication in thirty-eight countries. The journal mainly consisted of refugee accounts and reports culled from the Eastern European media, all of which was gathered into a monthly edition to illustrate negative aspects of life in the Soviet bloc. Sports were given some attention, none of it positive. "To be a good sportsman in present-day Czechoslovakia," read a quote from a refugee in a typical article, "is determined by one's political 'maturity' rather than one's athletic skill. Political 'maturity' is judged by membership and activities in the Communist Party and the Union of Czechoslovak Youth."[15] Overall, the general aim of the sport-related stories was to demonstrate the ideological nature of sport behind the Iron Curtain, its use for propaganda and indoctrination, its restrictive nature, its military leaning, its contribution to solidarity among communist nations, and the professionalism of communist athletes. As one column assessed, "To the Communists, sports are a grim and serious business. They form an integral part of the regimented Communist State System and are assigned a specific function in the Communist propaganda machine."[16]

At one stage or another, too, the NCFE also provided meager funds to a small number of refugee sports groups operating in Europe. The organization was linked to the Polish Sokol Union in Lens, France, the DTJ Czechoslovak Sports Verein in Vienna, the Hungaria Sports Club in Paris, and the Austria-based World Federation of Hungarian Refugee Sportsmen.[17] Nevertheless, the focal point of sport-related propaganda that received the committee's backing was on initiatives orchestrated, in most instances, with cooperation from the HNSF. Formed in 1949 under the auspices of the Hungarian National Council, the HNSF operated as "a popular instrument for propaganda against the enslavement of physical culture by international communism" and aimed to help refugee athletes to start a new life beyond the Iron Curtain and utilize their political potential.[18] As the organizers of the NCFE had already recognized, anticommunist propaganda was far more effective if it came from the voice of someone who had lived the experience. What the HNSF provided were athletes with intimate knowledge of the sporting culture in Hungary and a motivation to reveal what they saw as its abysmal flaws. All that the HNSF needed was financial help to pursue its goals, and a suitable forum in which to express them. The NCFE fulfilled the first of these requirements and sporting competition satisfied the second.

The individuals involved in the HNSF were dedicated anticommunists who hoped that their own small contribution would one day lead to the collapse of communism in Hungary. One name became synonymous with the group's work: the president of the HNSF, Count Anthony Szápáry. Descended from a distinguished Hungarian family, the count made his journey to the United States following some almost catastrophic experiences at the time of, and after, Hitler's attempt to master Europe. During the war Szápáry was an officer of the Hungarian Red Cross and helped to aid the Polish refugees who swarmed into Hungary. He was arrested by the Germans in 1944, imprisoned in the Mauthausen concentration camp, and condemned to die.

Count Anthony Szápáry,
President of the Hungarian
National Sports Federation.
Courtesy of Gladys and
Paul Szápáry.

To his considerable good fortune, an intervention by the king of Sweden
saved his life. He arrived in the United States in 1948, found employment
at the Chesapeake and Ohio Railroad, and later married the granddaughter
of Cornelius Vanderbilt, a descendant of the great commodore.[19] Szápáry
possessed a sound knowledge of international sport and was familiar with
the training methods in the Soviet Union and its imprisoned countries. He
was always keen to highlight the difference in ideology between sport in the
East and West, with the former always taking the brunt of his criticism. "In
these countries competitors and their performances are used for political
propaganda, athletes are forced to make political statements, to sign political
petitions and to solicit political funds," he complained.[20]

Aside from its base in New York, the HNSF had thirty-one affiliated sports
clubs worldwide, in locations such as Brussels, Buenos Aires, London, Paris,
Rome, and Salzburg. It claimed to have representatives in twenty-three countries, and it published sports newspapers in Canada and Argentina. In 1958
the HNSF was incorporated.[21] By the end of the 1950s, the NCFE was providing an office and regular funding for the group, but it is unclear in the records
whether Szápáry knew about the origin of the NCFE's financial support. That
said, he was a well-respected member of the Hungarian exile community and
familiar with other Hungarian groups that received money from the NCFE.

In light of that fact, it is worth considering the opinion of the former NCFE employee John Foster Leich: "The exiles without exception assumed that government funds were involved, and were glad of this evidence of United States interest in their cause."[22] It is also hard to be precise about the total amounts the NCFE funneled to the HNSF over the years. On multiple occasions it is indicated that the NCFE gave the HNSF funding from the outset. A confidential budget review for fiscal year 1959–60 indicates that the HNSF collected $18,486 (the equivalent of approximately $151,000 in 2014) for its program, and there is every reason to believe that it was given an allowance before that. It does appear, however, that the funding subsided in 1960 and was canceled by the NCFE in 1962.[23] In return for its investment, though, the NCFE gained access to the rich propaganda potential of sport.

The Idea for a Refugee Olympic Team

Entering refugee athletes into international competitions, a key component of the HNSF's aims, certainly presented Szápáry and his colleagues with a considerable obstacle. International sports federations, and the IOC, were organized around the primacy of the nation-state; individual sportsmen had to be affiliated with their national federations who, in turn, had to be recognized by the international governing body. In the case of the IOC, its charter dictated that athletes who wanted to compete in the Olympics were obliged to be members of the national Olympic committee of their respective nation. As refugee athletes were, in effect, without a national Olympic committee, their situation was difficult. There was, moreover, a further complication. It was not enough for stateless athletes to simply become citizens of a different country. The charter prescribed that if they had already competed for one country in the Olympics, then they were forbidden to compete for another.[24] For more than a dozen years after its foundation, the HNSF lobbied the IOC on its provision for refugee athletes, seeking a change in the rules, not just for the sake of émigré sportsmen, but also for the concomitant rationale of propaganda.

The germ, then, for the project that translated into the Union of Free Eastern European Sportsmen came from the HNSF. At first, Szápáry wanted Hungarian refugees to compete in international competition because he thought that the impact in Hungary would be disruptive. He probably never considered that it might cause a revolution, but he might have thought it could contribute to one. Being as this was the aim, it made sense that the HNSF would want its athletes to compete at the Olympic Games, an international athletic festival that drew great attention across the globe. It made equal sense that he should first contact the head of the USOC, Avery Brundage. Upon receiving his first letter from the count, Brundage was terse but encouraging. "I shall keep your organization in mind," he told Szápáry. "If at any time there are developments that might be of interest to you, I shall let you know."[25] Even though Brundage's response was vague, it made a mockery of his well-known beliefs on the separation of politics from sport. It is doubtful that he knew about the covert function of the NCFE, the reality of who directed the organization, and by whom it was funded. At no point in his correspondence does he even hint at possessing such knowledge. But he did know, because Szápáry had explicitly stated it, that the HNSF was political. If Brundage had followed his personal dictum, he would have thrown the letter away. But he did not, and in this case, he put his principles aside.

Although Szápáry referred only to Hungarian athletes in his communication, they were not the only sportsmen and sportswomen to defect from Eastern Europe in the early Cold War years. It became a regular occurrence, in particular, at international athletic events. In 1948, the *New York Times* commented on the presence of athletes amongst the "flight of refugees from behind the Iron Curtain," and observed that "they are merely the most noted participants in an exodus which has been going on since the end of the war and is now proceeding in a steadily expanding wave."[26] Many of these athletes were still willing and capable of pursuing their sporting ambitions even if the rules of many sports federations would not allow it. Szápáry, of course, would have been aware of this. He had already begun to assess the possibility of émigrés competing in international sport by writing to Brundage, and though the Olympic Games were not mentioned by either party, the implication was clear. It is also clear that the HNSF started to look beyond the participation of only stateless Hungarian athletes at the Olympics and began to consider an East European exiled team for the Olympic festivals of 1952.

By 1951, the HNSF started to broker this idea to the NCFE. Though the documents on this formative period are haphazardly dated, if dated at all, it appears that probably by April the matter reached the NCFE's staff. Andor Gellért of the NCFE proposed a meeting between himself; the secretary of the HNSF, Péter Zerkowitz; and another committee employee, Robert Cutler. Gellért explained to Cutler that the issue of stateless athletes was due to be raised at the IOC session in Vienna (which never happened) and that Brundage was in favor of the proposal. Gellért added that a refugee sports team, based upon the model of the HNSF, could be formed and "function in accordance with the guidance" of the NCFE. Clearly taken with the scheme, Gellért commented on the "tremendous propaganda" that "could be derived" in relation to "the countries behind the Iron Curtain."[27]

As the idea of a refugee sports team remained only an idea, Zerkowitz—a former vice president of the European Judo Federation—produced a memorandum to clarify what was needed to make it a reality. First, he stated the problem: stateless athletes could not compete in some official championships under the existing rules of international sports organizations. Nevertheless, the HNSF managed to identify a small number of precedents that proved that rules could sometimes be navigated or broken. The skater Kornél Pajor had competed as an exile at the World Championships in 1951 after defecting; the HNSF had been recognized by the International Sport Shooting Federation; and a refugee Hungarian soccer team had played some competitive games, even though the Fédération Internationale de Football would not give the team full recognition. Zerkowitz argued that a group would be more effective than trying to get individual entries at the Olympics, and that it was crucial that this group have the backing of both the NCFE and Brundage before it applied for official recognition from the IOC. Zerkowitz also produced an inventory of the most capable émigré sportsmen, to establish that such a team could hold its own at the Olympic Games. Among the athletes he listed were gymnasts, fencers, swimmers, boxers, wrestlers, more than forty soccer players, and Hungary's silver-medal-winning water polo team from the 1948 games. In sum, the aim of group would be (1) "Co-coordinating and developing the exiled national sports federations," (2) "Exploiting the tremendous propaganda value inherent in the activities of the organization," and (3) "Participation in international sports events." Finally, the group needed money.[28]

With the potential of a refugee Olympic team capturing the attention of NCFE staff, the project took form. As well, intelligence from behind the Iron Curtain pointed to the need for action. The story of refugee athletes and the Olympic Games was greeted positively in Hungary, for example. A report received from Budapest by the Hungarian desk of RFE called for more information on the subject because it had stirred a great deal of interest.[29] Without support from influential sports officials and the sanction of the IOC, however, the émigrés did not stand a chance, and so it was to this vital cohort that the NCFE turned.

There was reason for optimism. Brundage had been contacted early in 1950 and seemed responsive to the situation faced by stateless athletes, so the NCFE started to seek assistance from other U.S. sporting organizations. In June 1951, two representatives of the NCFE, one of whom was Frank C. Wright Jr., met with Daniel Ferris, the secretary-treasurer of the AAU and a member of the USOC executive board. They discussed the refugee conundrum over lunch. A week later, Wright informed Ferris that NCFE president C. D. Jackson was "very anxious to follow through with the matter," and that he wished to meet with Brundage.[30] Ferris tried, but failed, to arrange this conference. Ferris did, however, write a letter to Brundage intending to "pave the way" for a discussion on stateless athletes in the next session of the USOC executive board, scheduled for June 29–30.[31]

In spite of this reassurance from Ferris, Wright prepared a draft letter for Brundage. Since the letter was to be signed by the president of the NCFE, Wright asked Jackson for "any suggestion as to how we can squeeze the very last drop of publicity out of an opportunity which is, according to Brundage, almost inevitably going to result in a negative answer."[32] The final version of the missive, which is dated 30 January 1952 and signed by Jackson, contained several persuasive arguments. Jackson understood that the main problem for the moment was the IOC rules, and so he alluded to Article 1 of the Olympic Charter, which stipulated that no person should be barred from the games for reasons that are either racial, religious, or political. Jackson followed this point by arguing that the refugee athletes were not so much interested in representing "another country" but the "exile community" instead. Furthermore, Jackson reasoned, the rules were subject to some flexibility and cited the decision by the International Sport Shooting Federation to recognize the HNSF. He concluded his case by stating, "The National Committee for a Free Europe is anxious to place the question before your Committee [USOC] in order to bring it to a conclusion in the International Committee as soon as conveniently possible."[33]

By November 1951, Brundage was already aware of a general NCFE strategy, having received a further letter from Szápáry. "Negotiations have been initiated," Szápáry announced, "with the competent authorities of the National Committee for a Free Europe, who are willing to support—may be also financially—the plan of organizing a Free Europe Olympic Association under the auspices of which sportsmen escaped from behind the iron curtain would participate as a group in the Olympic Games." The NCFE, he claimed, intended to sponsor approximately thirty to thirty-five of the finest refugee athletes to compete in Helsinki. Szápáry asked Brundage for his support: "The realization of this generous initiative depends, in the first place, on you, Mr. Brundage." The count tried his best to veil the political motivation of the proposal. "Those sportsmen in exile are led by the true spirit of fair play," he wrote, "whilst Bolshevism takes sport for nothing but as a means of propaganda."[34]

Faced with an escalating situation, Brundage confessed to being "at a loss to know what to do."[35] He knew that there was no chance that the refugees could be admitted; the rules of the IOC forbade it. To further complicate the issue, the IOC presided over the reentry of the Soviet Union into the Olympic Movement at the 1951 IOC Session in Vienna. Still, he did not drop the issue and dispatched a letter to Szápáry to offer him at least a glimmer of hope. He reiterated to the count the sympathy he felt for their cause, while also reminding him that the "existing rules" of the Olympic Charter simply did not accommodate the émigré sportsmen. All that Brundage felt he could do was to place the issue on the agenda for the IOC session in Oslo, due to convene in February 1952.[36] This was the very approach recommended by the USOC executive, and precisely the approach Brundage followed. The decision led to the first success for what became the Union of Free Eastern European Sportsmen. Staff members at the NCFE were pleased at the international exposure. Wright wrote to Jackson, "Consideration by the International Olympic Committee should provide us with many handles to take hold of for propaganda purposes."[37]

The Union of Free Eastern European Sportsmen and the Helsinki Games

Although the organizers of the Oslo winter games confirmed that athletes without membership in a fully recognized national Olympic committee could not pursue a medal at the festival, the question of refugees was indeed raised for discussion at the Oslo IOC session.[38] Sigfrid Edström, the IOC president, explained to the assembly that many refugees, including former Olympic champions, had come together with the intent to participate at Helsinki and queried the members for any suggestions that might solve the problem. The most influential contribution came from Erik von Frenckell, the Finnish delegate. According to the minutes of the meeting, von Frenckell stated that it was too late to consider the application for the Helsinki games and contended that the refugees would be too old to enter the 1956 games in Melbourne.[39] Edström agreed with the argument, and thought—though with an unfortunate choice of words—that the "fugitive question" was "a passing problem that we must not pay too much attention to."[40] This line of thought, along with the rules of the Olympic Charter, became the standard IOC thinking on the problem of stateless athletes in relation to Helsinki.

Undeterred by the proceedings in Oslo, the plan for a refugee Olympic team continued. Running initially under the title Free Eastern European Olympic Committee, it soon evolved into the Union of Free Eastern European Sportsmen. In a geographical sense, the union purposed to represent the refugee athletes of ten nations "enslaved by the Kremlin": Albania, Bulgaria, Czechoslovakia, Estonia, Hungary, Latvia, Lithuania, Poland, Romania, and Yugoslavia.[41] From a financial standpoint, the NCFE paid for the cost of the project and for other items, such as mailing expenses and cables that could spread the union's story in the media.[42] The group also drafted a constitution, elected officials, and established an executive committee.[43] When it came to forming the union, though, Hungarians bore a considerable amount of the administrative burden, with Szápáry chairing the organization and Zerkowitz serving as general secretary.[44] Having completed these bureaucratic steps, the fledgling committee applied for official recognition from the IOC in May 1952 and then began its short but eventful campaign to compete in Helsinki.[45]

Not long after this application had been sent, the union made its first significant move to generate public exposure by arranging for a reception at the Weylin Hotel in New York City. Szápáry sent an invitation to Brundage, and another to John T. McGovern, the counselor of the USOC.[46] In a somewhat odd letter to Brundage two days previous, McGovern claimed that he had never heard of the group and was unsure of their intentions. Wary of any association being implied with the USOC, McGovern declined the invitation.[47] Even though McGovern had been part of the USOC's discussion on refugees earlier in the year, and even communicated with NCFE officials, he now did not want to endorse them. His actions failed to send the desired message, as the UFEES still claimed the backing of the USOC in the coming weeks. As for Brundage, he chose not to attend the soirée either; like his colleague, he was careful of making any official connection between himself and the IOC with the exiled Olympic committee. This, too, was a wasted gesture; Brundage had been painted as a supporter of refugee athletes for some time. In a letter to McGovern, he did not hide his admiration for the UFEES, extolling the "first class athletes" and the "high class individuals" who were associated with the group.[48] One U.S. sports official who did attend the reception was Daniel Ferris from the AAU. He was joined at the Weylin by Richard B. Walsh of the U.S. State Department, and the new chairman of the NCFE, Rear Admiral H. B. Miller.[49]

As Helsinki fast approached, the story behind the UFEES began to receive national publicity. On 21 May, an Associated Press release on the refugee athletes was carried by newspapers throughout the United States. The article acknowledged that the IOC session in Helsinki was the last chance for the UFEES. "We are more hopeful than confident," admitted Szápáry. "We realize that the time is short but even if we do not obtain approval to compete in Helsinki, we hope to obtain permission for our exiled athletes to participate in future events."[50] Another article on the union claimed that the number of world-class athletes associated with the organization grew by the day and included "16 Olympic, 20 World and 35 former intercollegiate champions."[51] One of them was Stella Walsh, a Polish-born track athlete who relocated to the United States. She was highly enthusiastic about the possibility of taking the Olympic stage for her third time as part of the UFEES team. Walsh correctly thought that Brundage favored the exiles' entry, but she acknowledged that the Soviet delegates in the IOC might quash the proposal. "For that reason," said Walsh, "I suspect that our chances are slim."[52]

It is not surprising that the newspaper coverage provided the UFEES with opportune moments to criticize the communist bloc. During interviews with the media, Zerkowitz openly disparaged what he saw as the Soviet Union's motivations for sending its athletes to Helsinki. He charged that Soviet sport records were falsified and that Soviet victories against the satellite nations were rigged by biased officials and played by dubious rules. He also drew attention to the systematic training and financial rewards given to Soviet athletes and even questioned whether the Soviet Union would attend Helsinki when faced with a superior U.S. team. "The Russians are like children," Zerkowitz told reporters, "they can't stand to lose."[53] Further accusations from Zerkowitz, combined with NCFE information on the close surveillance of Iron Curtain athletes by communist authorities, were also featured in U.S. newspapers. In addition, the whole issue was carefully manipulated by the U.S. government's propaganda machinery. RFE beamed information about the team behind the Iron Curtain, while stories on refugee athletes were featured in Voice of America broadcasts and in the State Department's international propaganda output.[54] It all added to the generally negative depiction of Soviet sport that filled column inches across the United States.

The Hungarian National Council (HNC), one of the national councils sponsored by the NCFE, also managed to expand the union's campaign through clandestine efforts to influence the IOC. This process started when Paul Auer, an HNC representative in its Paris office, communicated to Edström that the subject of refugee athletes had been raised at the January session of an organization named the European Movement in London.[55] Unbeknownst to Edström, he faced another front. Like other components of the state–private network, the European Movement aimed to prevent communist expansion by rallying support for a united Europe. With Winston Churchill among its leading advocates, it approached the U.S. government in 1948 to acquire unofficial funding, and a large portion of the $3 million that propped up the group from 1949 to 1960 arrived via the CIA.[56] But when Edström received Auer's communication, he was unmoved.[57] The matter did not halt there. One of the ideas that the European Movement strongly supported was the creation of the Council of Europe, yet another outlet for its pro-unity position.[58] Under advice from Auer, the Council of Europe (formed in 1949) subsequently contacted the IOC chancellor, Otto Mayer, to discuss the participation of stateless athletes in future Olympic Games. Mayer, however, rejected each query he received. "It has been considered that giving satisfaction to the exiles would mean changing the complete machinery of our whole world organization, and this is impossible," Mayer explained apologetically.[59]

The key, then, to a refugee team participating at the 1952 summer games rested firmly on the outcome of the IOC meetings scheduled for Helsinki. The IOC had received the official application for recognition from the UFEES, and Otto Mayer informed the group that the final decision would be made in the executive committee meeting in July, shortly before the games opened.[60] With that, Szápáry produced a lengthy letter to sway the minds of any members in the IOC's executive committee who might have been undecided. He asked them to consider the very nature of the Olympic Movement, the high ideals proclaimed in Article 1 of the Olympic Charter, and why, despite the rule violation, the Soviet Union was allowed to send its professional athletes to compete. Most of all, and on behalf of the ten nations the UFEES represented, Szápáry attacked the regimes from which each athlete had escaped: "These stateless athletes are barred from the most noble Festival of the youth, just because their political convictions were against a regime which took over each of their countries by force, and which will tolerate no political opposition whatsoever."[61]

So important was the IOC meeting in Helsinki that the UFEES decided on a last-minute plan to lobby its cause. Zerkowitz wrote to Wright with another request: money to send two representatives of the UFEES to attend the critical IOC meeting. Zerkowitz drew Wright's attention to the "attack launched against us by the Communist press and radio" as evidence of the group's effectiveness.[62] A final chance to speak with IOC delegates in Helsinki could only cause more disquiet in the Soviet bloc and increase the chance of recognition for the team. Miller compromised and cleared the way for one UFEES delegate to make the eleventh-hour journey.[63] The task fell to a Hungarian émigré named Thomas de Márffy-Mantuano.

This was not the first time Márffy had entered the plot. At the IOC session in Oslo, he had spoken discreetly to Brundage about refugee athletes and he had also written a passionate letter to Jackson on the same subject.[64] His past explains why. Márffy was a Hungarian aristocrat by birth and was educated at Cambridge. In 1929 he passed the examination to enter the Hungarian Foreign Ministry. This gave Márffy access to powerful people and high politics. He experienced for himself the hypnotic power of Hitler during a state dinner in Rome and was a helpless spectator in Poland, where he witnessed a Nazi airplane gun down an innocent peasant girl. He despised National Socialism. He also detested the Soviet influence in Hungary after World War II. When a communist suggested that Márffy join the party, he replied, "How could I? You stand for the destruction of my class, my ideals, my religion."[65] In the postwar years Márffy was relieved of his position in the Hungarian foreign ministry as his aristocratic lineage no longer suited a government increasingly dominated by the Communist Party. Nearly all of his family was released from Hungary by the persistent lobbying of his sister, the Countess of Listowel, a resident of Great Britain. Márffy took refuge in Vienna for a while and fought in diplomatic circles to join his wife and two of their three children in England. The countess eventually secured Márffy's entry, and some years later, that of his final sibling, Peter. Márffy's struggle to aid exiled sportsmen was motivated by his resentment of the communist regime in Hungary and a lifelong love of sports. He claimed that captaining the 1936 Hungarian Olympic field hockey team was one of his greatest honors.[66]

Upon arriving in Helsinki, Márffy distributed a pamphlet prepared by the HNSF for the Hungarian Olympic team and made efforts to speak with a large number of IOC delegates, claiming that most supported his arguments on refugee participation. Apparently Otto Mayer was "in all respects most helpful."[67] Márffy might well have gained this impression, but years later Mayer recalled that Márffy was a "nuisance" who "upset everybody."[68] Márffy was permitted to speak at the official IOC press conference and asked Mayer whether he could do the same in front of the IOC members at the general session. But first the executive committee deliberated the case. On 14 July, Brundage addressed the executive committee, outlined the problem, and confirmed that the rules did not permit refugees to take part. After a long debate, the executive could not reach a satisfactory conclusion and referred the case to the general session, due to convene two days later.[69] Márffy was told that he could speak before the plenum. The proceedings of the general session opened at 2 p.m. on 16 July. Following some introductory comments, and other business, the refugee issue took center stage. Edström summarized the problem and handed the floor to Márffy. Grasping the moment, Márffy appealed to the IOC members on the plight of stateless sportsmen. He asked that the IOC authorize the International Sports Federations to recognize the refugee athletes, or that the UFEES might be able to compete either under the banner of the International Red Cross, the Olympic Rings, or possibly even through "the intermediary of countries such as Switzerland or Greece." He asked for leniency in the interpretation of Article 1 of the Olympic Charter. He pointed to the decision to include China at the games and the example of the recent Wimbledon tennis championships, in which stateless players had taken part. Having completed his oratory, Márffy withdrew and left the decision to his audience. Edström explained that the executive committee had looked at the problem at length but could find no way of admitting the group. The assembly vetoed the entry and the session adjourned at 4:30 p.m.[70]

Days after the IOC announced its decision, Szápáry sent his reaction to the *New York Times*. Referring to the athletes of the UFEES, he wrote, "For 'choosing freedom' they are now banned from the greatest sports event of the world." Szápáry challenged the participation of the Soviet Union and the other countries behind the Iron Curtain, which were allowed to compete despite their professional athletes. Blame was apportioned two ways: The IOC was guilty of its adherence to an "obsolete rule," and the Soviet bloc was culpable for protesting against the participation of the refugees.[71] Whether the Soviets did in fact protest is unclear. The minutes of the IOC session in Helsinki reveal nothing on the subject and a later report prepared by Zerkowitz is no more illuminating. Publicly, the IOC stood behind the reasoning expressed in Oslo by Erik von Frenckell and the edicts of the Olympic Charter. What happened behind closed doors in Helsinki, we do not know.

In his final account on the Helsinki games, Zerkowitz expressed delight with the results of the UFEES campaign. He quoted an article in the Hungarian newspaper, *Szabad Nép*, which labeled the émigré sportsmen traitors, and noted that Radio Warsaw and Radio Prague had reported on the work of the union. The fact alone that the IOC voted to offer its sympathy to the refugees gave Zerkowitz reason to think that the efforts of the UFEES had been justified, and that the refugees had "the moral support of the free world." He continued, "Through our representative's conversations with officials and delegates as well as some of the Iron Curtain team members the propaganda value of the Union became clear which originates from its very existence." He called for a further intensification of activities by refugee athletes and a greater use of "sports as a means for propaganda" in broadcasts behind the Iron Curtain. The results of work thus far, concluded Zerkowitz, was "beyond expectations."[72] Wright agreed, stating that "it is considered by all to have been a fine investment, particularly in view of the wide syndicated news coverage given the petition in the press."[73]

Szápáry maintained contact with Brundage despite the setback of 1952. He even proposed a new idea to navigate the issue and suggested that international federations could nominate one or two athletes to compete at future Olympics, thus abandoning the idea of a refugee Olympic committee.[74] Szápáry hoped that the issue could be discussed at the 1953 IOC general session in Mexico City. Unfortunately, the international federations were not invited to Mexico and so could not be petitioned. Even if they had been present, Brundage predicated that "opposition in the Federations from their members who come from behind the Iron Curtain will prevent them from taking affirmative action."[75] A year later, Zerkowitz took one last stab on behalf of the UFEES for the next general session in Athens. He asked Wright whether the NCFE would pay for a delegate to be flown to Athens to speak to the IOC in person. Once again, Márffy was dispatched to cajole the IOC delegates and raise awareness in the media. The IOC declined to discuss the issue, striking what must have been a final blow to the UFEES.[76] From 1954 onward, letters from the organization ceased to arrive at the IOC, but the HNSF, which provided the main ballast for the refugee Olympic team, did not fold quite so easily.

5 A New Olympic Challenge

Shortly after Dwight D. Eisenhower took office, Joseph Stalin suffered a fatal stroke. The Soviet dictator died on 5 March 1953. A small cadre of officials assumed leadership in the Kremlin, until Nikita Khrushchev eventually manipulated his way into power. Almost immediately, Stalin's successors took steps to reconfigure Soviet foreign policy. They brought an end to the Korean War and mended diplomatic ties with Yugoslavia, Israel, Turkey, and Greece. They also displayed a willingness to negotiate with the United States. "There are no contested issues in U.S.–Soviet relations," announced Georgi Malenkov, the chairman of the Soviet Council of Ministers, "that cannot be resolved by peaceful means."[1] These changes in foreign policy were complemented by an eddying Soviet commitment to waging the Cold War in the realm of culture. More foreign visitors entered Soviet borders, and the Kremlin sent a barrage of cultural representatives from country to country to show that communism was not a fearsome and repressive force but a vibrant, creative, and friendly doctrine. By contrast, Washington's reluctance to accept Moscow's peaceful overtures left the United States looking like the greater belligerent of the two superpowers. As a man with a well-calibrated appreciation for propaganda, Eisenhower looked upon the Kremlin's strategy as a "new type of Cold War."[2]

The Soviet policy of winning favor around the world through an intensified cultural offensive could be clearly discerned in the escalation of sporting exchanges between the communist bloc and the outside world. U.S. officials claimed that communist athletes functioned as cultural ambassadors wherever they visited, perpetuating a softer image of communism and contributing to a broader Soviet policy of forming contacts and alliances. In addition, the Soviet Union's ongoing aim of achieving supremacy in international sport also presented the United States with a new problem in the post-Helsinki years. Stalin had allowed a Soviet Olympic team to enter the 1952 summer games because he thought they would win the most medals. The slender margin of defeat suffered at the hands of the U.S. team did not quell, rather it strengthened, Soviet resolve. The Kremlin poured more resources into the cultivation of elite athletes, and with equal haste it was rewarded. It became a clear possibility to the interested observer that the 1956 summer games in Melbourne might not see the victory for the United States that was witnessed by onlookers in Finland.

The U.S. government's psychological warfare apparatus certainly identified the 1956 Olympics as a potential pressure point for future action. After all, it was easier to defend the U.S. sporting culture when U.S. athletes were winning athletic events around the world and dominating at the Olympics. But what if the United States were to lose on the Olympic stage? In the end, government officials used familiar tactics to wage this Olympic propaganda war. Psychological warfare experts became even more involved in the activities of U.S. sports organizations, and began to press the boundaries of the state–private relationship. Indeed, the level of state interference in the country's sporting establishment led some U.S. sports leaders, particularly Avery Brundage, to push back and even condemn the government for compromising the ideals that underpinned the nation's athletic structure. A debate in the U.S. Congress over whether the U.S. Olympic team should receive federal funding in order to create a level playing field with the communist professionals signaled the lengths to which sport had been affected by the unique conditions of the Cold War. Still, the government kept within the boundaries of state–private cooperation established by the Truman administration. Washington would work with U.S. sports officials, but not over them. And much like the approach in 1951–52, the Eisenhower administration would disseminate propaganda to global audiences in a strategy to secure a favorable climate of opinion on the U.S. participation in the Olympics and aim to discredit the performance of the Soviet Union in the case of either victory or defeat.

Sport and the Soviet Cultural Offensive

It is clear, then, that the evolving nature of Soviet foreign policy in the aftermath of Stalin's death placed significant demands on policymakers in Washington. But other crucial dynamics that emerged during Eisenhower's presidency, notes Kenneth Osgood, "further accentuated the ideological, political, and symbolic dimensions of the Cold War." Osgood argues that the "accelerating pace of decolonization in the third world raised the importance of the nonmilitary dimensions of the Cold War, as both superpowers competed for the political allegiance and vital economic resources of countries in Asia, Africa, and Latin America." Osgood also points to the influence of nuclear weapons on strategic planning. As it turned out, the United States was not prepared to launch a bomb at the Soviets, and when the Soviets attained nuclear capability, they did not the push the fateful button either. Both sides accumulated a host of nuclear weapons, but it achieved only a stalemate. In 1953, when the United States tested the hydrogen bomb, an even more destructive weapon, it was clear that a nuclear war could end in the destruction not only of a country, or of a continent, but possibly of much of civilization. For all these reasons, Osgood asserts, "psychological factors seemed more important than ever to winning this total contest for hearts and minds."[3]

Cultural relations, a showcase for peoples and nations, were therefore vital in such a war. The post-Stalin powerbrokers in the Kremlin, keen "to undo the harmful effects of Stalinist rudeness, secrecy, bluster, and violence," quickly increased the Soviet Union's commitment to international trade fairs, exchanges in cultural activities (e.g., ballet troupes, musicians, performing artists), and international athletics.[4] At the same time, communist propaganda portrayed the United States as a nation bereft of creativity, taste, and high art. Eisenhower responded in 1954. "I consider it essential," he said, "that we take immediate and vigorous action to demonstrate the superiority of the products and cultural values of our system of free enterprise." Congress cleared the way for a supplemental appropriation of $5 million to finance the President's Special Emergency Fund, and this fiscal backing was secured permanently in 1956, when legislators passed the International Cultural Exchange and Trade Fair Participation Act. With this monetary boost, the Eisenhower administration was able to embark on its own cultural offensive to promote a positive image of the United States in foreign lands. The emergency money for cultural exchange was directed primarily into programs that worked through private groups and organizations so that government involvement could be kept largely hidden or at least shielded. The State Department organized the cultural presentations program, and the administration's newly established psychological warfare machinery, the United States Information Agency (USIA) and the Operations Coordinating Board (OCB), coordinated the propaganda aspects of operations. As a result of this interagency cooperation, the administration was able to send a plethora of U.S. cultural representatives abroad, with NBC's symphony orchestra visiting the Far East, the Martha Graham Modern Dance Company performing across Asia, and Louis Armstrong and the Dizzie Gillespie Band touring worldwide. These and a multitude of other presentations were designed by officials to "refute communist propaganda by demonstrating clearly the United States' dedication to peace, human well-being and spiritual values."[5]

As well, the sporting component of the Soviet cultural offensive was the subject of a number of USIA reports, many of which were widely circulated in the administration. On the one hand, it appears, government officials were alarmed by the achievements of Soviet athletes. "Soviet victories, in virtually every form of sport, are creating the psychological effect the Soviet seeks—impressing on the minds of youth everywhere that communist youth is the new symbol of athletic perfection and that the myth of American sports supremacy has been shattered," explained one USIA analysis.[6] Yet officials also recognized that Soviet participation in sports had "taken a new psychological direction, one designed to create friendliness among the democratic and other non-communist countries." They believed that the USSR was trying to build friendships through athletics, avoiding the flagrant denunciation of democracy typical of previous years.[7] Intelligence experts noted that in 1954, for instance, the Soviet Union organized 59 exchanges with free world countries. In 1955 the number climbed to 137, and Moscow's total program of exchanges, including other communist countries, amounted to 178 sports groups (consisting of around 2,000 people) visiting the USSR and 142 Soviet groups (consisting of around 2,186 athletes) traveling abroad. For the most part, these interactions were with Western European nations, but officials also recorded the rising number of communist bloc exchanges with countries in Asia, Africa, and Latin America.[8]

This intelligence did not go unheeded. A portion of the funds that Congress granted for the expansion of cultural exchanges was set aside for sport-related tours, signifying the government's increasing acceptance that sport was a highly effective means of promoting U.S. society to global audiences. "If we Americans are sincere and devoted to making this exchange of persons a two-way street then we must present all facets of our life," wrote Harold E. Howland of the State Department. "Not only must we exchange the professor, the lawyer, the trade unionist, the member of government, but also our athletes. Certainly, athletics is a major facet of American life."[9] With the assistance and guidance of the Amateur Athletic Union of the United States (AAU), the State Department funded a large variety of tours for U.S. athletes to destinations on either side of the Iron Curtain. Between 1954 and 1960, approximately forty teams or individuals competed, gave clinics, or appeared at social occasions in Africa, the Far and Near East, Asia, South America, and Europe. "American athletes on tours abroad have won immeasurable respect and abundant good will for the United States," Howland proudly announced.[10] Reports from overseas posts also praised the value of these exchanges in combating communist propaganda about the United States. For example, the tour of the black middle-distance runner Mal Whitfield to Europe, North Africa, and the Middle East received glowing reviews from information officers in the countries he visited. An officer in Belgrade noted that Whitfield had "indirectly but effectively made the point that the Negro problem in the United States is regional rather than national."[11]

At no time in U.S. history had the government invested so heavily in sports diplomacy. Yet the number of exchanges still paled in comparison to the Soviet program. Moreover, the AAU explained, U.S. athletes were still underrepresented in international competitions. Many in government, now more cognizant of amateur athletics than ever before, knew that more had to be done to counter the global reach of communist sport. In his role as special assistant to Eisenhower on Cold War planning, Jackson was giving this issue serious consideration in mid-1953.[12] It also bothered his old colleague from the National Committee for a Free Europe, Abbott Washburn, now deputy director of the USIA.[13] Typically, he suggested creating another front organization. "What is needed," wrote Washburn, "is a group of distinguished leaders, some of them sports figures, to form a committee to take on the responsibility for seeing that the United States has the best possible representation at the most important overseas competitions." He told Jackson that the "committee would work closely, though informally and entirely unofficially, with USIA, CIA, and State." Money would not present a problem. Private business would help and funds could be channeled via covert foundations. Aside from U.S. sports officials, prospective members included John Whitney, a wealthy businessman who worked closely with the intelligence community; William H. Jackson, the former deputy director of the CIA; the golfer Ben Hogan; and Ford Frick, the commissioner of Major League Baseball.[14] The managing editor of *Time*'s new publication, *Sports Illustrated*, wanted a representative on the committee and offered space in the magazine for stories on the committee's work. Jackson even intimated that Eisenhower was "personally interested in this project."[15] Unfortunately, however, Jackson and Washburn could not find a suitable chairman for the committee, and so the entire plan hit a wall.[16]

A New Olympic Challenge

Although the Soviet Union had lost the 1952 Helsinki games to the United States, the performance of Stalin's athletes had left an indelible mark on the U.S. sporting landscape. Just months after the summer games had ended in

Finland, Douglas Roby, the AAU president, was already defining U.S. participation at the 1956 Melbourne games in terms of the Cold War conflict: "We saw a red danger signal at Helsinki," Roby blustered, "and the red was Russia." He accepted that U.S. citizens had done well in the major events (i.e., track and field) but that they were "woefully weak" in others, such as gymnastics and wrestling. "If we are going to win the Olympic Games in Australia, we have got to start an intensive period of training right now," warned the AAU chief.[17] Following Roby's lead, in January 1953 the AAU announced that it would endeavor to raise five hundred thousand dollars to accelerate its athletic development program to help bolster the U.S. chances of defeating the Soviet Union at the next Olympics. "We must beat Russia," Jeremiah T. Mahoney, the chairman of the AAU national fund-raising committee, told reporters.[18]

The steadily improving results of Soviet competitors in international events added credence to these claims. When the Soviets overpowered the United States at the 1953 world weightlifting championships, Arthur Daley wrote an indignant piece on the event for the *New York Times*. "This is far more than a straw in the wind," he declared. "It's a full hay mow blown away by a gale." The Unites States had earned only a narrow victory in Helsinki and would surely be defeated in Melbourne. "The Soviet athletes are virtually a cinch to oust us from our perennial world leadership and win the unofficial team championship unless all signs and portents have been grievously misread," Daley forecast.[19]

U.S. sports officials were soon arriving at a similar conclusion. In 1954 *This Week Magazine* published an interview with the United States Olympic Committee's (USOC) counselor, John T. McGovern. He held little back. As "a man who has intimately participated in the administration of the Olympics for much of his life, I must warn you that as things stand now, the U.S. will obviously be beaten at the Australian games in 1956," McGovern said. "In all probability Russia and her curtained neighbors will be the victors." McGovern argued that the Soviets had "launched a sports offensive designed to sweep us from the boards" at the Melbourne games "by developing track athletes who can finally conquer the Americans." He complained that the state-sponsored athletes of the Soviet bloc had a distinct advantage in time and resources for training, but that U.S. citizens could compete if they were willing to "fight for their lives." This had to be done, McGovern said, "in our uniquely American way" with private funds for the Olympic team, an intensified effort by college track programs, and better use of athletes serving in the military. But he thought that the United States had a fighting chance, a chance that would be inspired by voluntary traditions and a "free spirit."[20]

McGovern's article was soon being read and debated by psychological warfare experts throughout the administration. Although some dismissed the importance of the matter, others thought it "might be developed into a target of opportunity."[21] In fact, the general interest across government departments in the Soviet sports offensive resulted in a gathering at the Pentagon in late September 1954, attended by representatives of the USIA, the Department of Defense, the Department of State, and an unnamed member from USOC. Those assembled discussed the forthcoming participation of U.S. athletes at the Modern Military Pentathlon in October 1954, the Pan-American Games in 1955, and the winter and summer Olympics in 1956. "All such international sports events are being treated as a propaganda device by the Russian Communists and their satellites to increase the prestige of the Communist world and add to their propaganda theme of the invincibility of Communists and Communism," the group determined. Equally, they maintained, the communist bloc had an advantage over the "nations of the Free World" in sporting competitions because "the Red Governments can support preparation for events with their full financial strength" and resources.[22]

Even if the U.S. government would not attempt to emulate the communist strategy, it did assist in the fundraising drive for the U.S. Olympic team. A proclamation issued by Eisenhower, and passed by Congress, had named 16 October 1954 as National Olympic Day, and the USOC hoped that it would help to reach a target of $1.1 million. *Life* magazine offered its assistance to publicize the day and suggested that the president should continue to put his weight behind the drive through public appearances and statements stressing the "tremendous value of the Olympic Games" in the U.S. "competition with the Communists."[23] He did both. Eisenhower publicly announced his support for the USOC and opened the drive himself during half time of a televised football game between the universities of Southern California and Oregon. As well, district associations of the AAU joined the cause by holding special races, parades, demonstrations, carnivals, collections, dinners, and luncheons across the country. The AAU asked forty thousand retailers to place Olympic posters in shop windows to stimulate interest in the Olympics, and the company that produced *The Bob Mathias Story* offered to donate the proceeds from the film's premier night to the fund. The USIA managed to exploit the voluntary campaign by disseminating news of Olympic Day in its overseas output, describing the national resolve to take part in the games as a movement to "promote peace, understanding, and sportsmanship."[24]

Olympic Day, then, was part of a national effort to transform elite athletics in the United States in order to keep up with the Soviet Union's immense progress in the post-Stalin years. The AAU, having already committed to a massive fundraising campaign to improve athletic standards in the United States and to financing the U.S. Olympic team, took further steps to strengthen U.S. participation at the 1956 Olympic festivals by organizing a series of Olympic Development Meets in 1955 and 1956. These meets were designed to "spark a revival of interest" in the "orphan" events in which U.S. athletes had struggled during the Helsinki games, such as distance running and walking, the decathlon, the triple jump, the hammer throw, gymnastics, wrestling, and water polo. The AAU also stressed the importance of enhancing the opportunities for women to take part in the development meets in order to "figure out why we have so far to go before the quality of our women's performances matches those of our men."[25] The campaign soon paid dividends. Although sports officials accepted that more needed to be done, the AAU was still quick to declare that "the goal of strengthening our chances for the 1956 Olympic Games has been reached." This nationwide program invigorated U.S. Olympic officials with optimism and provided a doubting public with a rather more positive outlook for the upcoming summer games.[26]

Between Freedom and Control

Meanwhile, the growing public anxiety about the Soviet Union's potential to dominate in Melbourne soon led to several heated discussions on the subject in Congress. Possibly the loudest voice on the issue was that of Republican senator John Marshall Butler of Maryland. At times, it seemed, he was unable to restrain himself. On the evening of 9 June 1955, he told an audience at the Friendship International Airport in Baltimore: "Are we in the United States . . . allowing the Soviet Union to pollute the Olympic Games; to use, with diabolic deceit, the spirit of sportsmanship itself as a velvet gloved iron fist to ruthlessly hammer out their Godless propaganda?"[27] Butler called for Congress to encourage U.S. Olympic authorities to press for the elimination of Soviet professional athletes from the Olympics or, if that failed, to demand that the U.S. team should participate in the games "under official protest."[28] This suggestion clearly compromised the concept of peaceful internationalism that guided the Olympic Movement and was not something U.S. Olympic officials would sanction.[29] Even the State Department determined that this action would be unwise and added that it "may very well result in our country getting considerable criticism from abroad."[30] Other members of Congress attempted to pass bills that would, among other things, provide official government funding for the U.S. Olympic team. Such a drastic alteration of the U.S. Olympic administration, however, was not ratified on Capitol Hill. Vice President Richard M. Nixon clearly agreed with this position. "Let us show the world," he said, "that America can field a team financed by volunteer private contributions which will hold its own with the world's best."[31]

Butler's outbursts were part of a national discussion on Soviet sport that had been brewing for some time. The U.S. media was filled with "the deep and constant cries of horror about the possibility of the United States losing to Russia" at the Melbourne games and the impact such an outcome could, or could not, have on world opinion.[32] For those who aired their views on this imminent national disaster, the question of what to do about it naturally entered the discourse. Congress had debated whether the U.S. team should receive federal funding and *Sports Illustrated* magazine put the same question to several public figures. "Currently, the Olympics are on an uneven basis," remarked J. Walshe Murray, S.J., a psychology professor at Le Moyne College. He challenged the "unrealistic . . . attitudes of our officials" on the process of raising money, and urged that federal grants should be used in conjunction with private donations. "To be truly realistic—to see what is really 'there'—is to be sane," added the psychologist with an appropriate choice of words. The former Olympic swimming champion Eleanor Holm was of the same opinion. She thought it was "ridiculous" that the "richest nation" could not pay the expenses of its athletes. It is not surprising that U.S. sports officials did not share their perspective. Edward P. Eagan, the chairman of the USOC Fund Raising Committee answered no to government financial support. He explained that the "public is privileged to contribute" to the U.S. team and that the popular participation "adds a great deal of interest to the Games." Asa Bushnell, the secretary of the USOC, also answered the question with a no. "The U.S. Olympic team belongs to the public," he said. "We want to keep it that way." Perhaps, however, Warren Lee Pierson, chairman of the board of Trans World Airlines, hit the nail on the head as far as U.S. Olympic officials were concerned when he contended, "Where the Government contributes, it also controls."[33] The USOC consistently rejected the possibility of allowing government money to galvanize the country's Olympic team and, in so doing, maintained its hold on the fortunes of the U.S. Olympic effort.[34]

One of the few sport-related items acted upon by Congress was to clear a total of eight hundred thousand dollars for distribution among each of the military branches to brace their Olympic programs. This certainly pressed the boundaries of the separation between athletics and the state, but the results proved that a fertile reservoir had been tapped. John McGovern told the Operations Coordinating Board that more than half of the male U.S. competitors at the Pan-American Games in Mexico City were drawn from the armed forces, and he praised their "performances and behavior."[35] The USOC president, Kenneth Wilson, was equally pleased at the invaluable impact of military personnel on the U.S. team and acknowledged that the USOC was "counting on them" for the summer games in Australia. To an outside observer, though, this approach was far from credible. The British government's ambassador in Mexico noted the "grim determination" of the United States to build momentum at the Pan-American Games as if a defeat in Melbourne "would apparently be equivalent to losing the first vital battle in the next world war!"[36] When the U.S. team did march into the Olympic stadium in Melbourne, nearly a third of its 338 athletes were from the military.[37]

Despite the pronouncements of many concerned lobbyists on the preparation of the U.S. squad for Melbourne, no official funding for the U.S. Olympic team was sanctioned by Congress. In this instance, tradition ruled the day. In another case, it had been reversed. During the Truman administration, the USOC had responded to the conditions of the Cold War by assisting the government rather more than it had done in the past. This closer relationship became apparent once again in the post-Helsinki years, when the OCB asked McGovern for inside intelligence on Olympic issues. The OCB wanted to know what influence the Soviet Union had in the IOC, what the IOC members from the free world thought about the Soviet Union and other Iron Curtain countries, and an update on the issue of two Germanies in the Olympic Movement. Though McGovern was not an IOC member, he had access to U.S. citizens who were and based his reports on information from those sources.[38] McGovern's first report gave the OCB two issues to consider, both raised at the IOC General Session in Paris. The first was the award of the 1960 summer games to Rome, and the second was the East German effort to form an independent Olympic committee. McGovern claimed that the decision made by the IOC to select Rome to host the summer games, and Cortina d'Ampezzo to host the winter games, had been influenced by the large presence of communists in Italy. "It was thought by many of the delegates that the award successively of Winter Games and Summer Games to Italy would create a favorable attitude towards the West and perhaps keep the Italian population pro West at least during the period covered by the Winter and Summer Games," wrote McGovern.[39] Though other factors undoubtedly entered the consideration of IOC members, McGovern felt that politics had swayed the voting and accounted for the U.S. delegation finally supporting Rome, even though a bid had been lodged by Detroit.

The possible entrance of an East German team into the Olympic Movement was a less conclusive matter. McGovern explained that the Russian delegates had raised the East German question but that the IOC members had not decided on anything definite. A later letter he sent to the OCB, however, was more enlightening. In it, McGovern outlined a new IOC proposal disclosed by Douglas Roby. East Germany would be allowed to participate at future Olympics, but only as part of a joint team with West Germany, which already had full recognition. McGovern reassured the OCB that the Russians would not control the East German athletes: that privilege lay instead with the West German Olympic Committee, which was the preponderant partner. On the strength of Roby's statements, McGovern reported that "if it should happen that Russia might dominate the situation . . . the I.O.C. is prepared to cancel the participation by East German athletes" in the games. "I am confident this information will be pleasant to you," McGovern noted.[40]

McGovern consulted four members who were present at the Paris meeting. Though he trusted Roby, McGovern built his case around the information of one very important contributor: the president of the International Olympic Committee and McGovern's friend, Avery Brundage. McGovern revealed that he spoke to Brundage—"the most powerful man in the whole Olympic family" who was "unswerving in his efforts to obtain observance of amateur conformity"—for some time about state amateurs. It transpired that Brundage did not hold the opinion expressed by many in Washington. On several occasions, Brundage had said publicly that the Soviets would enter only amateur athletes in the Olympics, a point of view that McGovern attributed to "delusions inflicted by the nature of his geographical observations."[41] McGovern's statement most likely referred to Brundage's visit to Russia the previous year. In any case, it oversimplified the situation. At the IOC General Session in Athens (1954), it was decided that national Olympic committees must be responsible for policing their own athletes on amateurism.[42] Articles were incessantly published on Soviet professionalism in newspapers across the globe, and many press clippings found their way to Brundage's desk. On the content of those reports, Brundage directly challenged the Soviet IOC member, Konstantin Andrianov. "I wish that you could give me some definite supporting evidence which might offset this growing indignation against communist methods which are alleged to be in violation of Olympic rules," Brundage told his colleague.[43] Each time Brundage asked for an explanation, he was given one. He knew as well as anyone that communist athletes were funded by the state, but if Soviet sport officials told him that they were conforming to Olympic rules, then what more could he do?

Brundage had always been a diligent warden of amateurism in the United States but his comments do, in some way, reveal the change in his position after becoming the IOC president in 1952. In private correspondence, he still exhibited a deep anticommunism. In public, however, he kept these feelings largely to himself, an approach that earned him a massive amount of criticism in the United States. When, for instance, the U.S. media attacked the Soviet Union's mission to win the Melbourne Olympics, Brundage would have none of it. "It is not the strength of other people that we in the United States need fear," he lectured, "it is our national complacency and the softness in life brought on by too much prosperity."[44] When U.S. newspapers complained about Soviet state athletes, he pointed out that military personnel on the Olympic team received privileged treatment and that the scholarships given to college athletes were "notorious" for "gross irregularities."[45] And Brundage's ire was directed not merely at the U.S. public and press. By taking aim at the personnel in the U.S. Olympic team, he was also picking a fight with the USOC. Kenneth Wilson publicly supported the surplus of military participants on the U.S. team and said that he would defend this position if the IOC challenged it. Brundage refused to back down and continued to assert that the practice was no different from the methods deployed by the communists. Moreover, the State Department's goodwill tour program was another serious issue for the IOC president. Brundage wrote a series of letters to the USOC to complain about the tours and then openly accused the State Department of using athletes for "political purposes" in an interview for *Sports Illustrated*.[46]

The U.S. government and public should perhaps have been satisfied that a U.S. citizen was elected to lead the IOC at a time when influence was required in Lausanne. But Brundage did not always prioritize his country over the Olympic mission he directed. He became less cooperative with U.S. officials and even, to a degree, with other members of the U.S. sporting establishment.

The OCB Working Group on the 1956 Olympic Games

As time pressed on, talk in government departments about the "possible" defeat to the Soviet Union at the 1956 games was sometimes replaced by talk about the "inevitable" defeat. In January 1956, Leslie S. Brady of the OCB produced an influential memorandum that emphasized the sheer symbolic value of the Olympic Games in a war of words and ideas. "'The struggle for men's minds' slogan has led to an accent on wordiness that is not always appropriate. . . . Some things are not explained away at all . . . and any attempt at alibis ends up looking like . . . alibis," wrote Brady. "A case in point is the Olympic Games, fast upcoming. If the Russians win them, no amount of words from us will convince the world that they did not win or should not have won." He reasoned that a Soviet victory "might not immediately demonstrate to intellectuals that Russians are now superior to Americans," but "it would have an immediate impact on the man in the street, the worker, the rural citizen who reads little, the maiden who admires brawn." Although Brady feared the broad appeal of the Olympics, he was not convinced that nothing could be done, and he laid out a contingency plan that could act as "insurance against the worst." Like other plans prepared before, Brady targeted a number of areas for a propaganda offensive: the U.S. could draw attention away from nationalism as it related to the Olympics; preach that Soviet sport was an instrument of the state; plant negative material on communist sport in various media outlets; and implore the IOC to form an official scoring system so that the final medal count could not be manipulated behind the Iron Curtain. Finally, Brady thought the U.S. should flood all events with U.S. athletes to maximize the chances of winning medals, or be sure to publicize events the U.S. would not compete in. Brady stressed the importance of action. "Time's a-wasting. The Winter Games await only snow in Italy."[47]

Elmer B. Staats, the OCB's executive officer, considered the Brady memorandum to be a "sufficient introduction to the problem," and it soon led to the creation of an interagency working group on the issue.[48] Chaired by Frank L. Dennis of the USIA, representatives were also assembled from the Department of State, Department of Defense, CIA, International Cooperation Administration, and OCB.[49] The working group aimed to "develop courses of action, and assure their coordinated implementation, to achieve a favorable 'climate of opinion' in connection with U.S. participation in the Games."[50] Disguising the government's role in actions, though, still remained paramount for policymakers. "It is the consensus," read an OCB report, "that the hand of the U.S. Government must not appear publicly in operations, sponsorship, or management of American Olympic participation."[51]

Yet establishing a strategy was fraught with difficulties and complications. In particular, the interpretation and application of the amateur rule perplexed the OCB, in much the same way as it had the participants at the Pentagon meeting a few years before. The working group wanted to "preserve or create for the U.S. the optimum world-wide benefits from participation in the 1956 Olympic Games by U.S. athletes" but realized after months of deliberation that the "situation is not so uncomplicated as it may seem at first glance." A strategy of simply accusing the Soviets of professionalism, a propaganda tactic used in 1951–52, now appeared to have serious flaws. Like Brundage, officials noted that U.S. athletes from the military received full pay while they trained, that college athletes probably benefited from similar arrangements through scholarships, and that even athletes employed by private businesses were still given some "concessions" while they trained or competed. The working group assessed that the ambiguous status of many U.S. athletes meant that using the theme of Soviet professionalism "would be almost sure to backfire." The propaganda campaign had to change. The final report recommended that information materials should "emphasize the positive approach of U.S. participation in the Games," how the U.S. Olympic team was funded by private donations, and the "background of American athletes." The working group added that propaganda should stress the "nature and scope of state control in the USSR of athletes who would participate" in the Olympics but principally through "unattributed channels."[52]

The USIA, which served as the main conduit for this tactic, was to "continue and increase output prior to the Melbourne Games" in radio, television, publications, films, and feature stories.[53] It was more than equipped for the task. By the end of the 1950s, the USIA had more than 200 information posts in ninety-one free world countries, all of which received a steady stream of material for distribution to local audiences. The USIA's considerable output included carefully prepared feature packets filled with stories, pictures, and cartoons on key demographic areas, such as labor, women, and youth. Through these features, propaganda experts tried to overcome Soviet accusations about civil rights and general inequality in U.S. society, dispel communist allegations that the United States had no culture, and obliterate claims that U.S. women were materialistic glamour girls.[54] Sports stories, it turned out, continued to serve as a powerful form of news to communicate these and other messages about U.S. life. In 1954, the USIA initiated a feature packet specifically dedicated to sports when overseas public affairs officers "almost unanimously" declared that it was an area of interest to local audiences in the free world.[55] In many ways, these packets mirrored the approach taken by information officers in the Truman administration, as the USIA painted an idyllic picture of the U.S. sporting culture and often contrasted it with the totalitarian model experienced under communism.

Starting in late 1955, the USIA sent feature stories, reprints, glossy photographs, and cartoons of U.S. Olympic athletes to all its information posts, and the volume of material grew with each passing month as the winter and summer games drew closer. Some of the earliest articles returned to the staple topic of Olympic amateurism. Repeating the tactics from four years earlier, one feature carried the remarks of Avery Brundage, this time quoting his warning to the organizers of the festival in Cortina d'Ampezzo. "Not only are non-amateur entries to be banned," announced Brundage, "but even those who are believed to be willing to exploit their participation in the Olympics in an indirect way." The USIA followed up this item with a piece on the comments of Dr. Karl Ritter von Halt, the president of the West German National Olympic Committee, who blasted the so-called "sham amateurs" of the communist bloc.[56] Upon the OCB's recommendations, however, the amateur theme soon ebbed away from U.S. propaganda in 1956 as the USIA focused on other areas of the country's Olympic image.

This output incorporated a steady stream of material on the role of the United States in upholding Olympic principles of peace and fellowship, as opposed to pursuing a political agenda. In one story, for instance, the USIA managed to capture this message by widely disseminating Eisenhower's comments to the U.S. team just weeks before it left for Melbourne: "Throughout the years of our participation in the Olympic Games we have striven for athletic excellence as an expression of the vitality of our people," stated the president. "At the same time we have always tried to keep before us the true spirit of the Olympics which motivated the Baron De Coubertin to revive the ancient competitions and which governs the behavior of honorable men and nations in their friendly rivalries. This spirit of the Olympics, embodying a high code of sportsmanship, reflects the ideas of our democratic society."[57] Other features celebrated the work of U.S. coaches and trainers in the preparation of foreign athletes and squads. Pictures and stories lauded the technical and motivational contributions of coaches such as Larry Synder in India, Dave Albritton in Iran, and Gosta Ericksen in Sweden. The USIA also publicized the University of Oregon's track and field coach, Bill Bowerman, who spent two months developing athletes in Pakistan. The story explained Bowerman's admiration for the steadily improving Pakistani athletes and that he was "impressed" by their "general ability and enthusiasm."[58] An additional article praised how the U.S. Chamber of Commerce in Japan was helping to raise funds for the Japanese Olympic team to get to Melbourne. It proudly revealed that U.S. businessmen were so "impressed with the spirit" of the Japanese athletes at the winter games that they were eager to donate to the country's summer effort.[59]

U.S. propaganda experts produced and distributed a wealth of material on individual U.S. Olympians. Multiple features depicted the sportsmen and sportswomen as well-rounded, energetic, determined, and accomplished products of the U.S. social system. A profile of the weightlifter Jim Bradford enthused over the "reserved" and "quiet" second-year student from Howard University. "He is a good-natured, well-educated boy who makes an ideal sports ambassador of goodwill when he goes abroad," gushed Bradford's coach. "It's a pleasure to have him around."[60] A biography of the hammer thrower Harold Connolly emphasized the fact that he had overcome the handicap of a withered arm to become one of the best in his discipline in the world. Connolly paid tribute to the influence of a German coach for his improved technique and spoke of the warm reception he had received from fans while competing overseas. "A friendly person, Connolly is quick to make friends," the feature added.[61] Other materials illustrated the various talents of many U.S. Olympians by highlighting their interests in art and music. A cartoon of the gymnast Karl Schwenzfeier noted that he "likes to play the drums and trumpet in his spare time and enjoys listening to records, both popular and classical."[62]

In keeping with a general government information theme, USIA material on the female members of the U.S. team directly confronted communist propaganda on the daily lives of U.S. women. A profile of the outstanding skier Andrea Mead Lawrence explained how she adored raising her three children and did not feel that it had hindered or lessened her excitement for sport. "Still as modest as she was as a teen-aged girl, she hasn't let sports fame affect her," the USIA reported. "She is a natural person who doesn't use make-up and she wears a single barrette to control her long, brown hair—unless she is wearing it in pigtails." Mead Lawrence liked "to read books, enjoys classical music, and relishes the fireside fellowship of other skiers, fierce competition, and the smell of the mountain air." When not in competition, she appreciated spending time at her Colorado ranch with her husband and children. "We have thousands of rabbits, deer, elk, and fish," she said. "I like to fish myself. But there are plenty of ranch chores to keep us busy."[63] Further materials restated that U.S. women were family-oriented, motivated, feminine, and cultured. A cartoon of the Olympic swimming prospect Wanda Werner highlighted the fact that she wanted to become a novelist and helped her mother with housework, sewing, and knitting.[64] Other illustrations included the recently married gymnast Judy Howe, who worked as stenographer at a telephone company and "enjoys cooking and other household duties," and the swimmer Carin Cone, an "earnest student" and "devotee of music."[65]

The USIA's sports packets also attempted to present an image of U.S. racial and ethnic diversity through portraits of U.S. Olympians. Overlooking the discrimination and segregation that perforated U.S. society and its sports, propaganda experts avoided civil-rights issues by claiming that all U.S. Olympic athletes were prime examples of the progress anyone could make in a democratic system. A cartoon of the soccer star Ruben Mendoza described how he learned the game in Mexico as a boy but was now one of the leading players on the U.S. squad. "He plans to open a barber shop after his graduation from barbering school," the USIA explained in a caption about Mendoza's ambitions beyond the soccer field.[66] In much the same way, information on African American Olympic athletes also was carefully constructed. A cartoon of the basketball star Bill Russell stated that he wanted to become an accountant when his playing career ended and noted that for recreation "he likes to drive an auto and watch motion pictures."[67] The long jumper Gregory Bell was supposedly yet another benefactor of the U.S. way of life. In addition to his aspirations of breaking Jesse Owens's long-jump record,

JUDY HOWE of Pittsburgh
U.S. OLYMPIC GYMNAST

JUDY, 20, IS ONE OF SIX GIRLS ON THE U.S. WOMEN'S GYMNASTIC TEAM WHICH WILL COMPETE IN THE 1956 OLYMPIC GAMES AT MELBOURNE. SHE IS FIVE FEET FOUR INCHES TALL AND WEIGHS 130 POUNDS.

JUDY WORKS AS A STENO-GRAPHER FOR A TELEPHONE COMPANY.

RECENTLY MARRIED, SHE ENJOYS COOKING AND OTHER HOUSEHOLD DUTIES.

A United States Information Agency cartoon of the gymnast Judy Howe. Courtesy of the National Archives. College Park, Maryland.

a cartoon indicated, Bell was an honors student who hoped to become a dentist.[68]

The civil-rights question remained an Achilles heel for U.S. propagandists, but they, in turn, were able to exploit gaps in the communist armor. In addition to highlighting state amateurism or publishing accounts from the Soviet bloc media, the USIA continued to produce articles on the defection of Eastern European athletes as a way to undermine communist doctrine. According to a Hungarian exiled athlete interviewed in one story, communist claims that sport was aimed at cultivating a healthy population was just "empty talk." The

BILL RUSSELL of San Francisco University

U.S. OLYMPIC BASKETBALL PLAYER

BILL IS EXPECTED TO BE AN OUTSTANDING PERFORMER
IN THE 1956 MELBOURNE OLYMPIC GAMES.

RUSSELL WANTS TO BECOME
AN ACCOUNTANT WHEN HIS
PLAYING DAYS ARE OVER.
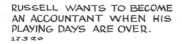
17320

FOR RECREATION, HE LIKES TO
DRIVE AN AUTO AND WATCH
MOTION PICTURES.
SP-376

A United States Information Agency cartoon of the basketball player
Bill Russell. Courtesy of the National Archives.

refugee asserted that sport behind the Iron Curtain was designed to isolate
and train elite athletes for propaganda purposes. "I knew I was being used as
a tool," he said. "It is questionable how long I could have stood the pace. They
(the communists) were driving me the way a bad jockey drives his horse. They
gave me shots—vitamin B and also ten cubic centimeter sugar shots." Yet the
USIA was able to provide audiences with a happy ending. "Now my life has
purpose again. I have a future, and if I should take part in sports, I shall do so
for my own pleasure," the Hungarian concluded.[69] Another USIA feature, this
time on Stella Walsh, echoed the point. Walsh, who competed for Poland at the
Olympics in 1932 and 1936, became a U.S. citizen in 1947 and wanted to qualify
for the U.S. national team. The IOC's rules prevented her from joining but she

declared that representing Poland was simply not an option. "The government which I represented does not exist," she said.[70]

In concert with a media blitz, the OCB working group sought to employ "all appropriate means to enlist maximum support" from the private sphere to further its objectives.[71] This strategy demanded that the government continue to pursue its ongoing, though sometimes muddled, relations with Avery Brundage. In compliance with OCB recommendations, Frank Dennis met with Brundage at the New York Athletic Club in order to communicate the propaganda problems of the Olympic Games and asked what the IOC president thought of them. Brundage felt that there was "less commotion" about Soviet sporting success in other countries, although the "Communists may . . . seek to utilize these victories in their propaganda."[72] A few weeks after their meeting, Dennis sent Brundage a newspaper clipping from the *New York Times*. The article considered the merits of altering the parameters of what counted as an amateur, something Dennis and other government experts believed might inject some parity in the competition between U.S. and Soviet competitors.[73] If the best U.S. athletes were in Melbourne, then perhaps the chances of the Soviet Union winning the Olympics could be vastly decreased. After reading the article, Brundage retorted that it must have been written by someone "who is not familiar with the Olympic Movement."[74] Rather than pushing to amend Olympic rules, Brundage suggested that the government should try to educate people in other countries about correct amateur standards. Dennis was, at least, prepared for the worst. An OCB strategy report had acknowledged the "anticipated difficulties of dealing with Mr. Brundage."[75]

Never afraid to air his opinions, the sports administrator also turned his attention to the ceremonial parade performed to open each edition of the Olympic Games. As national teams enter the Olympic stadium during the opening ceremony, it is considered respectful for each team to dip the flag of its country as it passes the seating position of the president, or monarch, of the country where the games are being staged. "That is," wrote Brundage in a letter to the State Department, "all except the United States flag."[76] Brundage thought the slight reflected poorly on the United States and simply asked for the policy to be amended. Though Brundage may have had good manners on his side, the State Department responded that the law of the land was not.[77] The matter of dipping the flag was included in the final working group report, but, when the U.S. Olympic team reached the Tribune of Honor at the Olympic Stadium in Melbourne, their flag remained vertical.[78] Brundage, no doubt, would have noticed this.

Brundage certainly noticed Eisenhower's selection of four personal representatives—Daniel Ferris, Bob Mathias, Sammy Lee, and Jesse Owens—to go to the Melbourne games. For Ferris, the mission was marred from the outset. He contracted pneumonia and spent most of his time in a hospital bed, watching the games on television. Owens, on the other hand, was commended by officials for his diplomacy during the visit, where he appeared at a range of social functions and made numerous appearances on television and radio. The U.S. consulate in Sydney heaped praise upon the Olympic legend for being able to "size up an audience and make the appropriate remarks in a most acceptable manner." A consulate official was especially pleased with the way that Owens had successfully dealt with the issue of race in one of his speeches, something that no doubt the athlete had been sent to address in one way or another in the first place.[79] Regardless, this was not the way that Brundage saw it. In his usual fashion, he groused to a colleague about how the United States had sent a delegation to the Olympics on a political mission.[80] Brundage, like many in Washington, knew that the games created a Cold War battlefield that reached far beyond the athletic events.

The widespread prediction of a Soviet victory in Melbourne held true. Despite all the preparation and fundraising, the United States simply could not defend its crown against the far stronger communist opposition. The Soviet athletes, now in uncharted territory, were given a hero's welcome when they arrived home and invited to join Khrushchev at a New Year's Eve Ball at the Kremlin. Kenneth Wilson, by contrast, searched for some perspective. "We don't consider ourselves the second sports nation of the world because of what happened here," he announced defiantly.[81] In truth, it was the outcome that he and many other U.S. citizens had prepared for. Between the close of the Helsinki games and the opening of those in Melbourne, the national media had produced story after story about the significance of the superpower rivalry under the distant Australian sky. To be sure, Soviet athletes had been the object of curiosity, conjecture, and suspicion in Finland. But propaganda about the superiority of the communist system was not such a threat when Soviet athletes finished second. Now they had finished first. And now, some believed, the rhetoric perhaps matched the reality. One thing is for sure, never before had the performance of the U.S. team at an Olympic festival been so widely discussed and scrutinized across government departments. If, as Osgood claims, "psychological factors seemed even more important than ever" during the Eisenhower years, more than ever before the same historical forces also thrust the issue of Olympic affairs into the corridors of Washington.

6   *Sports Illustrated* and the
Melbourne Defection

During his election campaign, Dwight D. Eisenhower had publicly criticized the Truman administration for "silently consenting" to Soviet rule in Eastern Europe and told voters that he would endeavor to restore freedom to the countries behind the Iron Curtain. Yet as his first term in the White House drew to a close, the United States was no nearer to fulfilling this goal. The government's aim of "liberating" Eastern Europe suffered perhaps its greatest setback in 1956, when riots in Poland and a revolution in Hungary failed to dislodge either country from the Soviet orbit.[1] In the aftermath of these events came the Melbourne Summer Olympic Games, and out of this festival emerged a story that dramatized the upheaval in Hungary. In an article published on 17 December 1956, *Sports Illustrated* described in detail how it had been involved in the defection of thirty-eight Eastern European athletes, coaches, writers, and sports administrators after the close of the Melbourne Olympics. Thirty-four of the group were Hungarian. André Laguerre, *Sports Illustrated*'s chief correspondent at the Olympics, not only wrote the story, he was also integral to arranging the whole defection. His article began

> Less than 48 hours before the Melbourne flame was officially doused, two men in ill-fitting civilian clothes walked for the last time through the Olympic Village. It was dusk, they spoke no word, and they trod by one of those dramatic coincidences which occasionally brighten the drab hues of reality—a road named Liberty Parade.
>
> In silence they were let through the guarded exit and in silence they climbed into a car waiting for them, by agreement, at the flagpole from which flew the Hungarian flag. They were driven to a private home on the outskirts of Melbourne.

> The two men were named Zoltán Török and Róbert Zimonyi. They were the
> first Hungarians to make the break from their teams, their families and their
> homes in the hope of finding a new life in a country which, for 10 years, their
> own government's propaganda had vainly sought to depict as the epitome of
> selfishness and vicious exploitation—the United States of America.

In the self-congratulatory piece, Laguerre claimed that the athletes were
"subjected to no pressure or propaganda. They had no contact with any U.S.
official. They sought out representatives of *Sports Illustrated*."[2] The magazine
did play the leading role in the defection; but these words were a little disin-
genuous. The whole project did not come together in quite the manner that
Laguerre suggested. The secret background of the Melbourne defection has
been examined once before, in a 1976 doctoral dissertation written by Thomas
M. Domer. Domer's short account of the episode showed that other actors
made equally important contributions to the effort, none more so than the
involvement of C. D. Jackson and the Hungarian National Sports Federation
(HNSF). Laguerre mentioned neither one. Without question, it was Jackson
who pulled strings at the U.S. State Department so that the refugees could
enter the United States with relatively little fuss. Likewise, Domer correctly
attributed the whole idea of the defection to the HNSF and not *Sports Illustrated*, but he had no inkling of the HNSF's connection to the Free Europe
Committee (as the National Committee for a Free Europe became known
in 1954).[3] Previously unexamined documents in the private papers of Count
Szápáry and the Radio Free Europe archives reveal an even more nuanced
picture of the HNSF's and Jackson's roles in getting the East Europeans to
the United States. This material also demonstrates that, despite Laguerre's
careful wording, it is impossible to overlook *Sports Illustrated*'s part in the
state–private network, or the element of "propaganda." The tumultuous circumstances of 1956 may have dramatically exposed the poverty of the U.S.
government's policy of liberation, but the defection of some of Hungary's
very best sporting assets at least provided Jackson, and to some degree the
administration, with a valuable propaganda sidelight.

Liberation?

Although the Truman administration had taken significant steps to shatter
Soviet control in Eastern Europe, the failure of these efforts would be used
by the Republican Party, rightly or wrongly, to keep another Democrat from
assuming leadership in the White House. As the Republican presidential
candidate, Eisenhower trumpeted a party platform that intended to brush the
"immoral" policy of "containment" to one side and to instead give "genuine

independence" to the "captive peoples" of Eastern Europe. This message was bold and clear. On the campaign trail, John Foster Dulles, who would become Eisenhower's secretary of state, affirmed that the United States "should activate stresses and strains within the Russian Communist empire so as to disintegrate it." In a similar fashion, Eisenhower regularly censured the Truman administration for allowing the Soviet Union to dominate Eastern Europe and for not securing a "positive, clear cut, long term action for peace." Eisenhower's comprehensive victory in the elections did not put an end to this rhetoric. Indeed, his chief adviser on psychological warfare, C.D. Jackson, was a stout supporter of rolling back communism in Europe.[4]

The limitations of this policy, however, were repeatedly exposed in Eisenhower's first term. In June 1953, for instance, workers in East Berlin's construction industry went on strike after news that a 10 percent increase in labor quotas would not be reduced by the government. Further strikes soon riddled the country. Protests turned to violence and Soviet tanks were required to restore order. The U.S. government's Radio in the American Sector encouraged the protesters to seek change in the political system of East Germany, while Jackson and other officials pushed for further U.S. action. The CIA, on the other hand, predicted that any military intervention in the region, which included arming the protestors, would only lead to greater "bloodshed." Eisenhower concurred. In lieu of a more forceful response, the administration provided the people of East Berlin with 4,500 tons of food relief and continued to expose and inflame the riots through propaganda. As Chris Tudda has noted, the White House was in the process of saying one thing and doing another. In public, Eisenhower remained attached to the rhetoric of liberation, but in high-level security meetings he exhibited no intention of military intervention within the Soviet bloc or of taking any other measures that could instigate a full-scale "hot" war.[5]

When the administration embarked on its "New Look" strategy (expressed in NSC 162/2) in October of the same year, it would aim to secure the nation, fiscally and militarily, from the Soviet threat by increasing the U.S. nuclear arsenal. This approach, designed to deter Soviet aggression, signaled the government's acceptance that the Soviet Union remained dominant in Eastern Europe and was not likely loosen its grip for the foreseeable future. At the same time, however, the New Look also advanced the use of nonmilitary methods and psychological warfare to counter the Kremlin's own propaganda tactics and challenge communist control in the satellites. This strategy, argues Scott Lucas, created a void of uncertainty that "allowed the network of psychological warriors to persist."[6] Without question, the National Committee for a Free Europe remained dedicated to stirring unrest in Eastern Europe, and Jackson did not stop pressing for the same revolutionary outcome at the time and long afterward. U.S. psychological operations also intensified in the "free world." The government countered the widening of Soviet efforts in developing countries with a range of covert activities, including "black" operations to "roll back" communism in North Vietnam by stimulating uprisings and encouraging defections. The interagency Operations Coordinating Board and the CIA manipulated elections in Thailand, and the CIA infamously organized coups to overthrow governments in Iran (1953) and Guatemala (1954). In spite of this, the liberation of Eastern Europe continued to be a lingering challenge to the administration. Indeed, Walter Hixson notes that as Eisenhower's first term came to a close "U.S. Cold War planners began to emphasize a gradualist approach over aggressive psychological warfare" to break the Soviet bloc. This policy became clearer in 1955, when NSC 5505/1 stipulated that U.S. strategy toward the satellites should "stress evolutionary rather than revolutionary change."[7] Yet even after this declaration, U.S. propaganda still retained a revolutionary tone for years to come.[8]

The riots in East Berlin, then, were part of a wave of strikes and unrest that occurred throughout Eastern Europe in 1953. It was a hangover from the Stalin era. People protested for economic reasons, which then translated into grievances against the regime in general. In fear of further unrest or outright dissolution in the Soviet sphere of influence, the leaders in the Kremlin made plans to reform their policies toward the satellites. The "little Stalins" in Eastern Europe were told to take a "New Course." In part, this meant putting an end to the "excesses of police terror" and providing "economic concessions" to the people. Moreover, in 1955, the Soviet Union embarked on another initiative to promote unity within the communist bloc, by way of the Warsaw Pact. As a reaction to the integration of West Germany into NATO, the Warsaw Pact was a political and military alliance that encouraged the satellites to increasingly promote Soviet goals in Europe and the developing world. Evidence of a relaxation in Moscow did not end there. In February 1956, Khrushchev, who now had control in the Kremlin, made a remarkable "secret speech." At the Twentieth Congress of the Communist Party of the Soviet Union, he emphasized the doctrine of "peaceful coexistence" and also denounced the crimes of Stalin. Rather than relaxing the mood of people in Eastern Europe, it created an atmosphere for change. This opened a door in Poland and Hungary which, in the case of the latter, the Soviet Union had to forcibly shut.[9]

Hungarian leaders were called to Moscow in June 1953 for instructions on implementing the New Course, with the Stalinist leader of Hungary, Mátyás Rákosi, demoted on the spot as punishment for his brutal regime. Rákosi thus fell to the position of first secretary of the party, and Imre Nagy rose to become the premier. But the New Course did not last long in Hungary. The battle for control in the Soviet collective leadership significantly affected the pattern of reforms in Eastern Europe. The decline of Malenkov's influence in the Kremlin shifted the dynamic of power to such an extent that in 1955 Nagy was called to Moscow and berated for implementing the policies that he had been ordered to implement in the first place. This time the Soviet leaders replaced Nagy with Rákosi, who subsequently directed the country away from the New Course and back to the old. Unleashed once again, Rákosi resumed the heavy-handed tactics that prompted his first demise, much to the despair of the weary and beleaguered Hungarian people.

Meanwhile, in February 1956, Edward Ochab succeeded the deceased Bolesław Bierut as leader of Poland. Ochab, as a "reliable Communist," was prepared to enact the reforms articulated by Khrushchev at the Twentieth Party Congress. The Polish population embraced this chance for political change, and the release of Khrushchev's secret speech abruptly inflamed these sentiments. In June, workers rioted in the city of Poznań, invading police headquarters, government buildings, and prisons. The Polish security forces managed to crush the rebellion, though not until hundreds had died as a result of it. From the midst of the crisis grew a movement to install Władysław Gomulka, formerly in disrepute for being a "Titoist," as the new leader. Once in power, Gomulka proceeded to strike a balance that gave concessions to the population but allowed Soviet troops to remain on Polish soil.[10]

Shaken by the events in Poland, the Soviets reoriented their approach in Hungary by once again relieving Rákosi of his charge. Still, the subsequent appointment of Ernö Gerö was not much better, as Gerö had worked under, and in compliance with, Rákosi. The Hungarian people were bitter and frustrated. Various student groups, who had already held a series of protests and rallies against the regime and the Soviet influence in Hungary, swelled around the Hungarian Parliament on 23 October 1956 in what began as a peaceful demonstration. When the Department for the Defense of the State (ÁVO) opened fire on the crowd, the kindling of the Hungarian Revolution was set aflame. Soviet tanks entered Budapest on 24 October, and Nagy was again installed as premier to appease the people. A further peaceful demonstration a day later was sprayed by bullets from the ÁVO, and revolt gripped the country. John Foster Dulles exclaimed that "the great monolith of communism is crumbling!" Yet the National Security Council warned against military intervention, and Eisenhower publicly stated the same thing. On 4 November, Soviet tanks moved back into Budapest and smashed the revolution. Eisenhower admitted that it was "indeed a bitter pill for us to swallow."[11] "It proved," writes Gregory Mitrovich, "that despite the years of public support for satellite liberation the United States would take no overt action to support an independent Eastern Europe."[12]

To make matters worse for the administration, accusations emerged from countries in both the East and West that U.S. propaganda had caused the turmoil in Hungary. Even though the Voice of America had toned down upon recommendations from the Jackson Committee, the same could not be said for Radio Free Europe (RFE). Fortunately for Eisenhower, RFE was not an official mouthpiece of the government, and this allowed the White House to distance itself from criticism. Nevertheless, the issue was unfortunate. Without question, RFE had been closely following the events of 1956 and gave extensive coverage to Khrushchev's secret speech. Studies of RFE programming during the changes in Poland have commended its "restraint," claiming that RFE called for "moderation" from the people of Poland rather than outright revolt. Much the same content was evident in RFE broadcasts to Hungary up until 23 October. There were no cries for violence, simply recommendations for "gradual reform." Policy guidance for RFE from the U.S. government followed the same general line. But as the revolution unfolded, the Hungarian Service of RFE exceeded its mandate. For although, as A. Ross Johnson argues, "the RFE Hungarian Service . . . could not have inspired, provoked, or by themselves prolonged the Hungarian Revolution or caused the Soviet Union to suppress it," it did contribute to and "nurture the hopes of Hungarians for Western military intervention that would never happen."[13]

Aside from the ruptures in Eastern Europe, there were further signs that the Cold War was spreading to encompass the "third world." Egypt, long under the protectorate of the British, encountered a nationalist revolution in 1952. It resulted in Great Britain withdrawing its forces from the country, though the British refused to relinquish control over the Suez Canal, a crucial transport link to the Middle East and beyond. Colonel Gamal Abdel Nasser, the Egyptian leader, sought preeminence in the Arab world and was willing to court both the Soviet Union and the United States to get it. He secured funding from the United States to build the Aswan Dam on the Nile, a vital economic project, and purchased arms from Czechoslovakia. Nasser then angered the United States by recognizing the People's Republic of China, causing the United States to cut off its capital for the dam. Unperturbed, Nasser simply brokered a deal with the Soviet Union and nationalized the Suez Canal. The decision drew an aggressive retort from the British and French, who, in league with the Israelis, planned an invasion of Egypt to secure the canal and topple Nasser. They did so, however, without conferring with the

United States. The attack took place in late October. Not wishing to lose the support of the Arab world, Eisenhower forced the British and French to cease the operation through a resolution in the United Nations. Khrushchev, after the fact, threatened an unlikely nuclear attack on the belligerents. Nasser remained in control of the canal. It was an example of how "nonaligned" states could manipulate the attention of both superpowers for their own gain.[14]

The Melbourne Olympic Games and the World Situation

The state of affairs in Egypt and in Hungary generated international condemnation. The 1956 summer Olympic Games were enveloped in this sentiment. Egypt withdrew from the festival in August in protest against British influence in the Olympic Movement. Lebanon and Iraq boycotted as a sign of Arab solidarity. The Netherlands and Spain withdrew from the festival over the Soviet intervention in Budapest. In an unrelated act, the Olympic committee from the People's Republic of China withdrew because athletes from Taiwan would be in Melbourne. Even the neutral Swiss got caught in the shuffle. They boycotted because of the actions of all the belligerent nations prior to the Melbourne Olympics, then rescinded, then realized it was too late to send a team. Otto Mayer, the International Olympic Committee's (IOC) chancellor and a Swiss citizen, was aggrieved "that a neutral nation and the very country where the IOC has its headquarters should set such a shameful example of political interference with the Olympic ideal."[15] Mayer tried his "utmost" to change the decision made by "hesitating countries," but with no success.[16]

Not without reason, the president of the Netherlands National Olympic Committee inquired, "How can sports prevail over what has happened in Hungary?"[17] The argument that sport and politics should not mix was far from convincing, but this did not stop the idealistic fraternity from making the point anyway. "Never before in the history of the Olympics have the games been staged under such difficult conditions," said W. S. Kent Hughes, the head of the Melbourne Games Organizing Committee. Nonetheless, he added, the "true spirit of the Olympics triumphs over international distrust and jealousies."[18] The IOC stuck to the same script. True to form, it approved a statement from its president, Avery Brundage, for release to the press. "Every civilized person is shocked by the massacre in Hungary," Brundage stated, "but that is not a reason to destroy international cooperation and the Olympic Movement. The Games are competitions between individuals, not between nations. We do hope the nations that decided to stay home might reconsider their decision. In this imperfect world there would be very few international competitions if the politicians violate the human laws."[19]

While the chaos unfolded in Hungary, U.S. officials considered a boycott of the Olympic Games as a form of punishment for the Soviet Union. Decades later, during the Carter administration, this idea was given full support. But on that occasion, the Olympics were in Moscow, and a boycott was thus viewed as a more dramatic affront. For government officials in 1956, it was not seen as a worthwhile or appropriate exercise. At an interdepartmental meeting on 6 November, a representative of the CIA asked whether withdrawing from the Olympics had been considered as a measure in response to the Soviet Union's actions in Hungary. "Not advisable," was the response from the State Department.[20] Primarily, the decision rested with the United States Olympic Committee (USOC), but the State Department also did not want to upset their "good friends" in Australia or appear to support the position of either "Red China" or Egypt. Certainly, in the case of Egypt, the action might be interpreted by "England and France as a widening drift" in their "traditional alliance" with the United States. Government "interference in our U.S. Olympic Committee affairs, at this time, would not have the abundant support of the American people," the State Department added, and there had been "no indication" that the USOC intended to withdraw its athletes in response to the "world situation."[21] The U.S. attitude to a boycott reflected the general, though not the uniform, international reaction.

While some countries debated whether to send a team to the summer Olympics due to the turmoil in Hungary, a decision also had to be made by the Hungarian Olympic Committee. Some athletes on the Hungarian Olympic team fought in the revolution, marched in protest against the Soviet Union, and wielded machine guns against Soviet troops. An Associated Press release in late October seemed to have clarified the matter when it reported that Hungary had withdrawn from the Olympics altogether. Commenting on the report, the *Daily Mail* of London observed that the absence of Hungary's "formidable" athletes would be a "major blow to the Games" and feared that athletes were part of the "corpse-littered streets" in Budapest.[22] RFE even announced that the Hungarian soccer star, Ferenc Puskas, had died in the fighting. Both stories, it turned out, were wrong. Further news releases from the communist press in Hungary told a different story. "The Hungarians are coming," declared a relieved Sir William Bridgeford, the executive officer of the Olympics in Australia.[23] The Hungarian National Olympic Committee sent a cable to the Olympic Organizing Committee to confirm that its athletes would arrive in Australia on 10 November, one week later than originally planned. The understated message blamed "unforeseen circumstances."[24]

In order to get the athletes safely out of Hungary, Otto Mayer managed to persuade the Swiss government to speak with Hungarian authorities on the

IOC's behalf. This diplomatic approach apparently worked. Shortly thereafter the Hungarian government conveyed its athletes to Czechoslovakia,
an outcome that inspired Mayer to claim that he had achieved an "Olympic
Truce."[25] While the team waited for a flight out of Prague, some of the athletes wondered whether they should return to the fray after hearing stories
about "Soviet reprisals" on the radio. They were given no choice. As the team
waited to depart on two flights, they were told by regime officials that they
"must go on to the Games."[26] The first group of Hungarian athletes landed
in Darwin before the final leg of their journey to Melbourne. When they
left Budapest it looked as if the revolution might succeed. Only in Darwin
did they learn that it had been broken by the Soviet army. Some of the team
spoke of not returning home. When they arrived at the Olympic Village a
day later, they noticed that the communist flag of Hungary was flying over
the entrance gate to the complex, a fact that proved deeply disturbing to the
travel weary team. Many were overcome with emotion and demanded that
the flag be replaced by the traditional Hungarian standard. "We can never
compete while the Communist flag flies," said one of the athletes. "If it is
not replaced, we will tear it down ourselves."[27] Two days later, the flag was
switched in time for the arrival of the second Hungarian contingent, who
were greeted by around two thousand members of Melbourne's Hungarian
community. The cheering crowd sang the Hungarian national anthem and
enthusiastically chanted "long live free Hungary."[28]

The Soviet Union's military intervention in Hungary also appalled many
of the IOC's members, but they would not take the matter any further. The
Soviets would participate in Melbourne and that was that. A portion of the
Soviet Olympic team flew to Australia in six chartered Pan American Airways
flights furnished with copies of the U.S. government's Russian language propaganda magazine, *Amerika*.[29] Perhaps the reading material was particularly
good, as the crew aboard the flight reported that the Soviets were extremely
"affable" throughout the journey. The athletes also appeared to enjoy the
opportunity to sip tea and eat American meals. On arrival in Melbourne,
Konstantin Andrianov, the president of the Soviet National Olympic Committee, could relax no more when challenged about his country's actions at a
press conference. One report—which described the Soviet official, somewhat
unflatteringly, as a "little, round-faced man with disheveled hair"—explained
that Andrianov gave little away. When questioned about the boycott of the
Netherlands, he replied, "I know of no grounds for a protest." When pressed
on whether he knew of the latest developments in Hungary, Andrianov said,
"Yes, we read the papers. But we are sportsmen, not politicians. That comes
under another bureau."[30]

The Defection

The subsequent involvement of *Sports Illustrated* in the Melbourne defection was indicative of how the U.S. government managed to cultivate a range of contacts with prominent journalists, newspapers, magazines, and television networks. The *New York Times*, for instance, granted "cover" for at least ten CIA officers, the Columbia Broadcasting Company helped to launder CIA funds, and the intelligence community also secretly funded or directed a host of publications and journals. Within the government's media arm of the state–private network, clandestine operatives also established an extremely close relationship with Time, Inc., a company run by the anticommunist crusader Henry Luce. Spurred on by religious zeal and a deep conviction in the U.S. capacity to lead the world, Luce pitted *Time* magazine against communism in a "private war."[31] Luce, a founding member of the Free Europe Committee, was well connected in covert circles. He was close with Allen Dulles, Eisenhower's director of Central Intelligence, and the presence of Jackson at the company meant that the media mogul had a further direct contact into the government's psychological warfare machinery. *Time* magazine assisted in various government projects, provided cover for CIA staff, and often published articles that gave the Eisenhower administration favorable coverage, with or without prompting from Jackson. In return, a grateful Dulles hosted dinners for *Time*'s foreign correspondents. Taking all this into account, historian Hugh Wilford has commented that "it was difficult to tell precisely where the Luce empire's overseas intelligence network ended and the CIA's began."[32]

Luce had indeed built himself a considerable empire. His company experienced a particularly marked period of success in the 1940s, and he looked to capitalize on this boom in sales by adding another magazine to his portfolio. Luce and some of his advisers decided that a weekly publication dedicated entirely to sport would fill what they perceived to be as a gaping hole in the marketplace. After a great deal of research and deliberation, Luce launched *Sports Illustrated* magazine in 1954.[33] But to what extent was *Sports Illustrated*, a subsidiary of *Time*, caught in the U.S. government's covert web? Thomas Domer was the first to suggest a clandestine connection. John Massaro, on the other hand, has posited that *Sports Illustrated*'s reporting was consistently anticommunist in 1956, but he doubts whether there was any government "conspiracy"; rather, it was merely a case of a "typical Cold War bias" that pervaded U.S. society.[34] Of course, *Sports Illustrated* may not have had reporters on the CIA's payroll, but there is evidence to suggest that the popular magazine was not an innocent or objective vessel. After all, the *Sports Illustrated* editors had already donated space in the publication when Jackson requested it in 1955, as part of a failed effort to form a front group to fund a greater U.S. athletic presence in international competition. The events that transpired before, during, and after the Melbourne Olympic Games indicate that *Sports Illustrated* was part of Luce's "private war" against communism, and that this war was not isolated by any means from the U.S. government.

The battle lines were soon drawn. On the afternoon of 11 November 1956, Count Szápáry and his wife entertained Whitney Tower (a relative of Szápáry's wife, Sylvia) at their home in Pound Ridge, New York. Also present was Dr. George Telegdy, the secretary of the Hungarian National Sports Federation. This was not a social gathering, however. It was just under two weeks before the start of the Melbourne Olympics, and Szápáry had just returned from Vienna, where he had been trying to organize relief for Hungarians in the wake of the revolution. The count had contacted Tower for a meeting primarily because the latter was the associate editor of *Sports Illustrated*. Szápáry inquired whether *Sports Illustrated* and *Time* could assist in the defection of Hungarian Olympic athletes, many of whom had decided not to return home upon the conclusion of events in Melbourne.[35] Tower agreed to help. He produced an "urgent and confidential" memorandum on the idea and submitted it to the eternally optimistic managing editor of *Sports Illustrated*, Sidney James. James reacted at once. He immediately sent the memorandum to C. D. Jackson, the "man behind the scenes" at *Time*—in Tower's words—and the "closest friend" of Henry Luce. Tower told Szápáry that "outside of top government officials there is probably no man who has more influence with Ike [Eisenhower] and the State Department than C. D. Jackson."[36] Within days, Tower wrote Szápáry that "things definitely look promising" and that "Jackson is at the moment probing deeper into the matter in Washington." He added in a handwritten note, "I cannot over-emphasize the importance of maintaining the closest possible secrecy on this subject."[37]

Plans developed rapidly. *Sports Illustrated* sent a reporter, Coles Phinizy, to Melbourne with a copy of the Tower memorandum for the magazine's chief correspondent in the Olympic city, the renowned André Laguerre.[38] Phinizy was also instructed by the leadership at *Sports Illustrated* to create a code so that communication between *Sports Illustrated*'s New York office and Melbourne could be kept secret. For instance, the Hungarian athletes would be referred to as "Australian rules football players," and Jackson as "Charles Johnson of Merion Cricket Club." Finally, Phinizy had to make contact with Telegdy who, "with an assist from Radio Free Europe," had already left for Melbourne. Indeed, the Free Europe Committee provided Telegdy with funding for the operation while he kept the organization abreast of developments as and when they occurred.[39]

George Telegdy had been associated with the HNSF from its early days, but gradually became a driving force in the organization. Born in Hungary in 1921, Telegdy graduated from the University of Budapest with a doctorate in political science. His professional career was spent in the Budapest city administration where, for a time, he was the personal secretary to the city's mayor. In 1948, he escaped from Hungary and eventually made his way to the United States. Telegdy enjoyed a prominent reputation in Hungarian sporting circles. He was an outstanding fencer during his time at the university and later became a member of the Hungarian Fencing Association and president of the Budapest University Athletic Club. He was characterized by an often misguided passion. This characteristic endeared him to some; not so to others. One Free Europe Committee employee described him as a "megalomaniac," prone to "exaggeration of his own importance."[40] Count Szápáry was told about the "incompetence" of his colleague, but the count looked past it. He appreciated Telegdy's "energy" and "dynamic personality," not to mention his "extraordinary ideas." When Telegdy set foot in the United States, Szápáry once recalled, "he continued his vocation, rather than his job . . . and that was fighting against communism."[41]

Telegdy arrived in Melbourne on 18 November and was immediately greeted with tragic news. His uncle had been killed by Soviet gunfire during the revo-

The Officials of the Hungarian National Sports Federation. From left to right, George Telegdy (Secretary-General), Count Anthony Szápáry (President), and Frank Chase (Vice President). Courtesy of Gladys and Paul Szápáry.

lution and his cousin seriously wounded. This intelligence steeled his resolve: "I decided to do all that I could to help those Hungarian athletes who decided not to return to Communism." He called the plan "Operation Griffin."[42] One of Telegdy's assignments in Melbourne was to report on events for Hungarian émigré newspapers, but he also found time to enjoy the Olympics and attended several events. He witnessed the crowd booing Soviet fencers during the saber tournament and watched the famous, and bloody, water polo contest between the Soviet Union and Hungary. But Telegdy was not at the Olympics to just report on the events. Authorities in Australia knew this. Telegdy claimed that he was quietly taken to one side by government officials and encouraged to work clandestinely so as not to disturb the conviviality of the Olympics. Through HNSF contacts in the Argentine and Italian Olympic teams, word of Telegdy's presence in Melbourne was conveyed to Hungarian athletes. Friends in the city found him private accommodation in North Brighton. "Within a few days," Telegdy wrote, "this became a second home for Hungarian Olympians, whom we welcomed at all hours of the day or night."[43]

The Olympic Games opened on 22 November. On the next day, the first coded message from Laguerre arrived at *Sports Illustrated*'s New York office. The experienced reporter had talked with Telegdy; the HNSF official intimated that between 20 and 50 percent of the Hungarian Olympic team was thinking of defecting. At this point, there was confusion over whether these athletes would stay in Australia, go to Europe, or request asylum in the United States. For the time being, Laguerre waited for developments; the Olympics had only just started and much could happen in the coming weeks.[44] His message had been calm and deliberate. In contrast, Telegdy wrote Szápáry from Melbourne with an "urgent" letter. He feared that if the Hungarian athletes stayed in Australia "the tremendous propaganda value they represent, would be lost for once and for ever." He needed assurances that the U.S. government would grant the Hungarians asylum. Telegdy implored his colleague: "I have all this on my shoulders, on my mind. . . . Do something, before it is too late. This is the last chance to do something for our sportsmen, and at the same time to gain a vast fortune for the free world."[45] Telegdy, abandoning secrecy and ignoring the code, cabled on 29 November that he had twenty-three athletes and three coaches who were prepared to defect. With assistance from local authorities in Australia they would be taken to a "safe place." Besides this promising news, Telegdy pushed for information on transport for the athletes to the United States and an update on whether they could obtain visas. He asked that fundraising begin for the defectors and that Szápáry "confer with Jackson" about granting the athletes asylum in the United States.[46] At the same time, Laguerre cabled James with the same questions, though in a more measured tone. James was happy to inform Laguerre that Telegdy "need not worry about money" and that Jackson was making progress with the State Department. Asylum in the United States looked probable.[47]

As soon as the Hungarian team reached Melbourne, rumors of possible defections quickly swirled in the press as some of the athletes talked indecisively about their future plans once the Olympics had finished. In Washington, a representative of the CIA mentioned that the Hungarian Olympic performers were preparing to defect "en masse" and, as the Olympics drew ever closer to a conclusion, newspapers in the United States increasingly reported that Hungarian athletes were unwilling to return home.[48] László Tábori, a celebrated middle-distance runner, told a journalist, "I cannot say definitely what I will do, but I am seriously considering staying in Australia."[49] The Hungarian Olympic team was composed of around one hundred forty athletes and approximately thirty government officials, and some reports guessed that two-thirds would "choose freedom." Others newspapers estimated the number to be only in the thirties.[50] The head of the Hungarian team explained that the athletes were under no pressure to return to Hungary. "Let them make up their own minds. They love their home and are free from politics," he said.[51] Some would stay in Australia, but the majority preferred to fly to the United States. "The United States would look with favor on any pleas for political asylum from any Olympic Games athletes—Hungarian or otherwise," the U.S. consul general in Melbourne, Gerald Warner, told reporters.[52]

One by one, the athletes began to disappear into the city of Melbourne. Just days before the Olympics closed, the first two to leave, Zoltán Török (a rowing coach) and Róbert Zimonyi (a coxswain), "strolled" out of the Olympic Village and "sprang," as Telegdy related, into a car bound for Telegdy's house. Telegdy and the two men later celebrated the moment with a glass of aged Hungarian apricot brandy.[53] Other athletes made similar plans once their athletic exertions were over. *Sports Illustrated* reported that members of the Hungarian water polo team "had barely dried themselves and tucked their gold medals into their pockets before they were unobtrusively driven off," while gymnasts were "whisked away" to a "safe and secret destination" just minutes after they had finished competing.[54] Noticing this phenomenon, the Australian media reported that several Hungarians had "vanished" from the Olympic Village.[55] Telegdy was even approached by László Nadori, the chief of staff of the Hungarian Sports Ministry, who no longer wanted to serve the communist regime. According to Telegdy, early one morning at 3 a.m., Nadori walked around the Olympic Village as though "indisposed" before climbing into a waiting car with the long jumper, Olga Gyarmathy. Both were taken to a nearby hotel, close to Telegdy's house.[56]

The Olympics were due to end on December 8. This left some undecided Hungarians precious little time to make an extremely difficult decision. Apart from leaving behind their country and loved ones, athletes feared government reprisals against family members and carefully considered whether their relatively privileged life as an athlete under communism was worth giving up. The *Sports Illustrated* team grappled as best it could with this key phase of the operation, but it was, naturally, a very challenging period. Laguerre, who had met with Hungarian athletes on three occasions, explained that a good deal of confusion hampered their decision making. Some lacked confidence in the abilities of Telegdy, and Laguerre even surmised that some were merely waiting for the most lucrative offer, be it from the United States or their home government. Laguerre did not feel comfortable negotiating on such matters, though he assured the athletes that they would be given help to start a new life in the United States and that *Sports Illustrated* would arrange for them to make a tour of U.S. cities. Finally, Laguerre reminded his colleagues that within a day or two a number of Hungarians were going to be the "moral" responsibility of *Sports Illustrated*, but nothing had yet been heard from the State Department.[57] James cabled his colleague a reassuring response. He understood that some of the athletes were struggling with their decision but emphasized that *Sports Illustrated* would not renege on its promises. "Luce himself just called to say this issue [is] a knockout," James added.[58]

Transportation to the United States remained an ongoing issue. All commercial flights were fully booked through the Christmas period, and the Hungarians wished to be in the United States to celebrate the holiday. Jackson, who appeared to be a whirlwind of activity, had continuously "needled" the State Department and worked on an "immediate special airlift" by Pan American Airways. But the State Department would not release this flight from the United States until the Olympians had registered with the Australian immigration authorities.[59] Furthermore, the number of defectors was far from established; some were scattered around Melbourne and not in a single location. The end of the Olympics approached and the situation remained fluid. By this point, too, the press was covering the story, and so Laguerre abandoned using the code. He also abandoned Australia, climbing aboard a scheduled flight to the United States. Roy Terrell, another *Sports Illustrated* representative in Melbourne, took over the chaotic operation. To add to the difficulties, Telegdy welcomed four Romanian athletes to join the defectors. "Telegdy now apparently gathering oppressed peoples like a dog gathers fleas," cabled Terrell in his first communication with the New York office. A further individual, Alexander Brody, was told by *Sports Illustrated* to follow Telegdy closely.[60] Brody, an employee of the marketing firm Young and Rubicam, was enjoying the Olympics as a tourist but appears to have been inadvertently embroiled in the defection. *Sports Illustrated* staff praised his assistance, and Brody stayed involved in the project for some time.[61]

Hungarian sports officials had made arrangements for the team to fly out of Melbourne immediately after the sporting events finished on December 7, the night before the closing ceremonies. The decisive day soon arrived for those who wavered over defecting. To further complicate an already tense and fragile situation, Telegdy reported that other "foreigners" were "bidding" for the allegiance of the athletes. He claimed one such "foreign group" was the International Rescue Committee. This is plausible. The International Rescue Committee was a refugee relief organization that focused on refugees from Eastern Europe and the Soviet Union. At one time or another, it had received CIA funds. But Telegdy would not let the athletes slip from his grasp and spoke to them about "a life without fear in the world's greatest democracy." He promised them that "America awaited them with open arms." Telegdy's promptings and Laguerre's promises were enough for many of the Hungarians. Nearly half of the athletes from the full Hungarian Olympic squad chose to stay in Australia, and a large portion of this contingent intended to fly to the United States.[62]

With the Olympics finally over, the "freedom"-bound Hungarian athletes either stayed in the Olympic Village or found places to hide out in Melbourne for the next two nights. Olympic authorities allowed those due to fly to the United States to stay in the U.S. quarters of the Olympic Village from 10 December onward. Some of the athletes proceeded to this location under their own steam and others were rounded up by the Australian police. On the same day, Terrell revealed that "Australian immigration officials decided to take the mountain to Mohammed" and entered the Olympic Village on their own initiative to process the athletes. A crucial phase of the operation was over. The Hungarian National Olympic Team, as Telegdy referred to them, would stay in their new accommodations until their departure, watched over by Australian security agents. The *Sports Illustrated* team in Melbourne started to disperse. As Terrell departed, Stan Eskell, a *Sports Illustrated* correspondent based in Sydney, took over the task of coordination. Laguerre, now back in New York, started to send cables in the other direction. Personnel at *Sports Illustrated* sent money to Telegdy to buy the athletes clothes and for other living expenses. Everyone waited for confirmation from Washington that the Hungarians could legally land in the United States and that the Pan American flight would arrive in Australia to take them there.[63]

But problems unexpectedly arose within the State Department. As a result of the revolution, more than two hundred thousand Hungarians fled their country. In the first week of November, fifteen thousand escaped into Austria. More followed. The Eisenhower administration, ineffectual thus far in dealing with the revolution, moved to admit some of the refugees into the United States. The government relaxed the strict immigration rules of the U.S. Refugee Relief Program, which started in 1953, and allowed five thousand Hungarians to enter the United States by the end of the year. It increased the number as thousands continued to pour into Austria. An Eisenhower directive attempted to expand the intake by way of admitting an alien into the country on "parole." This option was offered on an "emergency" basis, whereby refugees could enter the country if it "served the public interest," although the alien had no official status and no visa.[64]

Jackson phoned Tracy Voorhees, who had been appointed by Eisenhower to coordinate the Hungarian refugee program. Even though Voorhees did not believe "that State has been asleep on this one," and that "between them and CIA there has been a lot going on," he admitted that the defection of the Hungarian Olympic athletes was "not such a clear-cut matter as . . . first understood."[65] When representatives of *Sports Illustrated* also hounded Voorhees, the government official lost his temper. Simply putting the Olympic athletes on an airplane and flying them to the United States meant avoiding standard procedures. The *Sports Illustrated* team argued that the athletes could be brought to the United States as part of the Refugee Relief Program. Voorhees retorted that the relief program was first and foremost for those people "who have had their horses shot out from under them." He underscored that the Hungarian athletes were not in the same desperate need as the refugees in Austria.[66] During a meeting of the Operations Coordinating Board on 14 December, the same points were discussed. One participant explained that "haste had been urged" to get the athletes to the United States, but that "normal visa procedures" did not apply. There was even doubt about whether some of the team qualified for a visa in the first place. When another participant suggested that the athletes be brought in under "parole," the point was countered with the assertion that this had only been authorized for refugees in Austria. A decision needed to be made whether the "admission of the Olympic escapees on parole would be in the national interest."[67]

Jackson spent a weekend exerting his influence in Washington and the red tape loosened. On 18 December, Laguerre sent a cable to Telegdy with the good news. The U.S. government had granted "immediate" asylum to the Hungarians. They would enter the United States on parole, a status that came back to haunt them in their future Olympic ambitions. A special Pan American flight would carry them to San Francisco, via Honolulu, where they would land on Christmas Eve.[68] *Sports Illustrated* feverishly made preparations for the arrival of the refugee athletes, arranging for photographers and maximum publicity. Dick Neale, an assistant publisher at *Sports Illustrated*, was responsible for the Hungarians the moment they hit U.S. soil. Before they even landed, Neale delighted in the "great national interest in [the] returning athletes."[69] All told, thirty-eight athletes and officials stepped off the Pan American flight arranged by Jackson. Four were from the Romanian water polo team; the rest were Hungarian. Notably, they included five fencers, three of whom were part of the gold-medal-winning saber team; five swimmers, two divers, two from track and field, a canoeist, and a rowing coxswain. There were four gymnasts, two of whom, Andrea Bodó and Margit Korondi, took gold in the team exercise on apparatus. Five members of the gold-medal-winning water polo team were part of the group, along with six coaches, one of whom was the famed Mihály Iglói, the mentor of another defector, László Tábori.[70] Telegdy congratulated himself on the achievement: "I delivered to the people of the U.S.A. the world famous Hungarian athletes who henceforth would serve the cause of American and Hungarian freedom in this greatest of democracies."[71]

The defection certainly had an effect in Hungary. When the remainder of the Hungarian Olympic team returned to Budapest, the minister of state, Gyoergy Marosan, offered his congratulations. "We know you had to fight lures and temptation in Melbourne," stated Marosan. "We know that the civilized west tried to lure you away by false rumours and big financial offers." He told the Olympians that during their time away, "we here at home conducted a hard fight against the counter-revolution. I can tell you with pleasure that we have won."[72] A communist newspaper, *Nemzeti Sport*, wondered whether the athletes made their decision with a "calm mind." In general, however, the Melbourne defection sufficiently troubled Hungary's government, sporting establishment, journalists, and academics to a degree that few wrote about it in the country for years to come. Hungarian sport historians lingered over the 1956 Summer Olympics in only the briefest manner.[73] In the United States, the reaction to the defection was far different. The athletes were greeted as heroes when they reached U.S. soil. "Fleeing from Red oppression," commented the *Los Angeles Times*, the athletes "arrived here today to start a new life in a land of freedom."[74]

A few months after the Olympics concluded in Melbourne, the Soviet publication *Literary Gazette* ran an article that accused Allen Dulles and the CIA of various covert activities at the 1956 Summer Olympics. The *Gazette* claimed that Dulles and his "provocateurs" had "created a threatening atmosphere for the Soviet sportsmen" by spying on the athletes, attempting to plant "secret documents" on them, planning to kidnap them, stealing their belongings, plying them with anticommunist propaganda, and even trying to entrance them with women who offered "to give them a good time for the evening." Dulles was also allegedly guilty of organizing meetings where "venal emigrant leaders" depicted "the Soviet people along the lines of the darkest characters in American detective novels." In spite of all these efforts, the *Gazette* was able to boast that the "Allen Dulles commandos suffered a thorough defeat."[75] Perhaps on this occasion, the *Gazette* deserves some credit for exhibiting its own creative license. Still, Dulles was keeping an eye on the events in Melbourne. He, like Jackson, was eager to see that the Hungarian defectors were able to secure safe passage to the United States.[76]

Jackson had watched the events unfold in Hungary with a sense of deep frustration. He accepted the fact that the United States could not march a military force into Budapest, but he believed that Eisenhower could at least have done more to censure the Soviet Union. Eisenhower, for his part, knew that Jackson was profoundly involved with the Hungarian situation. "I know that your whole being cries out for 'action' on the Hungarian problem," the president told Jackson. "But to annihilate Hungary, should it become the scene of a bitter conflict, is in no way to help her."[77] Eisenhower's words failed to ease Jackson's anguish. Years later he would still recall that "hope was the controlling word from 1950 to 1956. But when October–November 1956 came around, which as far as the Hungarians and the Poles were concerned represented the climax of 'hope,' with the results we all know—and I repeat for good and sufficient reasons—that word 'hope' took a terrible beating, a beating from which it has not yet recovered."[78]

At a time when U.S. foreign policy lacked the purpose that Jackson demanded of it, the defection of Hungarian athletes in Melbourne provided him with a much-needed sense of accomplishment. He referred to the "highly successful operation" as "part high adventure and part dangerous long shot."[79] Jackson knew that the decision of the Hungarian athletes to live in the United States had shone a light on the actions of the Soviets in Budapest. He also understood that athletes in the communist bloc were prized cultural representatives and often celebrated in state propaganda. This is precisely why he then dedicated a great deal of his energies to making sure that the athletes stayed in the United States and did not return home. Moreover, for the next few years, Jackson and *Sports Illustrated* enlisted the defecting athletes in a nationwide campaign to reinforce anticommunist sentiments and convince the people of the United States that the vast influx of Hungarian refugees across U.S. borders as a result of the revolution was a bonus to the country, as opposed to a hindrance. Jackson also kept alive the hope that some of these refugee athletes could compete at the next Olympic Games, only this time for the United States.

7 Symbols of Freedom

One year after the Melbourne defection, members of the Hungarian National Olympic Team assembled in San Francisco, the city where they first set foot on the U.S. mainland. The athletes who, as one newspaper put it, "refused to return to their communist-dominated homeland," sipped drinks and reminisced about what happened at the time of, and also after, the 1956 summer Olympics.[1] To mark the occasion, the group sent letters of appreciation to a host of individuals involved in the defection. A letter, of course, was conveyed to C. D. Jackson. "We will always be grateful to you for your support," wrote representatives of the group in a communication to the publicist.[2] Jackson responded in effusive language. "The members of your Team," he commented, "represent the very best of Hungary's tradition through the excellence of their performance in sports, and through their demonstrated love of freedom. All Americans who have witnessed the Hungarian Team in competition must think also of that brave and oppressed land itself—in terms of admiration for its bravery and hope for its ultimate victory and freedom."[3]

It had been a remarkable year. Once the Hungarian National Olympic Team reached the United States, a triumvirate of parties had taken responsibility for their welfare: *Sports Illustrated*, the Hungarian National Sports Federation (HNSF), and Jackson himself. This triumvirate combined to accomplish two aims. First, they paraded the team around the country in a nationwide tour, an exhibition that provided U.S. newspapers and the United States Information Agency with an opportunity to depict the athletes as symbols of freedom, both in their choice to flee from communism, and as living proof that the people of Hungary wished to be released from Soviet control. Second, they took steps to make sure that the athletes transitioned to life in the United States in the smoothest manner possible. This fell in line with an overall propaganda strategy devised by the U.S. government, which was itself trying to ease the way for a further thirty-eight thousand Hungarian refugees into U.S. society, just months after Soviet tanks rolled into Budapest, destroying the revolution. The triumvirate secured housing and employment for nearly all members of the team, but, in a few cases, special actions were required. It was here that Jackson made his decisive impact. When, for instance, Mihály Iglói (a coach) and László Tábori (a runner), threatened to return to Hungary, Jackson contributed to finding them a place to work and train at an athletic club in Santa Clara, California. He also made arrangements for the Free Europe Committee (FEC) to pay most of Iglói's salary. Jackson hoped that the Hungarian coach might be able to develop a batch of U.S. distance runners who could challenge for honors at the next summer Olympic Games, to take place in Rome. He also hoped, as did others in government, that members of the Hungarian National Olympic Team, along with other refugee athletes in the United States, could be permitted to compete at the Olympics as representatives of the U.S. squad. Unfortunately for Jackson, and even more so for the refugee athletes whom he lobbied for, the International Olympic Committee (IOC) and the U.S. Congress quashed their efforts.

The Freedom Tour

After a long and momentous journey, the thirty-four Hungarians and four Romanians who defected after the Melbourne Olympics arrived in San Francisco on Christmas Eve. A little more than two weeks had passed since the Olympic flame had been extinguished in Australia. In that time, U.S. officials had determined that the Hungarian team's case served the "national interest," a decision that allowed the defecting athletes to avoid the standard screening process for U.S.-bound refugees of the revolution in Camp Kilmer, New Jersey. For a couple of days the group was able to sample the sights and sounds of the San Francisco Bay area before flying to New York.[4] They spent their first day on the East Coast registering with the United States Immigration and Naturalization Service—which Jackson later praised for performing its duties with a "total absence of bureaucratic red tape"—and then moved from location to location for a series of interviews and public appearances.[5] A dozen of the athletes even spent the evening of New Year's Day at the home of Jackson "for dinner and general discussion." Jackson led the conversation, using the opportunity to gather some firsthand knowledge of life in Eastern Europe by probing the opinion of the athletes on "radio broadcasting in Hungary" and "the root causes of the revolution."[6]

The Hungarian National Olympic Team stands in front of the United Airways plane that flew them from California to New York. Courtesy of Gladys and Paul Szápáry.

The dramatic and intriguing story of the Hungarian National Olympic Team had captured the attention of the world's media, but it was not uncommon for athletes in the communist bloc to exploit the advantages of foreign travel and take the opportunity to defect. Newspapers in the United States were more than happy to print these stories, thereby fanning the flames in the United States about the horrors of life under communism. The "satellite countries are losing their top performers faster than they can replace them," an editorial in the *Milwaukee Journal* declared with some satisfaction, while a steady stream of articles published across the country congratulated the "performers" and celebrated what they deemed to be a "victory" for the West.[7] If that were not enough, some of these athletes readily spoke to reporters about their experiences of living under communism and their dislike for the centralized sport system in the Soviet bloc. The *Chicago Daily News*, for instance, carried an article about how the Czechoslovakian ice skater Miroslava Nachodska seized a moment to flee at the 1955 world ice-skating championships in Vienna. "It was my big chance," she said, "because I was not considered politically reliable and had not been permitted to perform in the West since 1947." Nachodska admitted that life for an athlete in Czechoslovakia was full of material benefits, even national prestige. "I had everything but freedom and security," she lamented.[8] For the Western media, then, refugees became, in essence, walking and talking propaganda.

In time, the U.S. press would also exhaust a great supply of ink over the story of the Hungarian National Olympic Team's nationwide tour. Indeed, the idea for an athletic exhibition had emerged in the throes of the Melbourne defection and *Sports Illustrated*, for its part, had accepted the responsibility of organizing it. The "Freedom Tour," as it became known, was largely directed by the magazine's assistant publisher, Richard Neale, but he did receive cooperation from several powerful U.S. sports administrators, including Daniel Ferris and James Greene of the Amateur Athletic Union of the United States; Lyman Bingham, executive director of the United States Olympic Committee; Edward P. Eagan, president of the People-to-People Sports Committee; and José R. de Capriles of the Amateur Fencers League of America. In order to advertise the event, Neale sent a letter to sports editors around the United States to provide background information on the endeavor. He outlined the three main aims: "First, fund raising for Hungarian Relief; second, a living demonstration of the Free Hungary story, and third, resettlement and jobs for the athletes themselves." Neale also was keen to make sure that the media coverage of the tour was kept under a modicum of control. If the athletes complained about something or expressed "dissatisfaction," then it should not be hidden. By the same token, quotes from the team had to come from the mouth of the athletes in the presence of an interpreter. Neale warned against "second hand" reporting or the crafty work of agents spreading "false rumors." The *Washington Post and Times Herald* published one of his letters but carefully omitted a crucial sentence that was present in the original copy. "For your information, and not for the public record," wrote Neale, "the Freedom Tour has, of course, enlisted the active support of the State Department and CIA."[9]

Neale and his collaborators divided the six-week tour into three parts. The fencers journeyed with the gymnasts, the water polo team joined the swimmers, and Tábori had the stage to himself. Only on two dates, one in New York, and one in Philadelphia, did they all appear together. The Hungarian and Romanian athletes boarded two blue-and-white Greyhound Scenicruiser buses in New York on 10 January before traveling from "coast to coast" for ninety-five performances at fifty-nine locations. The gymnasts and fencers started out in Connecticut on 11 January and performed almost every other day with contests against teams from Harvard and the Massachusetts Institute of Technology in Cambridge, Notre Dame in South Bend, an Air Force Academy team in Denver, the Milwaukee Fencers Club in Wisconsin, and the San Francisco Fencers Club in California. The water polo and swimming teams moved across the country at an unrelenting speed. They gave demonstrations at Yale University, Springfield College (Massachusetts), Northwestern University, the University of Oklahoma, Texas A&M, and further shows in Phoenix and Las Vegas. Elsewhere, Tá- bori competed in indoor track meets in New York, Boston, Philadelphia, Washington, Chicago, Milwaukee, and Cleveland.[10]

The U.S. media had been covering the story of the Hungarian National Olympic Team from the moment they reached the United States, but the tour stimulated a further wave of interest from journalists across the country. Local and national newspapers contained advertisements, cartoons, pictures, and stories on the defecting athletes as they moved from the East Coast to their final stop in California. There "is something unforgettable about the story of the 34 Hungarian athletes who are not returning to their Red battered land," read an editorial in the *Mason City* (Iowa) *Globe-Gazette* as the tour commenced. "To them the Olympics was not only an athletic test but the beginning of a new life."[11] Other newspapers enthusiastically reported on the exhibitions and marveled over the athletes' skills, personalities, and resolve. The *New York Times* eagerly explained how the diver Joseph Gerlac, "thrilled the crowd" at Yale's Payne Whitney Gymnasium "with spectacular efforts seldom seen in America."[12] The *Washington Post and Times Herald* told readers how the "hand- some" Hungarian water polo player Miklos Martin had attracted the "most attention" from female fans at the University of Maryland because of his "bright brown eyes" and "radiant personality."[13] In a YMCA facility in Beverly Hills, noted *Sports Illustrated*, spectators were so impressed by the performance of the gymnast Attila Takach that they were moved to honor the performer with a "standing ovation."[14]

Although the Hungarian National Olympic Team may have garnered a great deal of popular appreciation as they performed in towns and cities across the country, the admission of more than thirty-eight thousand Hun- garian refugees into the country was a matter that the U.S. public did not greet with equanimity. Outspoken members of Congress charged that the relaxed screening methods, especially for parolees, presented an opportunity for communists to enter the United States. Soon enough, the Eisenhower ad- ministration took steps to arrest these fears. After all, the world had to see that the refugees were welcomed in the United States with open arms even if, in many instances, they were not. On 12 December 1956, Eisenhower created the President's Committee for Hungarian Refugee Relief to run a public relations campaign to "sell" the notion that the new inhabitants would be valuable, productive members of society and that they were opponents of commu- nism. Historian Carl Bon Tempo explains that the committee was formed to "coordinate the refugee-resettlement efforts of the voluntary agencies, the federal government, and private-sector contributors." Tracy Voorhees led the operation. The bulk of the public relations for the President's Committee was undertaken by two private firms: the Advertising Council and Communications Counselors (CCI). In order to silence the cries from doubters and critics, the Advertising Council pressed radio and television networks to air positive coverage of the issue, while the CCI launched an extensive drive to "assist in creating an atmosphere of public acceptance" of the refugees. Aside from courting television networks, the CCI encouraged newspapers and magazines such as *Look, Reader's Digest, Time, Life*, and *Sports Illustrated* to publish stories that would help to promote the assimilation of refugees into U.S. society.[15] Neale, in fact, visited the White House at the midpoint of the tour to speak with Voorhees. "In Washington, the importance of this tour, both for keeping the story of Hungary's fight for freedom alive in America, and for its impact behind the Iron Curtain, was again impressed on me," he wrote.[16]

As it turned out, data assembled by *Sports Illustrated* magazine's staff also seemed to suggest that the U.S. public had embraced the story of the defection and the Freedom Tour. In a random assessment of nationwide news outlets, *Sports Illustrated* found nearly eight hundred references to the tour in forty-eight states and, moreover, it recorded that radio, television, and newspapers were filled with stories of the athletes from the time they left Melbourne, with "human interest interviews," coverage of athletic performances, and the progress toward resettlement. Each and every time the athletes competed on the Freedom Tour, argued Neale, it "dramatized" their story. Movie and television newsreels across the country showed the Hungarian athletes arriving in San Francisco, landing in New York, and departing for the tour. The team appeared as guests on *The Ed Sullivan Show*, and Neale was interviewed on several occasions, twice by the sportscaster Howard Cosell. One contestant on the *$64,000 Question* even donated some winnings to the Hungarian fund.[17]

Sports Illustrated played its part in the media fanfare by carrying an assortment of stories on the team and by publishing supportive letters from the U.S. public. To commemorate the Freedom Tour, the magazine also produced a special edition booklet that profiled each of the thirty-eight refugee athletes, and Neale composed a wrap-up piece, titled "Across a Free Land," chronicling the journey of the refugees from start to finish. "They had spent Christmas in the West, New Year's in New York. They had touched the Liberty Bell in Philadelphia, visited the Capitol in Washington and scrambled playfully along the upper rim of the Grand Canyon. They had rested at quiet school and college towns like Andover and Middlebury. They had lived at the great universities of Michigan and Ohio State and

Notre Dame. They had watched Cadillacs being built in Detroit, broncos being busted in Texas," Neale gushed. "In turn, they brought three things to America: a living demonstration of the obstinate, furious idea of Free Hungary; the superb skill of Olympic champions in sports unfamiliar to Americans; and, not least important, they brought themselves and their talents and aspirations." He also underscored that the athletes were "urged to go back, in letter after letter from Budapest." From this evidence Neale concluded that "The tour, successful in America, had apparently been a sensation behind the Iron Curtain."[18]

Neale sent his article to Voorhees. After reading the story, Voorhees offered his sincere congratulations: "Sports Illustrated has performed a public service of genuine value in bringing these athletes here and arranging for the tour. This came at a time when the favorable publicity for the Hungar-

A United States Information Agency photograph shows U.S. and expatriate Hungarian swimmers enjoying each other's company during a Freedom Tour performance at the University of Maryland. From left to right the athletes pictured are Dick Amen, Ferenc Siak, Stapler Shields, and József Gerlach. Courtesy of the National Archives.

ian refugees which was generated by the presence of these Olympic athletes, was of particular usefulness in assisting in American acceptance of the . . . Hungarian refugees who have already come to our shores."[19]

The Eisenhower propaganda apparatus spun the same line. Individual experiences of refugees were carried on Radio Free Europe, the Voice of America, and in the output of the United States Information Agency (USIA).[20] Even prior to the events in Hungary, though, the USIA consistently referred to refugee Eastern European athletes living in the United States. These stories presented the athletes as exemplars of freedom, who, having chosen to leave a life under communist rule, were now integrated into the democratic ways of the United States and prospering in a system where anyone could succeed. The USIA depicted the Hungarian National Olympic Team in a similar way. A feature on László Tábori explained that he was among the Hungarian athletes and officials "who chose freedom rather than return to their Kremlin-dominated homeland." The article described Tábori as "engaging" and "pleasant," and a quote from the runner read, "I am grateful I was permitted to come to the United States. I should like to remain and work in my own field and compete in track when I have time."[21] Other USIA features described the Freedom Tour in the same tone and manner. One article boasted that the defecting athletes "have made many friends during their coast-to-coast exhibition tour of major U.S. cities. . . . Everywhere they went the athletes were greeted with warm enthusiasm and understanding." Propaganda experts were able to reinforce these claims by sending photographs of the tour to information posts in the "free world," which showed the Hungarians smiling and enjoying their interactions with U.S. competitors.[22]

After hearing a long debriefing from Neale, Jackson was extremely pleased with the "logistical triumph" of the Freedom Tour. "[D]espite all the built-in hazards it has turned out to be a truly happy end," he noted agreeably. The costs incurred by *Time* for the defection, the tour, and the resettlement of the athletes came to thirty-five thousand dollars, far below original estimates. The tour even made a profit, some of which was donated to First Aid for Hungary, and some set aside for a special relief fund for the families of the athletes.[23] Gradually, too, the role of *Sports Illustrated* in the orchestration of the team's affairs receded. But, on the other hand, the HNSF assumed a greater responsibility for the lives of the Hungarian National Olympic Team, in much the same way as it attended to the well-being of other refugee athletes, inside and outside the United States. For Jackson, his attachment to the project did not dwindle either and, at times, the refugee athletes turned to his aid when all else failed.

Resettlement: Operation Eagle

On the eve of the Freedom Tour, Whitney Tower sent a congratulatory letter to Count Szápáry: "Without your inspiration I don't think anything could have been accomplished—and the fact that it has been accomplished is, I am quite sure, largely a reflection on your strong will-to-succeed." In his remarks, Tower went on to make one apology and to give one warning. He bemoaned the fact that some people at *Sports Illustrated* were using the defection to raise the profile of the magazine. Tower claimed that he himself, and most of the editorial team, had attempted to stem this practice, but, he said, "one has to expect and accept a few warped mentalities in a journalistic empire whose rank and file live and breathe the words TIME, INC, 24 hours a day." Tower also gave a sour account of Telegdy's involvement in the defection. The *Sports Illustrated* staff in Melbourne, including André Laguerre, reported to Tower a "tale of terrible confusion" due to the work of Telegdy. Australian authorities confirmed this. "Frankly," finished Tower, "it was agreed by all who had a hand in the business, that he is incompetent for this sort of organizational work."[24] Incompetent Telegdy may have been, but he remained a pivotal figure in the HNSF. He continued to aid refugees, and irritate collaborators, for some time to come. In particular, Telegdy became immersed in the long-term process of resettling the Hungarian National Olympic Team in the United States, a process he called "Operation Eagle."

Sports Illustrated, Jackson, and the HNSF were reasonably successful in this final stage of the operation. By April, most of the athletes were placed in jobs or given a scholarship at a university.[25] For example, the fencer Jenő Hámori found work and an apartment in Philadelphia; the diving coach, Bálint Papp, accepted a job offer in Florida; and Gábor Nagy, the Romanian water polo player, was awarded a scholarship at the University of Southern California.[26] Yet this was not the case for all of the defecting athletes. While the fencer Béla Rerrick was in Melbourne, his wife and two daughters fled to Austria and were then resettled in Sweden. He naturally wished to be with his family, and so Jackson asked Voorhees for "guidance and/or help."[27] Jackson admired the multilingual Rerrick and felt that he could be "most useful in this country for the promotion of the cause of freedom behind the Iron Curtain" and in his capacity to "communicate with all kinds of people." Jackson continued, "I think it would be a definite loss, not to C.D.J.'s Olympic project, but to the United States, if this man were to leave. . . . And after all, what is he asking? Not for the moon or a million dollars, but simply to be reunited with his wife and daughters."[28] Voorhees moved to assist the Hungarian, but the problem only magnified over time. Rerrick was allowed to leave the United States and travel to Sweden, whereupon he was to meet with his wife and children and bring them back to the United States. Jackson worked on the visas and *Time* footed the bill. At the last minute, however, Rerrick announced that he and his family had decided to stay in Sweden to avoid more upheaval. Jackson was mystified. It transpired that Rerrick was suffering from a bout of mental frailty and harbored a desire to return to Hungary and resume his fencing career. The whole family eventually made it to the United States, but Rerrick then abruptly returned to Europe. His wife and children remained in the United States; Rerrick eventually moved back to Hungary.[29]

For various reasons, other members of the team also left the United States. Zoltán Török, the rowing coach, learned that his mother was deeply ill and flew home. László Nádori, the sports administrator, received letters from his family, pleading for his return. He could not, and did not, ignore them. The swimmer László Magyar and two of the water polo players, László Jeney and György Kárpáti, all "redefected." Others talked of doing the same thing. Coupled with personal and unforeseen dilemmas, Szápáry underscored that the communist regime was "desperately" trying to entice athletes back to Hungary. Telegdy even claimed that as a result of his prompting, a separate branch of the Federal Bureau of Investigation was "engaged in supervising the affairs of the Olympic athletes and of other sportsmen" in order to prevent the Hungarian authorities from "luring" the athletes back to Eastern Europe.[30]

The triumvirate, then, worked assiduously to keep the athletes in the United States. One strategy involved looking after the dependents of the defectors still living in Hungary by sending them goods and medicines only available in the United States. The HNSF dispatched more than fifty packages on four occasions to family members in Hungary and later received word that they "meant a great deal" to the dependents. Szápáry also wanted to make sure that the athletes who wanted to keep competing had the financial backing to do so, whatever the competition. He believed that keeping the athletes active might help in the process of resettling. "Now we have the chance to use the appearance of the Hungarian athletes as well as their results in the service of the Hungarian national cause and the athletes themselves are anxious to serve this cause," Szápáry added.[31] Some of the athletes were already taking part in local, regional, and national competitions around the United States, and the HNSF set up a "Campaign Fund" so that the practice could continue.

Szápáry made the first donation and FEC put four thousand dollars into the pool. By this stage, it appears, the FEC began to intensify its support for the HNSF and the Hungarian National Olympic Team. Perhaps spurred on by the level of public awareness directed at the athletes who had defected, the FEC supplied more money to the HNSF than it ever had before. The period from 1957 to 1960 were the golden years of the relationship.

One of the competitions the HNSF isolated for special attention was the 1958 World Fencing Championships, scheduled to take place in Philadelphia. Not only would the refugee fencers stand a good chance of winning, but representatives of the Hungarian regime also were sure to be there. It also served as a reminder that grave problems still had to be overcome with regard to the immigration status of the team. Although the Hungarian athletes who defected could compete in the United States at various national or state competitions, international events were a different matter altogether. The athletes that fled Melbourne entered the United States on "parole" and were thus not U.S. citizens. Initially, the participation of the defecting Hungarians in the World Fencing Championships was doubtful. The athletes had no country to compete for and the International Fencing Federation was reluctant to permit the entry of the refugees. The refugees had to provide evidence of their "statelessness." Through *Sports Illustrated*, Jackson, and contacts at the State Department, preparations were made to obtain the necessary documentation.[32] It was enough for the time being. The long-term challenge remained. Jackson could not hide his frustration with the laws of the land. "These are important people in the eyes of the world, particularly in the world behind the Iron Curtain. They have sought asylum in this country, which has been granted, but at the same time they are important specialists in an international field. Inevitably they will be invited to participate in athletic events outside the country, which at present they cannot do," he remonstrated in a letter to the State Department. "Does the Government of the United States, under constant attack for inadequate handling of the cold war problem, consider it important enough to go through the necessary bureaucratic motions to arrange for these people to do for the United States and for the West the thing at which they are supremely competent—something which will make headlines throughout the world."[33]

In July 1958, Congress passed a law that allowed parolees to apply for permanent residence if they had been living in the United States for two years. These first two years were then retroactively deducted from the five years of residence it took to apply for citizenship.[34] Unfortunately, citizenship was not enough for the IOC. The members of the Hungarian National Olympic

Team had competed for Hungary or Romania at the Melbourne Olympics, and this disqualified them from representing another nation.

The "Iglói-Tábori Mission" and the Santa Clara Valley Youth Village

As the case of Béla Rerrick clearly demonstrated, there was a complex human element to the Melbourne defection that accounted for inconsistent or unsettled behavior by some of the Hungarian refugees. The United States was a foreign land with an unfamiliar culture. Adjusting from a life of relative stardom, to relative obscurity, was not without challenges. Some of the athletes and coaches wanted the treatment they had received in Hungary and were not content to settle for random employment. The HNSF would have expected this. Jackson himself intimated that perhaps he and *Sports Illustrated* were less prepared for it.[35] At any rate, the strains of resettlement were once again revealed, this time in relation to Mihály Iglói, an internationally renowned coach of middle distance runners, and László Tábori, one of the few athletes of his time to break the four-minute mile. The two wanted to work together; the one to train, the other to coach, preferably in California. After the Freedom Tour, the University of North Carolina gave both men part-time jobs and invited them to lodge at the campus on a temporary basis. Once their sojourn in North Carolina ended, the two Hungarians reverted to their original plan and moved to California in the hope of forging something more permanent at a university athletic program. Instead, they found no openings. Tábori eventually secured a job in a shoe factory. The work itself did not considerably bother the runner, but the hours did. Beginning at 7 a.m. and finishing at 6 p.m. allowed little time for training. Much to his dissatisfaction, Iglói performed manual labor. He wanted to train Olympic-caliber athletes, and nothing else would suffice. The two men grew increasingly disenchanted with the U.S. sporting establishment. By the winter of 1957, they considered returning to Hungary.[36]

When Jackson became aware of the situation, he scrambled to find a solution. "Having been involved in psychological warfare work for a number of years, and having made somewhat of a speciality of the Eastern European countries, I cannot stress too strongly the impact that the return of either of these two men would have," he stressed. "In Hungary they are national figures as well-known as any of America's top personalities, and their return would therefore be a tremendous prize for the Communist regime, to be heralded and paraded as a great victory." He asked the dean at Princeton if he would

Pictured from left to right: László Tábori, Mihály Iglói, and George Telegdy.
Courtesy of Gladys and Paul Szápáry.

employ both Hungarians, but to no avail.[37] Two of Jackson's colleagues in San
Francisco, Richard Pollard, an employee of *Time*, and Alexander Brody—a
"special agent for SI and *Time*"[38]—tried to make other arrangements but
could do only half the job. They found Tábori a more accommodating position at the San Jose Steel Company that allowed the runner to train in the
afternoons. Then, to the deep relief of all concerned, a small AAU-accredited
athletic club administered by the Santa Clara Valley Youth Village stepped
into the picture and offered to employ Iglói as its coach and to have Tábori as
a member of its track team. The Santa Clara–based organization would take
the pair until the 1960 Olympic Games and provide Iglói with a chance to
train a team that "will beat the Soviet Union and, for the first time, establish
American supremacy in distances over 1500 meters." The only impediment,
as ever, was funding.[39]

The Santa Clara Valley Youth Village was established in 1944 by a priest
named Walter E. Schmidt. Born in San Francisco in 1911, Schmidt was
ordained in 1941. Gregarious and well-liked, he was once given an award
in San Jose for being the Optimist of the Year. Under his energetic leadership, the Youth Village grew in popularity during World War II and soon
required a large facility to serve as its base. Schmidt raised money for the
building of the Youth Village center by inviting celebrities such as Frank
Sinatra to perform at benefits, and he encouraged businesses and corpora-

tions to support the project. J. Edgar Hoover, director of the FBI, gave the Youth Village two commendations and respectfully observed that it "serves as a guidepost to moral living and is a dynamic force for good among young people." In 1953, Schmidt organized the Youth Village track team in tandem with an athletic coach named Mike Ryan. The team largely consisted of athletes who were no longer eligible to compete at a college or university and individuals who were refused sponsorship elsewhere because of their race. Although the Youth Village was not an educational institution, it competed against universities and colleges on the competitive track-and-field circuit. After fifteen years of work, the Youth Village produced fourteen athletes for the U.S. Olympic team, eight of whom won medals.[40] Indeed, some of these athletic heights could not have been reached without the considerable expertise of Iglói.

Before the great coach could start his tenure, however, a few logistical issues had to be resolved. Schmidt estimated that around ten or twelve thousand dollars a year would be needed to pay Iglói's salary and to keep the track fund at Santa Clara operational. "If this meets with your approval we will do all we can to help Mr. Iglói and László Tábori realize their ambitions in and for track in this country," he told Jackson.[41] Jackson was more than satisfied. "This situation had gotten so hopelessly complicated and emotional," he replied to Schmidt, "that I did not think a solution could be found, and now it has been thanks to your understanding."[42] Although the last year had been taxing, Jackson took it all in stride and good humor. "By now I think it would be less trouble to liberate all of Hungary than to take care of these Hungarian Olympic athletes, and am seriously thinking of suggesting this to the President," he quipped.[43]

At first, Jackson and his colleagues thought that they could fund the "Iglói-Tábori Mission" through private donations. They arranged for the 6 January edition of *Sports Illustrated* to contain a letter from the Hungarian National Olympic Team (which it did). In the next edition, *Sports Illustrated* would then publish a letter to the editor from Schmidt (which it also did), referring to the Hungarian athletes and alerting the readers that two of the defectors were part of the Youth Village program. Jackson believed the exposure in *Sports Illustrated* would stimulate contributions and act as a "handy reference piece" with which to approach larger investors.[44] In January 1958, Jackson began a personal effort to solicit funds. The first contribution came from Jackson's friend, Sigurd Larmon, the president of Young and Rubicam. "It is a worthy project," commented Larmon, who donated a thousand dollars.[45] *Time* gave a further thousand dollars, and

Walter E. Schmidt, S.J., pictured with young members of the Santa Clara Valley Youth Village. Courtesy of the Department of Archives and Special Collections, Santa Clara University.

a few smaller amounts arrived from other private sources.[46] Jackson was pleased with the early success. "This is one of those cases where you are actually helping not only a couple of Hungarians, and an athletic association, and our chances in the 1960 Olympics, but also the U.S., which would have suffered a terrible black eye if things had not been worked out as they have," he said to one of the sponsors.[47] Still, these few donations were well short of the twelve thousand dollars required to keep the Iglói-Tábori Mission afloat.

Jackson's confidence faltered. He wrote to Neale that "neither you nor I should have to be beating our brains out trying to find $12,000 for Father Schmidt in Santa Clara Valley."[48] By April 1958, Father Schmidt was worried that the money had dried up and, to further complicate things, he had employed Tábori as a part-time worker at the Youth Village. The financial situation, as Father Schmidt described it, was "precarious."[49] Jackson concurred: "I myself do not like this hand-to-mouth, month-to-month living."[50] As the project demanded an immediate injection of money, Jackson contacted another friend, the director of the CIA, Allen Dulles. "It clearly fits in to your psywar charter," he wrote in a letter to Dulles after discussing the issue on the telephone. Jackson asked for five thousand dollars right away.[51] "As you know," responded Dulles, "the welfare of defectors and refugees in this country is of the utmost importance, and the case which you cite in your letter is of special interest."[52] A month later the money arrived in Santa Clara. Yet even with these funds, Schmidt struggled to keep the athletic program afloat. Part of the reason he was able to do so was because the FEC donated five thousand dollars in 1959 and the same amount again in 1960.[53]

In many ways, Iglói earned his money. Although Schmidt admitted that the Hungarian was, at times, arrogant and difficult to work with, the impact of Iglói's coaching on Santa Clara's athletes was clear to see. One of the most prominent products of the Santa Clara system, Jim Beatty, improved dramatically under the guidance of the mercurial coach's strict training regimen. Beatty, who called Iglói the "world's greatest running coach," eventually became the first athlete to break the four-minute mile indoors.[54] Moreover, Tábori continued to capture the media limelight with impressive performances in race after race on the U.S. circuit and in European events. Jackson was proud of this exposure, but the Iglói-Tábori Mission was only a short-term plan. Jackson had used the Rome Olympics as a "sales point" for contributors and doubted whether he could arouse the same interest once the Olympics passed. He hoped, nonetheless, that the publicity given to the Hungarians at the Youth Village might attract other sponsors.[55] For his part, Schmidt recognized this. He had known all along that the "1960 Olympics made a natural breaking-off point." The two Hungarians were also, it appears, under no illusions about the situation. "Igloi understands," wrote Schmidt, "and always has, that the end of 1960 would bring an end, also, to the arrangements under which he worked here." Being no stranger to fundraising, Schmidt vowed to keep the program running.[56] Jackson's donations to Santa Clara ceased in 1961.[57]

The IOC Stands Firm

Even though the Melbourne defection had been a sensation in the United States, it did not register to any considerable degree in the IOC. This reaction is understandable. With the sheer controversy of the Hungarian Revolution, coupled with the Suez Crisis, Avery Brundage and his colleagues had to focus on promoting a united front, while trying, as ever, to insist that political incidents should not impinge on the Olympics. After the Olympics, Brundage casually mentioned to the Hungarian IOC member, Ferenc Mező, that some of the defectors were touring around the United States but did not seem to have been vocal about it.[58] On a further occasion, Brundage displayed no animosity to the HNSF or the Hungarians who defected when it came to a request for Olympic diplomas. In a letter to Otto Mayer, George Telegdy listed the athletes who had finished either first, second, or third in their respective event and asked that the appropriate diplomas be sent to the HNSF, who would distribute them accordingly. "Should the diplomas be sent to the Communist Hungarian Olympic Committee, the just owners of the diplomas would never receive them," Telegdy averred.[59] Brundage had no objections: "I see no harm in sending diplomas from Melbourne to this organization, since they are in touch with the athletes who have left Hungary."[60] Mayer replied to Telegdy that the IOC agreed with the request and Mayer told the Melbourne Organizing Committee to forward the relevant articles.[61] Telegdy was thrilled with this minor success.[62]

This case aside, however, the bigger issue of stateless athletes entering the Olympics remained unresolved. In 1957, Brundage confidentially told a colleague, with his usual choice of words, that the IOC could do nothing about the Hungarian refugees. "Furthermore," he went on, "we would be in endless difficulties if we permitted ourselves to become involved in political questions of this kind."[63] Telegdy and Szápáry had heard this explanation many times before, yet it failed to persuade them to accept it. Prior to the Rome Olympics, Szápáry again attempted to revive the debate with Brundage. The count thought it "absurd" that proven competitors like Tábori were excluded from the Olympics and told Brundage that the IOC should consider altering its rules "which were fashioned in another era" and by leaders who "could never have foreseen the circumstances existing in our world today." Offering a possible solution to the problem, Szápáry suggested a team could be formed that could compete "under the flag" of the United Nations. "I cannot imagine anything which could be more in the true spirit of the Olympics," he wrote.[64] In his response, Brundage repeated that the problem of defecting athletes had been debated at length but that no resolution had been forwarded that did not require reorganizing the basic structure of the IOC. At any rate, the idea of a team representing the United Nations appeared to inspire confusion in Brundage, as opposed to optimism. He offered to discuss the issue at the Rome General Session.[65] There is no currently known record to indicate that this transpired. Thomas de Márffy-Mantuano tried to rekindle the topic in the IOC by also writing to Brundage and Mayer. It was not received well by the latter, who thought that he had heard the last of the Hungarian in Helsinki. "He wants to interfere again," moaned Mayer; "if we begin again [to correspond] with that nuisance of a man, we shall not get rid of him."[66] In a calmer moment, Mayer told Márffy that the IOC could do nothing more.[67]

The IOC was also forced to consider the problem of defecting athletes beyond the protestations of émigré groups sponsored by the U.S. intelligence establishment. Various private groups, individuals, and organizations also sent communications to Lausanne, requesting Olympic leaders to reconsider the IOC's rules on national representation. It is not surprising that the message from the IOC remained the same. In a typical response to one interested activist, Brundage explained, "While the International Olympic Committee was very sympathetic toward the predicament of displaced persons, insofar as competition in the Olympic Games is concerned, no way could be found under existing rules to allow them to participate."[68] Nothing, it seemed, could be done to alter the situation. Jackson even hired a lawyer, Jack Dowd, to investigate the specific case of two Hungarian female athletes who, after defecting, were living in the United States. Dowd discovered nothing new. The only way the two ladies could participate for the U.S. team would be if they married a U.S. national and then applied for full citizenship. Having received the same advice from the USOC, Jackson commented, "I would love to see these fine athletes qualify for the Olympics, but [I] am not prepared to become a marriage broker in order to accomplish it."[69]

But the IOC's reluctance to accommodate stateless competitors was only a part of the larger problem. While Jackson pondered the possibility of Hungarian refugee athletes participating for the United States in Rome, it was still essential for the refugees to have U.S. citizenship. He had already berated the government for not following through with the "necessary bureaucratic motions" to expedite citizenship for refugee sportsmen, and the FEC, the HNSF, and the AAU had also been investigating ways to force special legislation.[70] They were not alone. In 1959, Texas Senator Lyndon Johnson submitted a bill to the U.S. Senate for the purpose of speeding up the immigration process for a Polish-born athlete who relocated to the United States. Johnson argued that it was an exceptional case. The individual could compete for the United States at the 1960 Olympics if he were granted citizenship in advance of the standard five-year waiting period. The Senate passed the bill in May. When it reached the House Judiciary Committee, it was given to a subcommittee on immigration. Here it faltered. The chairman of the subcommittee, Congressman Francis Walter of Pennsylvania, said he would "use every effort to block its approval."

Walter charged that if the United States were to pass such legislation, then it could be accused of "bootlegging" communist athletes.[71] Four other bills, this time for Hungarians, received the same treatment. Walter later added that the subcommittee did not recommend the bills to the House "because we believe it would be highly improper and totally out of line, both with the American tradition in sports and with the true spirit of the Olympic games."[72] Acknowledging the validity of this point, *Sports Illustrated* concluded, "In the field of sport, it is possible for the U.S. to try too hard."[73]

With the end of the Freedom Tour and the gradual resettlement of the Hungarian National Olympic Team more or less complete, the involvement of *Sports Illustrated* in the lives of the refugee athletes began to recede. The magazine had spent a large sum of money in all its efforts, not to mention the enormous cost of the time taken up by its staff. The intentions of the *Sports Illustrated* employees involved in the defection also reveal a great deal about the nature of the state–private network. No doubt there was a motivation to sell copies of the magazine or, at least, to advertise the brand in an innovative manner. As Whitney Tower admitted to Szápáry, many at the magazine wanted to exploit the situation for commercial, as opposed to political, gains. Still, this was not the only reason for the pivotal contribution of *Sports Illustrated*. It is hard to look beyond the Cold War mentality of individuals such as Neale, Tower, Pollard, and Jackson. Neale, for instance, understood the broader psychological aspect of the Freedom Tour, and Brody was not called to San Francisco simply to protect the reputation of a magazine. In a report on Iglói and Tábori, Brody wrote, "Their significance from a political and propaganda standpoint is too obvious to need explanation."[74] The Freedom Tour and the resettlement of the Hungarian National Olympic Team was about more than simply sales figures for *Sports Illustrated*. It was a case of private citizens and private groups doing what they could for a cause they believed in, and a cause that often complemented government policies.

8 Operation Rome

Throughout the second term of the Eisenhower administration, the United States remained fixated upon its global confrontation with communism. The "total" contest for international preeminence continued to spill unrelentingly, it seemed, outside the parameters of traditional diplomacy and ever more into the boundless activities of the human race. When the Soviet Union launched an artificial earth satellite into space in 1957, what could have been hailed as a moment of technological progress for all to share was instead viewed as a considerable setback by the U.S. public and its federal government. *Newsweek* magazine called the Soviet breakthrough a "defeat in three fields: In pure science, in practical know-how, and in psychological warfare."[1] The unsuccessful attempts by the United States to compete with this Soviet scientific achievement elicited further cries of concern from the U.S. public, who worried that communism was expanding not only on earth, but also toward the stars. While U.S. citizens contemplated and considered this worrisome predicament, another cultural defeat intensified the already alarmed atmosphere, as the Soviet Union outperformed all its rivals at the 1960 winter Olympics, deepening the sense of crisis in the reeling nation. One congressman, clearly troubled by the situation, felt compelled to ask, "Have we Americans lost the old competitive spirit?"[2]

In some respects, nothing appeared to have changed. In one area, though, there was a promise of détente. The Soviet Union had closed its borders and shielded its people from Western influence in the early years of the Cold War, but the leadership that followed Joseph Stalin started to press for greater East–West contacts with the United States, and, after some reluctance, the Eisenhower administration acquiesced. In 1958, the two countries signed a cultural agreement, signaling a new era of reciprocal technical, cultural, and scientific exchanges. The agreement also revealed the shift in U.S. policy toward the Soviet bloc under Eisenhower. With the prospects of "liberation" seemingly in abeyance, Washington looked to induce "evolutionary" change in the Soviet satellites through "cultural infiltration."[3] This strategy of "parting the iron curtain" would also rely on sporting diplomacy, with U.S. athletes traveling to Eastern Europe and the Soviet Union to provide the "captive peoples" with an opportunity to see and to meet representatives of their Western enemy.

Aside from the continuation and expansion of sports exchanges, the Eisenhower administration would still run into familiar problems when it came to the Olympic Movement. In the lead up to the 1956 Melbourne Olympics, the public discussion of federal funding for the U.S. Olympic team had been greeted with very little enthusiasm by U.S. sports officials and, moreover, on Capitol Hill. Yet in the aftermath of Melbourne, the communist challenge in the medals race prompted the same cries of frustration from state and private actors, although the balance of power would not be tilted into the hands of the former. In fact, psychological warfare experts had, by this point, started to accept the severe limitations of what they could and could not achieve through propaganda. They reluctantly accepted that the Soviet Union would likely win the most medals in 1960 and the symbolic power of that would be hard to refute or even to discredit. U.S. propaganda actions for the 1960 winter and summer Olympics, in Squaw Valley and Rome respectively, would follow, in many ways, the routine agenda established in 1952 and again in 1956. For Rome, in particular, the Olympic venue, rather than the athletic events, would offer covert operators with another platform to destabilize and unhinge the regimes in the Soviet bloc. Adhering to the U.S. government's new direction in policy, the Free Europe Committee (FEC) sought to increase "contacts" between exiles and the people of Eastern Europe by targeting the Rome Olympic Games with a multifaceted plan that exploited the propaganda potential of the hosting city and the tourists who visited it.

East–West Contacts and the Cultural Agreement

U.S. and Soviet cultural relations had quickly soured upon the conclusion of World War II. The spirit of cooperation, embodied in the Grand Alliance, gave way to mutual fear and distrust. As the Cold War set in, so did Stalin's insularity. In a move to purge the Soviet Union of Western culture, Stalin sealed the nation's borders, jammed the signals of foreign broadcasters—including the Voice of America and Radio Free Europe—and persecuted

Soviet writers, musicians, magazines, and scientists who displayed sympathy with the West. Cold War hysteria also affected censorship and immigration laws in the United States. In 1950, the Subversive Activities Control Act basically barred all unofficial Soviet bloc citizens from entering the United States. Two years later, the Immigration and Nationality Act, otherwise known as the McCarran Act, added further restrictions. From then on, all Soviet bloc persons applying for visas to enter the United States had to be fingerprinted. It is notable, therefore, that while both superpowers slowly embarked on cultural programs that reached far and wide, they ignored interactions with one another.[4]

The death of Stalin altered the situation. The collective leadership that took charge of the Kremlin enacted liberalizing policies within the Soviet Union and pursued a more welcoming policy toward the outside world. "This was an offensive strategy," Nigel Gould-Davies has explained, "designed to propagate the successes of the socialist system and attract new adherents and sympathizers" to what Soviet leaders thought was a "relentlessly growing international movement."[5] All of a sudden, U.S. citizens were granted visas to enter the Soviet Union and, once inside its borders, were given relative freedom to roam. This spirit of openness was not reciprocated by the United States. Although Eisenhower believed that educational and cultural exchanges with the Soviet Union would have a positive impact on superpower relations, the State Department, and especially the secretary of state, John Foster Dulles, feared that the United States would be exposing itself to espionage and negative propaganda. A few Soviet citizens were allowed into the United States in the 1950s, including a highly publicized visit of Soviet delegates to learn farming techniques in Iowa, but, in general, the fingerprinting law obstructed the progress of cultural relations beyond these narrow limits.[6]

Soon, however, resistance in the State Department would be broken. As the National Security Council had assessed in 1955, to foreign observers it appeared that it was the United States, not the Soviet Union, that had erected an "iron curtain." Even Dulles came to admit that "nothing catastrophic was going to happen as a result of the adoption of this new policy" of cultural contacts with the Soviet Union. Although, for a period, the Hungarian Revolution interrupted any progress on the matter, Congress soon abolished the fingerprinting requirement and, in January 1958, the two countries signed a cultural agreement that allowed all manner of reciprocal exchanges in science, agriculture, medicine, television, film, scholarly research, tourism, and sport. At the same time, the U.S. government sought to widen its cultural contacts with willing Eastern European regimes, thus "breaking down the isolation of the captive peoples from the West." This, and the cultural agreement, were

symbolic of the Eisenhower administration's evolving policy toward the Soviet bloc. "Liberation" may have remained the ideal goal, but it would have
to be achieved by "gradualist" means and with an "evolutionary approach,"
by penetrating the Iron Curtain with ideas and culture.[7]

On the U.S. side of the cultural agreement, sport exchanges were organized,
for the most part, through and under the auspices of the Amateur Athletic
Union of the United States (AAU). Indeed, the AAU and Soviet sports officials
had been negotiating on and off for athletic exchanges for several years, but
political and structural differences prevented an accord. As Joseph Turrini
has noted, the AAU preferred an "exchange of individual athletes to compete
in non-team-scored meets," while the Soviet Union "desired scored dual
meets between the two national squads." These structural problems were
eventually resolved. The political aspect was nonnegotiable.[8] Soviet sports
officials judged that the fingerprinting requirement in the McCarran Act
was a "humiliating procedure" that had to be removed before any meaning-
ful progress could be made.[9] A few isolated sporting interactions occurred
between the superpowers, such as the appearance of two U.S. wrestlers in
the Soviet Union, yet these were few and far between until the signing of the
cultural agreement. Once this legislation had been passed in 1958, the AAU,
at the request of the State Department, began to organize athletic exchanges
with the Soviet Union, and soon thereafter U.S. men's and women's basketball
teams visited the Soviet Union and Soviet wrestling and weightlifting teams
competed in the United States. "All of these tours were highly successful,"
opined the AAU.[10] Also that year, U.S. and Soviet sports officials agreed to
instigate an annual track-and-field meet, with the first competition set for
Moscow in July 1958, and the next in Philadelphia in 1959. The Olympic
decathlon champion, Rafer Johnson, later said of the first leg in Moscow,
that it "was not just man-on-man for the unofficial title of World's Greatest
Athlete, it was Communism vs. the Free World."[11]

It is not surprising that Soviet and U.S. sports exchanges attracted a huge
amount of publicity on either side of the Iron Curtain. On a few occasions,
too, the State Department arranged for U.S. athletes to compete in Eastern
Europe "to remind the captive peoples of U.S. interest in their ultimate freedom" and to in some way correct the "distorted image of the West as mirrored
in communist propaganda media."[12] In 1956, for instance, three U.S. athletes
attended a track-and-field meet in Bucharest, an appearance that occasioned
a glowing report from the U.S. embassy in the Romanian city. An embassy
official noted that the U.S. athletes were greeted with a "tumultuous" ovation as they marched into the stadium, whereas the applause for the Soviet
competitors amounted only to a "polite ripple." "There is no question," the

official added, "that the participation of these American athletes in this Track Meet did a great deal to maintain the prestige of the United States among the Rumanian people and gave them a rare opportunity of publicly exposing their warm feelings and admiration for the United States."[13] Two years later, the performance of a U.S. track-and-field team in Poland garnered more enthusiasm from diplomats. The U.S. embassy in Warsaw praised the "highly successful exchange," which drew huge crowds and "whetted" the Polish appetite for more frequent sporting contacts between the two countries.[14]

While the State Department continued to work in concert with the AAU, and to suggest valuable political destinations for U.S. athletes to tour, an additional government project also contributed to increasing the number of U.S. athletes traveling abroad. In 1956, the People-to-People Sports Committee was established as part of another state–private initiative, the People-to-People Program. Created as a further avenue to encourage ordinary U.S. citizens to make friendly contacts with other like-minded people around the world, the program was based on a host of independent citizen committees, with each focused on a particular area or segment of society, such as hobbies, fine arts, advertising, health, and insurance. The U.S. people, Eisenhower asserted, were needed to tell the world that the United States was dedicated to peace and understanding, not war and conflict. Although the individual committees were intended to be financially self-sustaining, the imprint of the U.S. government on the whole program was obvious, with psychological strategy overseen by the Operations Coordinating Board.[15]

The People-to-People Sports Committee emerged as one of the many committees that Eisenhower hoped would promote the image of the United States at home and abroad. Chaired by Edward P. Eagan, it aimed to promote exchanges with schools, universities, and amateur and professional clubs, provide sports equipment to those that needed it, and work with and stimulate other sports organizations to try and use sport as a way to break down social and cultural barriers between the United States and other nations.[16] "The significance of our billions of dollars of foreign aid is not readily understood by the man on the street abroad," Eagan pronounced, "but a little sports equipment which he or his son or daughter can use and enjoy with others is understood and helps erase the all too prevalent impression that we are cold, aloof, heartless, dollar-hungry people."[17] The U.S. Information Agency (USIA) furnished the People-to-People Sports Committee with a seed fund of eighty-nine hundred dollars and Eagan quickly enlisted the support of prominent sports, health, and recreation organizations. In its early years, the group arranged for U.S. representation in yacht races, boxing tournaments, and horse shows; facilitated tours in lacrosse, handball, rugby, field hockey, soccer, basketball, and lawn bowling; shipped thousands of dollars' worth of sports equipment to numerous countries; facilitated pen-pal correspondence between foreign and U.S. sports enthusiasts; and formed connections with sports associations and clubs across the globe.[18] Attempts to hide the political aspect of the committee were merely subterfuge. Cuban sports officials, for example, bitterly complained to the International Olympic Committee (IOC) about the anticommunist material distributed by the group at the 1963 Pan American Games and the 1964 Tokyo Olympics. For these transgressions, Brundage sternly reprimanded Eagan and threatened to ban the Sports Committee from operating at future Olympic or regional games.[19]

On the reverse side, U.S. statesmen also remained sensitive to communist sports propaganda and, equally, overseas perceptions of U.S. teams participating in various international competitions. One particular incident prompted a flurry of diplomatic activity. In 1959, an understrength U.S. basketball team lost to the Soviet Union at the world basketball championships in Santiago, Chile. The outcome of the contest, a 62–37 drubbing, was reported in newspapers across Latin America, a fact that greatly disturbed U.S. information experts. "As a result of this victory," wrote a public affairs officer in Lima, "the Soviet Union has again scored an important psychological advantage and, as far as the average, non-too-intelligent-man-on-the-street is concerned, it is another indication of Soviet 'superiority' over the U.S."[20] His colleague in Santiago also was irate. The official complained that the U.S. defeat backfired in two respects. Not only was the loss a blow to national prestige, but it also was a "slight to Chilean pride" in that the United States did not deem it necessary to send its best team. He argued that the basketball tournament had "a psychological importance which transcends the frontiers of sports" and that this aspect should be taken into account for future U.S. participation in sports events.[21]

More Olympic Controversy

As the Chilean basketball imbroglio tends to suggest, the attitude of the U.S. public to Soviet sport had in no way altered from the first half of the 1950s to the second. While U.S. diplomats were fretting over athletic results, the U.S. media was still filled with stories on the remarkable achievements of communist athletes and still debated the legitimacy of the communist sports system. Yet, in many ways, the tone of the discussion had changed. The Cold War rhetoric had cooled somewhat, even if it had not completely dissipated. With the advent of the dual track series, for instance, writers and sports officials increasingly acknowledged the cultural diplomacy of the events rather than their propaganda value.[22] The same attitude began to prevail in relation to the Olympic Games. The hue and cry that marked the public discourse in the aftermath of Helsinki had, for the most part, receded. Even U.S. propaganda experts, having feared the fallout of a Soviet victory in Melbourne, do not appear to have replicated their anxiety in the years that followed. In some sense, this outlook was based upon cold, hard reality: Come what may, the Soviets had the best host of athletes in the world and would most likely win the most medals in 1960. The U.S. people, whether they liked it or not, now knew what to expect. Perhaps, too, the dwindling of the anticommunist hysteria that so gripped the United States in the early 1950s had provided some perspective on the relative importance of athletic competitions.[23] Without question, the U.S. public still worried about the psychological and symbolic significance of the medals table at the Olympic Games, but they did not apply the same sort of exuberance to the issue as they had only a few years earlier.

Be that as it may, when the U.S. Olympic Committee (USOC) embarked on its fundraising drive for the 1960 winter and summer Olympics, it gave a familiar nod to the political significance of the U.S. athletic performance. "There never has been a greater challenge faced by the United States in its bid for continued Olympic Games prestige," declared the USOC president, Kenneth L. Wilson, "and we must redouble our efforts to produce a team which can compete successfully against all other nations in 1960 and in the future." U.S. Olympic officials drafted plans "to improve the efficiency of future" teams by molding clinics for male and female athletes of all abilities, reinvigorating grass-roots interest in a wide array of events, organizing local, regional, national, and international competitions, and facilitating greater cooperation between clubs and sports organizations. In addition to promoting and implementing a national development program, the USOC and the AAU determined that $1.5 million would be needed to fund it.[24] The FEC and the HNSF made their own "private" contribution by organizing a gala night of entertainment for a thousand guests at the Tavern on the Green in New York City's Central Park.[25] Yet the question of congressional appropriations did not gather the same momentum as it had before Melbourne. The financial burden would depend, as it always had, upon the generosity of the U.S. people.

With federal funds out of the question, for the second time Eisenhower announced a special "Olympic Week" to stimulate private donations and help the USOC reach its lofty target. The AAU's official publication, *Amateur Athlete*, applauded this "proper and most wholesome" approach to funding the national team through subscriptions from "patriotic individuals and organizations."[26]

Eisenhower agreed. During a news conference, he compared the U.S. athletic structure with that of the Soviet Union and attempted to seize the moral high ground. If the Soviets find an athlete, he lectured, "they take him, and it's a national responsibility to train him and build him up until he's the best there is in the world, if they can make him as such." In contrast, added the president, "we have a free enterprise; we place above all other values our own individual freedoms and rights, and we believe, moreover, that the operation of such a system in the long run produces more, not only more happiness, more satisfaction and pride in our people, but also more goods, more wealth."[27]

Even if many people in the United States would doubtless have concurred with the way Eisenhower connected sports with laissez-faire economics, they still demanded more than just the moral high ground, or at least what they perceived it to be. The apparent inability of the United States to gain an advantage in its athletic rivalry with the Soviet Union also was complicated by the rapid improvements of other communist and noncommunist nations. The average U.S. sports enthusiast might have wanted to defeat their greatest ideological enemy, but they also wanted to be first on the medals table, ahead of each and every other country. Observers noted, however, that British and West German athletes were "closing the gap" on U.S. and Soviet competitors, and Poland appeared to be improving by leaps and bounds.[28] In interviews and speeches, Brundage asserted that the "European countries are progressing much faster than we are" and spoke in complete admiration of Australia's achievements when considered on a per capita basis. "We are becoming a nation of spectators," inveighed the IOC president. "We're all lazy. I'm lazy."[29] These comments, and others like them, reinforced and blended into lingering worries that the nation's youth were physically inferior to children in Europe. In 1956, Eisenhower established the President's Council on Youth Fitness to study the issue, but it was hardly the sort of problem that could be solved very immediately.[30]

Public and private discourse on the state of the U.S. health and the nation's relative position in the world athletic order would rumble on for the remainder of the Cold War. Individuals on either side of the debate would also gather grist for their arguments at each of the 1960 Olympic festivals. But before the athletes would take center stage at the winter and summer Olympics, the policies and procedures of the IOC challenged and compromised U.S. diplomatic interests. The first in a farrago of incidents came as a direct result of the IOC's 1957 session in Sofia, Bulgaria, a country with which the United States had broken diplomatic relations in 1950. During a working trip to Europe, Brundage heard "rumors" that the U.S. government would deny him the opportunity to travel to Bulgaria, a possibility that greatly troubled him. In a communication to the State Department, Brundage insisted that the "Communists would make capital of my absence and only we would suffer by lack of representation."[31] The State Department eventually sanctioned the visas for all U.S. Olympic officials on the IOC, with particular attention to the passport of Douglas Roby, whose "experience and strength would be absolutely needed to properly protect U.S. interests at the international meeting."[32] Far from being an isolated act of détente, other U.S. citizens would be granted the same rights if the government deemed it to be in the "national interest." Not missing the significance of the situation, the *New York Times* assessed that the government's approach to Bulgaria represented a "general easing in policy on contacts with the Communist world."[33]

At about the same time as this matter ground its way through the government's bureaucracy, another related problem brewed with even more intensity. On this occasion, the issue stretched beyond U.S. and Bulgarian relations and pivoted upon the question of whether communist member nations in the IOC would be allowed unimpeded passage into the United States for the 1960 winter Olympics in Squaw Valley, California.[34] Konstantin Andrianov, the Soviet IOC member, wrote to Otto Mayer to point out that visits of Soviet sportsmen to the United States "were several times cancelled because they could not agree with a humiliating procedure of fingerprinting when getting the American visas."[35] There also were some communist countries, particularly China, with whom the United States did not even have diplomatic relations. On this point, Mayer agreed with the Soviet objections and suggested Brundage approach the State Department for assurance that "ALL athletes without distinction of countries get their visa to enter" the United States.[36] In the end, Brundage issued Washington an ultimatum. If the United States would not admit athletes from "all" IOC-recognized countries for the winter Olympics, then the event would be moved to a site outside the United States.[37]

Even though the question of visas for communist countries had escalated into a high-stakes game, as evidenced by the apprehension displayed by Squaw Valley organizers, for some the solution was straightforward. With his usual anticommunist gusto, Senator John Marshall Butler accused all communist sportsmen of being propaganda agents and "strongly urged" John Foster Dulles to "rule against any admission of the Red Chinese 'athletes.'"[38] But Dulles could ill afford to see the problem in such simplistic terms, and other officials shared his unease. The State Department assessed that the "Communists would have a propaganda 'field day' should the Games be taken away from the United States; they would revel in depicting the new 'American Iron Curtain.'"[39] For the image sculptors in the government, then, U.S.

actions had to be guided by psychological considerations. Dulles indicated to his staff and the press that the administration was in favor of eliminating the fingerprinting requirement altogether, and of approving legislation that would "specifically" apply to the Olympic Games.[40] As it turned out, the U.S. government acceded to the IOC's demands just days before the committee's meeting in Sofia, no doubt saving Brundage from an extremely awkward predicament. Moreover, the State Department explained that no communist athletes would be fingerprinted, but the government wanted the names of each athlete in advance so background checks could be completed.[41] With the issue seemingly resolved, another soon emerged when East Germany, as part of a joint team with West Germany, attempted to attain visas for extra officials and journalists beyond its quota. The State Department refused to issue visas to the suspicious complement, to which the East German Foreign Ministry retorted that the United States was "carrying the policy of cold war into the Olympics."[42]

To some degree, these incidents proved that the Olympic Movement was powerful enough to influence U.S. foreign policy. But the reverse was not really true. Perhaps no other incident illustrates the relative inability of the White House to force its will on the IOC in the early Cold War years than the 1959 China/Taiwan episode. China had been an ongoing and highly volatile problem for the IOC after Mao Tse-tung's communist revolution essentially split the country into two geopolitical entities, with the defeated National-ists fleeing to the island of Taiwan (Formosa). In 1954, the IOC accepted this reality and recognized two Chinas in the Olympic Movement, one on the mainland, the other on Taiwan. Mainland China (the People's Republic), however, never accepted the situation and lobbied Brundage to drop the committee in Taiwan. Brundage refused, and in 1958, the People's Republic of China cut ties with the Olympic Movement. After a lengthy discussion between its communist and noncommunist members, the IOC then ruled at its 1959 Munich session that because Taiwan did not govern Olympic mat-ters on mainland China, it should not be known as the "Chinese National Olympic Committee." The IOC subsequently asked the Taiwanese Olympic authorities to reapply for recognition under a name that made no reference to China.[43]

When UPI broke the story, it reported that the IOC had "expelled Na-tionalist China from the Olympic movement" and "opened the door for the readmission of Communist China."[44] Neither claim was strictly true but the impact in the United States was considerable. Without sufficient evidence to form a balanced opinion, many in the United States consumed the tale in the newspapers and concluded that the entire affair was a communist conspiracy.

Equally aghast, the USOC and the AAU were keen to distance themselves from the ruling and wrote strong letters of protest to the IOC membership, demanding a reversal of the decision.[45]

The U.S. government's reaction mirrored the public outcry. In fact, the ever-reliable Douglas Roby had informed an embassy official in Munich of the situation right after the vote on Taiwan had taken place. Roby then flew to Washington to provide the State Department with a full account of the IOC meeting. He revealed that the China issue had been put on the session's agenda by the Soviets in a strategy to reinstate the communist Chinese. Defending his own part in the whole affair, Roby justifiably claimed that he had made a counterproposal to keep the Taiwanese in the Olympic Movement while they changed their name, but it was supported by no one, and that included the two other U.S. IOC members, Brundage and John Jewett Garland.[46] The State Department immediately "censured" the IOC for its ruling and called upon the organization to restore the Nationalist Chinese to full membership under the correct name.[47] Brundage was bewildered. He told a colleague, "I found that we were being charged with having 'kicked out' the Formosa Chinese (which we did not do) in order to take in the Communist Chinese (which we did not do), as a result of Communist pressure (there was none)."[48] Brundage reacted to the furor by publicly denouncing the State Department's accusations and restated that the IOC "recognizes only sports organizations and not governments."[49] When Roby later told the media that the vote had not been anywhere near as "unanimous" as the IOC president had claimed, Brundage responded by admonishing Roby in a circular communication to all IOC members.[50]

With two of the three American IOC delegates providing conflicting accounts of exactly what happened in Munich, Karl Harr, the U.S. president's latest special assistant on psychological warfare, met with the third. Garland's recollections of the Munich meeting were far closer to those of Brundage than to those of Roby. He told Harr that the committee had not intended to exclude anyone from the Olympics, that there was no communist pressure, and that he had not even heard Roby's counterproposal (even though there was one). Nevertheless, Harr still suspected a communist conspiracy. "All in all," he ruminated, "this seems to have been a clear case of the inability of those motivated solely by an honest non-political approach to resist, or even to understand, the machinations of those who seek to pervert such forums to political purposes."[51] The State Department concurred, calling the name alteration "an attempt by Communists in the IOC to deny the existence of the Republic of China and thereby pave the way for the re-admission of the Chinese Communists."[52] When the media asked for a comment, Eisenhower said that "it seems to me that the Olympic Committee has gotten into politics rather than merely into international athletics."[53]

As soon as the news of the Taiwan ruling had been made public, the Operations Coordinating Board assessed that "it would be a great mistake for the U.S. to allow the action of the IOC to go unchallenged."[54] But what exactly could be done? The IOC had a long history of ignoring government interference in its global mission, and Brundage was hardly the sort of leader to deviate from this policy, even if the government in question represented his country of birth and citizenship. Still, the United States made some moves to reinstate Taiwan under the title of China. A resolute Congress voted to prevent the use of army personnel and equipment at Squaw Valley and to hold back a further four-hundred-thousand-dollar appropriation from the military for the winter Olympics if any country were denied the chance to send competitors.[55] In an additional lobbying tactic, the State Department "informed" various embassies to keep the issue alive in their respective countries and to maintain that Nationalist China could not "accept limited geographical designation as part of its title."[56] Roby promised to speak with various IOC delegates on the subject, but the State Department conceded that nothing could be done to influence Brundage. From its "past experience" with the IOC president, the State Department reasoned that "such efforts would probably have [a] negative effect."[57]

As it turned out, however, the public outcry did force the IOC to make a compromise. A little while after the initial explosion, Brundage admitted to U.S. officials that he was startled by the reaction to the committee's ruling and emphasized that there had never been any intention to expel Nationalist China from the Olympic Movement. In fall 1959 the IOC decided that the Olympic committee in Taiwan could retain China in its title (Republic of China Olympic Committee), but in international competition, it would compete under the name of Taiwan.[58] Eventually, the State Department was forced to accept the fact that it could do nothing more.

Making Plans, Making Contact

After years of debate about how or whether U.S. foreign policy would ruin or elevate the winter Olympics, the IOC was probably keen to see that the festival would open and distract the cynics from their usual political preoccupations. Largely funded by the state of California and congressional appropriations, the 1960 Squaw Valley Olympics turned out to be an extremely successful sporting event surrounded by "amity" and congeniality. Situated only seven miles from Lake Tahoe, Squaw Valley hosted one of the largest winter Olympics up to that point in time. Athletes and spectators enjoyed the new purpose-built facilities, marveled at the technological innovations, and watched the "entertainment, pageantry, ice statues, and daylight fireworks" organized by Walt Disney. Proud of the entire event, the publisher of *Amateur Athlete*, Harold Zimman, gushed that it was "the finest and most extraordinary winter sports festival in history."[59] Even the Soviet publication *Pravda* praised the "exceptional friendship and comradeship" at the Olympics and thanked the "American people for their hospitality and goodwill."[60]

Aside from these organizational triumphs, the spirit of psychological warfare and Cold War propaganda was still evident in and around the hosting city. One journalist observed that "the Russian athletes, amid alternate impassivity and inscrutable smiles, quietly distributed Moscow-printed brochures on 'Sports in the Soviet Union,' which aver, with all the subtlety of Niagara Falls, that athletic achievements were 'rare' in Czarist Russia, while 'Soviet power has helped the people unfold their talents in every field of human activity.'"[61] Not to be outdone, Radio Free Europe (RFE) prepared "special coverage" of the Olympics by producing stories designed for audiences in Hungary, Bulgaria, Poland, and Czechoslovakia. Working on strict deadlines, RFE "scooped its communist competitors not only in most instances by several hours, but actually succeeded in giving listeners coverage the night before they learned about [the results] from regime sources." An RFE report explained that the radio "succeeded in giving its audiences the satisfaction of being 'on the spot' and of having the sports events told to them and commented on by internationally known sports reporters who, as natives from the target countries, command a wide personal following" in the Iron Curtain nations.[62]

Anxious fans in the United States still took note of the medals table. Even though the United States was able to celebrate several triumphs in Squaw Valley, including the remarkable victory of their men's ice hockey team, the Soviet Union again won the most medals, this time for the third successive Olympics. Congressman Samuel S. Stratton of New York thought the result had a particular symbolic resonance. "Mr. Speaker," Stratton admonished in Congress, "does this not look like the same thing that we seem to be running into also in the race for space and the construction of a superior military?"[63]

Telegdy would probably have concurred. Early in 1960, he rolled out his latest Olympic plan. He estimated that between fifteen and twenty-five Hungarian athletes would defect at the Rome Olympics, and he wanted assurances that they would receive asylum in the United States, be helped to resettle, and possibly even be sent on an exhibition tour.[64] When C. D. Jackson read Telegdy's proposal, he reacted with indifference. "I think he is over optimistic," he told a colleague. "The atmosphere in the summer of 1960 is unfortunately quite different from the atmosphere of December 1956."[65] The report also landed on the desk of André Laguerre at *Sports Illustrated*. The veteran journalist, so influential in the Melbourne defection, thought that the magazine could be part of a committee to assist the athletes in the United States after the defection, but nothing more. "Journalistically," he informed Jackson, "the defections would not be anything like the story for us they were last time, and indeed I think we should be striking a false note in taking the lead again in this situation."[66] Although there were doubts whether anyone would, in fact, defect, and there were reservations about immigration procedures, Telegdy's plan, soon titled "Operation Rome," was given a far warmer reception by the FEC. An FEC memorandum underscored that Telegdy and the Hungarian National Sports Federation (HNSF) "have become recognized by the Hungarian regime as the greatest thorn in their side concerning sports propaganda." If Telegdy were not in Rome, it was added, "his absence would be considered a great victory for the [Hungarian] regime."[67]

The FEC's willingness to support Telegdy's plan also illustrates the organization's evolving approach to winning the Cold War in the late 1950s. Shattered by the failure of the Hungarian Revolution, the FEC followed the pattern of change in Washington and moved away, to some degree, from the policy of liberation.[68] Still, FEC officials accepted the fact that the United States would not go so far as to tolerate the "status quo" in Eastern Europe and concentrated instead on the "loosening of ties between the satellite states and the USSR by . . . maintaining the captive peoples' sense of identity with the West." This process of "stimulating a gradual evolutionary change of a liberalizing nature" through cultural infiltration would become an "interim goal on the way" to the satellites achieving "national independence on democratic foundations." Although the FEC acknowledged that liberation would not come from U.S. military action, the "residue" of the policy remained, as the organization continued to press toward ending Soviet hegemony.[69] A "broadening" of the FEC East–West contact program was therefore promoted with the view that "personal encounters" could possibly "achieve political objectives by . . . non-political means." In the spirit of this strategy, encouraging defections was not viewed as a productive exercise, for it might threaten the plan of "inducing cooperation" on the part of communist regimes.[70]

Even if the new policy of "liberalization" had a degree of vagueness that worried some quarters in the FEC, the organization tried to "strengthen" its commitment to East–West contacts as the next Olympic year approached. Committee officials acknowledged that in the aftermath of the 1952 Helsinki Olympics, the Soviet Union had expanded its "all-out drive" to dominate international sports competitions. "That the Soviet athletes continue to win and to increase the margin of their victories over the free world athletes is terribly important to the USSR, not as a feather in their cap, but as a strong (because popular) psychological argument in their ceaseless assault on the morale of the free world as they push toward their goal of total world domination," one report warned. "Thus," assessed the FEC, "we may expect at Rome the most intensive effort ever on the part of the USSR and all its satellites to dominate the Olympic Games and prove to the attentive eyes of . . . the world the superiority of their system." Moreover, the FEC predicted that the Soviet bloc would be able to create a false sense of popularity for its athletes by importing "cheering sections"—including "Italian communist toughs"—to "boost the morale of the communist nations."[71]

There were, nonetheless, obvious limits to an FEC response. Nothing could be done to alter the outcome of the sporting events, and nothing could be arranged to stop communist tourists from cheering or booing from the stands. But something could be done in other respects. Converting hard-line communists was unlikely, given the short time span of the Olympic festival, but the FEC would aim to make "contact" with "East Europeans who already feel themselves committed to the West and against the communists."[72] In order to achieve this aim, the organization approved a variety of émigré-run contact projects to take place in the Eternal City. Thus, as the sporting events of the 1960 summer Olympics captured the spotlight, in the background the U.S. government was supporting a host of secretly funded propaganda operations on the periphery of the athletic spectacle.

Operation Rome

The historical significance of the 1960 Rome summer Olympics has become somewhat of a contentious issue for writers and historians. Some have called the festival a turning point in the history of the modern Olympic Movement. They have claimed that in Rome the IOC started to grapple with the increasingly complex problem of television revenue, that performance-enhancing drugs were thrust into the public eye for the first time after the suspicious death of a Danish cyclist, that international politics undermined and overshadowed the festival on a scale never seen before, that commercialism reached new heights in and around the Olympic city, and even that Rome witnessed the last vestiges of Olympic amateurism. David Maraniss has gone as far as to assert that the Rome Olympics "changed the world."[73] Others, however, have been more cautious in their assessments. Rather, they argue that Rome merely marked a continuation of developments that had, for the most part, been brewing in the past and would change more dramatically in the future. The 1960 summer Olympics were large and expensive, and they did have more nations in attendance—noticeably from Third World countries—but they represented, in the words of one historian, "evolution, not revolution."[74]

From a political standpoint, the Rome Olympics were certainly not held in the same tense atmosphere as those staged in Melbourne four years earlier. Even so, the Cold War still lingered in the background. On 1 May 1960, the Soviet Union shot down an American U-2 spy airplane that had been gathering intelligence on Soviet military capabilities. Though at first Eisenhower denied violating Soviet airspace, he was forced to admit U.S. culpability when Khrushchev produced the airplane and the pilot. The incident curtailed the chance of détente, but it made far less of an impact on the Olympics themselves than the Hungarian Revolution and the Suez crisis had. U.S. fears about a communist "sports offensive" also were not so pronounced. Scholars have noted, too, that the Cold War rivalry had, at this stage, lost some of its bite. Under the sweltering heat of the Roman sun, for slightly more than two weeks U.S. and Soviet athletes congratulated one another after events, laughed and joked, exchanged pins, and sat on "lawn chairs sipping Cokes and munching on potato chips."[75] A journalist in Rome commented that there was "precious little of the bickering that has marred other Games," and the *New York Times* "happily" reported that "there has been less emphasis on nationalism in the Rome Olympics and less attention paid to the unofficial and meaningless team point standings."[76]

Although the interactions of athletes from East and West may have represented an easing of Cold War tensions on the track, the Olympic city hummed with U.S.-sponsored propaganda operations. U.S. athletes passed out "reading material" to Soviet competitors, and the People-to-People Sports Committee, working out of facilities in Rome donated by the YMCA, distributed various government propaganda publications, employed multilingual hosts to speak with tourists and athletes, served free refreshments and souvenir kits, showed motion picture programs, and arranged for evening music and dancing.[77] Yet the Soviet bloc regimes were far more irritated by other U.S. activities in Rome. Well aware of the broader FEC contact program, the Soviet publication *Trud* accused "reactionary émigré circles," the U-2 flights, and Allen Dulles of attempting to "destroy the friendly atmosphere of sportive competition at the Olympic Games." Czechoslovakian newspapers carried stories on U.S. plans to facilitate defections, and the Soviet bloc press linked these plans to a conspiracy with the Vatican. A USIA official in Rome reported on communist claims "that priests and nuns, speaking several languages, were receiving special training so that they could move actively during the Games to encourage defection." Although these charges were rather extreme, the official did admit that even though the Olympics were held in an "atmosphere which seemed on the surface to be confined to international sports competition," there were "propaganda undertones."[78]

Before Telegdy was able to contribute to these "undertones," he had spent nearly a month in Europe trying to "iron out differences" in the exiled Hungarian sports community and promoting the cause of stateless athletes. The FEC agreed to fund this part of his journey—with stops in England, France, Germany, and Austria—but reminded him to keep focused and to stay on track. FEC officials sent letters to the organization's representatives in Europe, instructing them to watch over the Hungarian and prevent him from attracting "undue attention."[79] These measures reveal the general concerns that many had about Telegdy's personality. "The only way he can be brought to heel," one committee employee sternly commented, "is to convince him that he does not, in fact, have the unqualified support of the FEC or the Hungarian sports world that he would like to have, and that unless he cooperates with the many other persons involved he and his Sports Federation are finished."[80] Robert Minton, vice president of the FEC, was a touch more diplomatic and wrote that "despite certain natural tendencies [Telegdy] has to over dramatize his and the Federation's importance, we place a great confidence in him personally as a conscientious and sound person who has the best interests of his athletes and the Free World at heart."[81] Even so, the FEC sent a special assistant, Anne Campanaro, to Rome in order to monitor Telegdy's movements and to prevent him from taking "any unilateral action."[82]

The FEC had advised Telegdy to "target" only the Hungarian athletes who wished to defect at the Olympics and to provide them with "information" about how their defection would be handled in the "smoothest and quietest possible way."[83] He was to offer advice and at no point to encourage athletes to flee. In Telegdy's earliest plans for Rome, he had estimated that there would be several defections at the summer Olympics even if he would not go so far as to predict anything on the scale of Melbourne. In fact, intelligence received from Eastern Europe suggested that communist authorities would double their guard over regime athletes and that they were well aware Telegdy would be stirring up trouble in Rome. These circumstances, coupled with the "large communist influence" in Italy and the more relaxed political climate, left the FEC to ponder whether the dramatic events of 1956 could be repeated in any way. Undeterred by this news, Telegdy continued to approach his task with a positive attitude and was joined in Rome by two other Hungarians in exile: the first, Géza Super, lived in Toronto and edited the HNSF publication,

Sporthiradó, and the second, István Moldoványi, was a former official in the Hungarian sporting administration who resided in New Jersey. Soon the three men, with Campanaro in tow, were circulating around the city and moving freely throughout the Olympic Village. Although the communist athletes were under close surveillance and ordered to travel in groups, they greeted and spoke with Telegdy and his associates, or found opportune moments to meet in private. These contacts appeared to have gleaned results; Telegdy soon handed Campanaro a list of nine athletes who had stated that they wished to defect.[84] Shortly before the Olympics ended, however, Campanaro reported that the communist sports authorities had tightened their "grip" on the regime athletes and it had become "impossible to speak" with them alone. Those who had made appointments to meet with Telegdy had not shown up and others were apparently "indifferent" to defecting in the first place. "I believe that Telegdy is now convinced that the situation has changed and that this will not be another 'Melbourne,'" added Campanaro. In the end, Telegdy was right. No Hungarian athletes defected.[85]

This disappointment aside, the team in Rome achieved somewhat more success in their efforts to raise awareness for the situation faced by stateless athletes in relation to the Olympic Games. The time appeared ripe for action. Having never competed for their nation at the Olympics, dozens of exiled Hungarians would be in Rome either participating for their new country of citizenship or operating as coaches and trainers. This alone would be symbolic. But before the Olympics had even started, a statement by Member of Parliament Christopher Chataway, an Olympian himself, had created a ripple of interest in the subject upon British shores, much to the satisfaction of the FEC and the excitable Telegdy. "This question of admitting stateless athletes has been put to the International Olympic Committee again and again in the past decade, but to no effect. Surely it should not be beyond the wit of these administrators to devise a formula by which athletes in this category are permitted to compete," Chataway complained in an article published in *The Times* of London.[86] Chataway's statement also led to the creation of small movement in England, which Chataway joined, when a group called the Committee for the Admission of Stateless Athletes to the Olympic Games pressed the IOC to alter its charter.[87] The Western media began to cover the issue as a result of these developments, usually pointing an accusatory and critical finger at Olympic leaders. Riding this current of publicity, some of which his own actions may well have stimulated, Telegdy sent a telegram to the IOC before arriving in Rome and continued to promote the very same cause for the duration of his stay in Italy.[88]

In one sense, then, this campaign was bolstered by the mere presence of exiles in Rome. As well, László Tábori and Mihály Iglói had been flown to Italy by the FEC to partake in exhibition races in the Olympic city. But these plans collapsed when the Italian Olympic organizers refused to sanction any "situations" that "might prove 'embarrassing' to the communists." Instead, the world-famous runner and his coach communicated with Hungarian athletes in Rome and spoke frequently about stateless athletes at press conferences, in media interviews, and on the airwaves of RFE and the Voice of America.[89] Yet the same sort of restrictions did not apply to a Vienna-based exiled Hungarian water polo team named Hungaria Heimatlos. The FEC paid for the team of "former top" Hungarian maestros to practice in France for a week and then shuttled them to Rome to compete in unofficial contests against Japan, the United States, Brazil, and France. The FEC argued that these games aroused sympathy and "admiration" for exiled athletes and raved about the fact that foreign newspapers sent correspondents to watch and report on the team's exploits. In a further attempt to advertise the predicament of the Hungaria Heimatlos, and the exile issue in general, the HNSF helped to organize a press conference at the Piccolo Budapest restaurant, whereby journalists were invited to meet the team's players and to hear about the Hungarians who could and could not participate in the summer Olympics. A host of Italian and overseas newspapers subsequently published articles on the event and noted the names of those Hungarians who would be competing for a second country of citizenship in Rome.[90] Regardless, the IOC was, for the time being, unmoved.

Although the sport-related aspects of the Rome contacts program did not always meet their stated goals, some of the other FEC initiatives overcame their obstacles. One of the largest and most effective of the FEC projects in Rome was a Polish information center on the Via Piemonte, a short drive from the Olympic stadium. Staffed by ten young recruits from England and France and some "reliable" Poles, the center consisted of a two-room apartment furnished with armchairs, a television, and facilities to serve light refreshments. The FEC estimated that around four thousand Polish tourists, in three waves, would arrive in Italy for the Olympics, the majority of whom were on excursions organized by state travel agencies. Wary of the "émigré provocators," though, Polish authorities in Rome worked hard to "protect" the tourists from mingling with undesirable Western elements or from visiting the FEC center. In order to "break the atmosphere of a spy scare," the staff at the center sent information leaflets to the hotels where the Polish tourists were staying and even bribed hotel porters to assist in getting the reading material to the appropriate rooms. The results were immediate. Soon Polish tourists and athletes started to frequent the FEC facility to indulge in the services that it had to offer. They took free sightseeing trips and bus tours to Monte Cassino, Pompeii, and Naples; they read or took free pamphlets, magazines, and books of the "highest political, historical and educational value" they attended a special FEC Mass at St. Peter's Basilica; and they gladly took the opportunity to sell goods and wares from home to the center's staff in order to make extra spending money. The staff, in turn, was able to exploit these opportunities to speak with the tourists in what was an ostensibly relaxed and enjoyable environment. In fact, it was sometimes the case that the visitors, often acting with caution and using fictitious names, asked most of the questions, always keen to gather information on life in the West and the standard of living in the "free world." So much attention did the center receive in the communist media that a trio of curious Soviet journalists also wandered in, browsed the literature collection, and questioned the staff on their aims. With the inspection complete, the three writers left the building clutching a batch of publications and a copy of *Dr. Zhivago*, a book banned in the Soviet Union. By the end of the Olympics, the FEC estimated that seven hundred fifty tourists and sportsmen visited the center and fifteen hundred people were contacted outside the premises.[91]

Other FEC projects also went ahead as planned. A Polish student operation, in conjunction with the Italian student group Foccolarini, handed out exile publications, showed movies, and operated as guides and translators to young Polish tourists.[92] And another CIA-sponsored group, the Assembly of Captive European Nations, established an exhibit in a centrally located building on the Via del Corso to contact the "thousands of spectators from the subjugated nations." On the night before the exhibit opened, however, the building was broken into and the signs for directing tourists to the location were stolen. The Assembly of Captive European Nations, which the communist media had already listed as one of the groups in Rome operating under the auspices of the U.S. "secret service," suspected that communist stooges had inflicted the damage.[93] For the remainder of the Olympics, plain-clothed Italian police watched over the building.

Elsewhere, a camp run by the Union of Free Hungarian Students experienced a steady turnover of inhabitants at its site near Castello di Magliana, donated for the duration of the Olympics by the Knights of Malta. This facility, which could accommodate three to four hundred people, served as a base for extensive contacts with youth from all continents and countries to prove that the West took care of refugee students, a matter challenged in Soviet propaganda. "The existence of the camp and so many active Hungarians," added the FEC, "will also be a reminder to free world visitors to Rome of the unresolved Hungarian situation" in the aftermath of the failed revolution.[94] Indeed, Telegdy would have seen for himself that the flag of the Hungarian Freedom Fighters fluttered over the camp during his visit to the grounds. Although the total number of guests at the site did not surpass three hundred, the FEC praised the valuable contribution of the Union of Free Hungarian Students to the whole operation in Rome. Far from limiting their movements to the campsite, the students made frequent contact with the three waves of Hungarian tourists in the city, offering information and advice for whoever sought it. They distributed publications, provided transportation, served as translators, helped tourists sell goods brought from Hungary, assisted RFE, spoke to regime athletes, and helped to organize the press conferences held with stateless sportsmen. Like other FEC projects in Rome, the "spyscare" lingered in the background. The Italian police provided a "special security service" to watch over the property and twice intervened when unauthorized persons tried to enter the grounds. The Union of Free Hungarian Students suspected that communist spies were intently watching and noted that a nearby news vender jotted down the license plate numbers of cars that stopped at the camp.[95]

Not for the first time in the early Cold War years, the hearts and minds of spectators, tourists, and athletes were being endlessly targeted by state and private actors as they roamed the streets and the sights of the Olympic city. The FEC, an unabashed participant in this phenomenon, had much to celebrate. Eastern European tourists had been communicated with en masse, propaganda materials had been dispersed and possibly taken through the Iron Curtain, exiles had demonstrated that the West still cared about the future of the satellite regimes, and the predicament of exiled athletes, an issue both of politics and of sports, had been placed at the door of the IOC and in the court of public opinion.[96] Yet for all of these behind-the-scenes efforts, the gaze of the world fell as always upon the athletes themselves and the countries they represented. In Rome, the Soviet Union swept its way to another resounding victory in the medals table. Before the Olympics started, a confident Kenneth Wilson had announced that the USOC would send its "strongest" ever team to the Olympics. It would not be enough. U.S. sports officials were once again left to reassess the nation's athletic structure and what could be done to overcome the burgeoning number of countries with vastly improved training techniques and performance.[97] Arthur Daley of the *New York Times* ruefully acknowledged that the athletes of many other nations were making medals far harder to come by. "The United States scares not a soul anymore," he said. For Daley, though, the communists were still the biggest threat, both athletically and politically. "The totalitarian powers have the ability to marshal their youth for what they regard, among other things, as part of the propaganda war. They have said so, bluntly and unashamedly. And the Rome Olympics, on that basis, represented a resounding victory for Soviet Russia."[98]

This indeed was the problem that the U.S. government struggled to reconcile. At the end of the year, the President's Committee on Information Activities Abroad (otherwise known as the Sprague Committee) assessed the state of the government's propaganda strategy and the place of sport in the Cold War battle. "The recent Olympic Games have aroused considerable public discussion about the political and psychological implications of such contests between athletes from the various Free World and Communist nations," the committee noted. "The Soviet Union obviously attaches considerable propaganda importance to these events as a means of projecting an image of its dynamism and progress. It spends large resources and marshals hundreds of thousands of its youth to dedicate themselves at governmental expense to becoming international sporting champions. It heralds its triumphs as proof that the Soviet system represents the wave of the future." Propaganda experts believed that Soviet victories did have a psychological impact on global audiences, particularly with younger persons and "those not ordinarily concerned with international political issues." Having outlined the problem, the committee admitted that it could find no solution to it. Strategists argued that "Free World efforts to remove the factors of national prestige and ideological significance from international athletic competition are not likely to succeed in the foreseeable future."[99] Ultimately, the United States could only gain ascendancy in an Olympic propaganda war if its words were backed up by its athletic deeds.

Conclusion

The late 1950s had been a difficult and challenging period for the Free Europe Committee (FEC). In 1956, the Hungarian people looked to be on the verge of a revolution that could, some thought, have led to dramatic social and political changes across Eastern Europe. The portents were promising, but they were wrong. The Soviet bloc had been shaken, but it had not been turned upside down. Shocked and demoralized by these events, the FEC struggled to regroup. It was riven by internal squabbling and disputes. Central Intelligence Agency officials even wondered whether its days of usefulness had passed. In 1961, however, the organization entered a phase of renewed fortunes under the leadership of a New York investment banker named John Richardson. A gifted and ruthless manager, Richardson streamlined the operation, giving it direction and purpose.[1]

While the FEC recovered, the reputation of the CIA declined. In 1961, the agency's clandestine attempt to overthrow Fidel Castro in Cuba was a complete and embarrassing failure. The incident, now infamous, forced government officials, members of the U.S. Congress, and the media to reconsider the value of covert operations and other such "harebrained escapades." To make matters worse, if that were possible, U.S. newspapers also began to dig up evidence of the CIA's secret network of front organizations. In 1967, the counterculture magazine *Ramparts* carried a story revealing the CIA funding of the National Student Association and followed it with an article that examined the CIA's use of dummy foundations to funnel money to private groups. The name of Radio Free Europe was among those mentioned in the exposé. Even though the FEC was, for a time, able to dodge the media's bullets, a 1971 speech by Senator Clifford Case was far more devastating. "Several hundreds of millions of dollars in United States government funds have been expended from secret CIA budgets to pay almost totally for the costs" of Radio Free Europe, Case told the Senate, and at "no time was Congress asked or permitted to carry out its constitutional role of approving the expenditures." In an exercise of damage limitation, Congress shut down the nonradio operations of the FEC and turned Radio Free Europe into an officially administered arm of government. The years of covert funding had ended. In more than two decades of work, from 1949 to 1971, the FEC had received well in excess of $300 million dollars from the CIA.[2]

A small portion of this sizable amount of money had been channeled into the account of the Hungarian National Sports Federation (HNSF). But well before the FEC was dismantled, the funding for Count Anthony Szápáry's organization, like that for several other émigré groups, fell victim to Richardson's efficiency. As of January 1962, regular payments to the HNSF ceased.[3] In a desperate letter to C. D. Jackson, Szápáry attempted to recover the situation. He argued that the discontinuance of FEC funds might cause "panic" in the HNSF's affiliated clubs and "greatly affect" the "morale and spiritual resistance of Hungarians in Hungary." The end result, the count added, "would only satisfy the Hungarian Communist regime."[4] Jackson did what he could. "Is this over the dam, or can something be done?" he asked Bernard Yarrow, vice president of the FEC.[5] In a somewhat optimistic response, Yarrow explained that "there is no assurance as yet that we will get the necessary funds to keep it going at its old level, but we shall try to do our very best."[6] For a time, the HNSF received a few more installments, but they soon ground to a halt.

The HNSF continued its operations on a smaller scale. Even if its main source of funds had been largely severed, it was at least rewarded for years of lobbying on behalf of stateless athletes. At the Sixtieth International Olympic Committee (IOC) Session in Baden-Baden, the organization's members voted to allow an athlete to compete at the Olympics for a second country of citizenship after "he has become naturalized [in a new country] and a period of at least three years has passed since he applied for naturalization."[7] In June 1964, the IOC executive committee acknowledged that Hungarians who defected in 1956 could compete for the U.S. Olympic team if they qualified under the new amendment.[8] With the change to the Olympic Charter ratified, three former Hungarian citizens took part in the Tokyo Olympics wearing the colors of the United States. Jenő Hámori and Attila Keresztes participated in fencing, while Róbert Zimonyi was the coxswain in the eight-oared shell.[9] Although it cannot be said that the HNSF compelled the IOC to change its rules, the group was certainly at the vanguard of the protestors and lobbyists for more than a decade. It must have been a moment to savor for Szápáry, who retained a copy of the ruling in his records.[10] With this battle fought and won, his correspondence with Olympic leaders ebbed away.

As for George Telegdy, the FEC paid him a wage until 1963.[11] One of his final acts, fittingly, was to write an article for *East Europe* (formerly *News from behind the Iron Curtain*) about the Melbourne defection and its place in his "own personal odyssey." To hide his identity, the story was published under a pseudonym, Peter Kovacs. In the treatise, Telegdy charged that in Hungary, athletes, "like industrial workers and peasants" were "mobilized to set new records and produce more trophies" in the post–World War II years. They "quickly learned," he said, "what was required of them as perform-ers and politicians." The Olympic Games "no longer meant sportsmanship or individual accomplishment. Their jobs, their salaries and the standard of living of their families depended on winning." Telegdy boasted that the Hungarian authorities had made "elaborate plans" for the national team to succeed at the 1956 summer Olympic Games. "What happened when they got to Melbourne was a catastrophe for the communist sports program," he trumpeted. For Telegdy, the "great exodus of 1956" was a defining moment in his personal anticommunist crusade. When he died of cancer in 1984, the defection was mentioned in the first line of his obituary.[12]

As the work of both these men demonstrates, one of the most prevalent aspects of many government initiatives directed at the Olympic Games was the level of cooperation it received from private groups and individuals. Much of the time, the motivation to do so was mutual. The leaders of the HNSF, of course, already had plenty of reasons, personal and political, to work with the U.S. intelligence community. With the onset of the Cold War, U.S. sports officials also began to see that the precarious state of international affairs, coupled with their own ideological beliefs, necessitated a partnership with Washington, as opposed to a mutually agreed upon isolation. Even though the traditional separation of the state from sport was generally maintained, par-ticularly in the case of funding, other lines of demarcation that the Amateur Athletic Union of the United States (AAU) and the United States Olympic Committee (USOC) usually upheld and defended became blurred. In the early 1950s, U.S. sports officials began to aid the government in the plan-ning and the execution of propaganda operations, something they had not done in the past, something they would have criticized other countries for doing. Sometimes, too, they also cooperated without knowing. Believing in the same anticommunist cause, U.S. Olympic leaders exchanged several communications with the HNSF and spoke to representatives of the FEC.

In one report, Telegdy referred to Daniel Ferris, the secretary-treasurer of the AAU, and Lyman Bingham, the executive director of the USOC, as "my good honorable friends."[13]

These state–private relations, then, were nuanced and complex. At times they were also far from harmonious. Covert operators accepted, to some degree, that the private sphere might not always echo the message of the state, and that a level of independence could even help to veil the hidden hand of Washington. As propaganda planners acknowledged, the "gain in dissemination and credibility through the use of such channels will more than offset the loss by the Government of some control over content."[14] Some scholars therefore insist that the lines of communication and cooperation between the U.S. government and the private sphere should not be reduced to a simple formulation of master and servant. In a study of CIA front groups during the Cold War, Hugh Wilford disagrees with those who suggest that the CIA was always the "dominant partner" in these covert relationships. "The CIA might have tried to call the tune," he reasons, "but the piper did not always play it, nor the audience dance to it."[15] It was often the case, moreover, that the impetus for action came from the private side.[16] After all, the HNSF approached the FEC for assistance, not the other way around.

The same give-and-take often defined the government's relations with U.S. sports authorities. The AAU and the USOC, for instance, were, and always had been, sensitive to any interference in their general affairs. For the most part, these two giants of the U.S. sporting establishment retained control over the organization of U.S. participation in international athletics, and this arrangement was never seriously disputed or compromised. In fact, government experts generally agreed that this had to be the case for the United States to project an image, real or imagined, of moral superiority. Sometimes, too, U.S. members of the International Olympic Committee (IOC) failed to represent the best interests of the U.S. government at IOC meetings, and Avery Brundage was hardly the type to be easily manipulated or told what to do. His personal compulsion to critique amateur violations in the United States would continue to be the cause of headshaking in Washington for years to come. On a similar note, Telegdy was not always the most popular figure in the eyes of staff at the FEC. He frequently spent his operational budget haphazardly and was often unpredictable. Yet these transgressions were just part of the price that had to be paid for the things he could do to unhinge the regime in Hungary.

The IOC was, without question, also caught in the Cold War crossfire. The archives of the IOC contain several letters from various U.S. and Soviet front organizations, each looking to find a useful affiliation. In general, Brundage and his colleagues could identify the origins of the Soviet-sponsored groups.[17] But when it came to U.S. front organizations, they detected no such irregularities.[18] Had Brundage and other IOC members been "witting," doubtless they would have kept the FEC and the HNSF at more than arm's length and would not have given an audience to Thomas de Márffy-Mantuano in Helsinki. Yet in order for the state–private network to function, few could know it existed. The secrecy of the FEC and the HNSF allowed their cause to be debated in IOC meetings, which, in turn, was converted into valuable propaganda in the world's media. If Brundage had known that the U.S. intelligence community was behind these organizations, it is unlikely that his correspondence with them would have been quite so civil or quite so voluminous.

As well, the design and distribution of propaganda was wracked with challenges. Even if, as Philip Taylor has asserted, it is no longer possible to dismiss the part played by propaganda and psychological warfare in the Cold War as a mere "sideshow" to the "political, military or economic strategies of the period," the appropriations for the U.S. government's propaganda program still paled in comparison to the expenditure on the nation's military. Selling the American way of life was a constant fiscal headache to the leadership of the U.S. information program under both Harry S. Truman and Dwight D. Eisenhower.[19] There was also the pivotal problem of what could or could not be achieved through propaganda in the first place. By the end of the 1950s, government planners had come to realize that when it came to Olympic competition, words could do only so much. If and when the Soviet Union won the most medals, little could be done to prevent onlookers from admiring the achievement, and it was a practical impossibility to downplay the "ideological significance" of the festival itself. People around the world believed that the Olympics provided a stage for proving national strength, and the U.S. public was no different.

Working under such restrictions, U.S. officials tried to fight an Olympic propaganda war as best they could. And while much of the material they disseminated was designed to promote the merits and values of the American way of life, much of it, too, was intended to mute Soviet accusations and "lies" about the United States.[20] This defensive, or reactive, element is apparent in the entire campaign against communist sport. Although U.S. Olympic athletes were undoubtedly presented as ideal representatives of freedom and democracy, other themes countered Soviet accusations about race, women, capitalism, and inequality. The same is true of the broader picture. The aim of exploiting the Olympic Games came on the back of growing apprehension about the effectiveness of communist sport as a diplomatic weapon and the subsequent entrance of the Soviet Union into the IOC. Propaganda experts discerned the sporting aspect of the Soviet "cultural offensive" and then tried to formulate a strategy to counter it. One is thus inclined to agree with Thomas Domer's assertion that "a large part of America's official governmental interest in sport since World War II can be considered a reply to Soviet overtures."[21]

Regardless, it cannot be disputed that the emergence of the Cold War and the rise of Soviet sport led the U.S. government to view the Olympic Movement as an ideal platform on which to wage psychological warfare. This had not been the case since the birth of republic. Even if U.S. efforts were dwarfed by the sheer size and scope of those undertaken by the communist nations, the period from 1950 to the 1960 Rome Summer Olympics was still transformative. Never before had the U.S. government taken such a keen interest in the Olympic Movement or been so compelled to wield it. Never before had it so deeply delved into the affairs of the nation's sporting establishment or so ardently promoted the U.S. Olympic team to foreign audiences. Never before had the White House been so preoccupied with the U.S. performance at the Olympics or as concerned about the prowess of another nation's athletes. For the first time, U.S. foreign policy experts sat down and talked extensively and repeatedly about how the Olympics could damage or enhance the image of the nation in the eyes of overseas observers. For the first time, propaganda warriors considered the philosophical nature of sport and the Olympic Movement and how it could be tied to democratic principles and used to gain a Cold War advantage. All this, therefore, was unique to the post–World War II years.

In many ways, then, the 1950s set the stage for the remainder of the Cold War. The superpower sporting rivalry continued to elevate the political significance of athletic exchanges, track meets, and a range of other competitions and interactions between sportsmen and sportswomen from the East and the West.[22] For the U.S. public, the Olympics were still the source of much debate as each festival arrived on its quadrennial orbit. "Part of a nation's prestige in the Cold War is won in the Olympic Games," attorney general Robert F. Kennedy famously wrote in 1964. In "this day of international stalemates nations use the scoreboard of sports as a visible measuring stick to prove their superiority over the 'soft and decadent' democratic way of life. It is thus in our national interest that we regain our Olympic superiority—that we once again give the world visible proof of our inner strength and vitality."[23] The same sentiments were repeated by Vice President Gerald Ford two years after another Olympic defeat at the 1972 Munich summer Olympics. Do "we realize how important it is to compete successfully with other nations?" wrote Ford in an article published in *Sports Illustrated*. "Being a leader, the

U.S. has an obligation to set high standards," he lectured. "I don't know of any better advertisement for a nation's good health than a healthy athletic representation."[24] One of the main reasons for the repeated U.S. inability to defeat the Soviet Union in the Olympic crucible, argued both men, was the ongoing and frequently bitter struggle for power over the country's amateur sports between the AAU and the National Collegiate Athletic Association. This feud, and other bureaucratic problems besides, were finally resolved by the Jimmy Carter administration when it passed the Amateur Sports Act (1978), thereby placing the nation's Olympic fortunes firmly under the purview of just one organization, the USOC. This intervention also solved the longstanding financial conundrum by handing the USOC the highly lucrative commercial rights to the five ring Olympic symbol in the United States.[25] After decades of defeats by the Soviet Union, the federal government had finally taken steps to improve the nation's athletic deeds at the Olympic Games. Nevertheless, the act did not lead to any consistent state funding for the U.S. Olympic team.

Victory or defeat at the Olympics clearly remained important to the public and to the White House. Declassified documents also suggest that in the post-Eisenhower years the government was still deploying the Olympics in the service of psychological warfare. At the 1964 winter Olympics in Innsbruck, the FEC targeted Soviet-bloc tourists visiting the Austrian city in a small-scale program of making contacts. In the same year, the Lyndon B. Johnson administration organized a satellite broadcast of the Tokyo summer Olympics because of the "psychological impact" it could have on "maintaining the U.S. image of space supremacy." Yet the usual obstacles got in the way of a larger effort. When it was suggested that the U.S. Information Agency (USIA) develop an "all-out program of coverage" for Tokyo, the USIA director, Carl Rowan, responded that "the Games have relatively little relevance to USIA psychological objectives so that only limited selective coverage is regarded as justified."[26] This reflected the general ambivalence displayed by the Johnson administration to the role of sport in the cultural Cold War, as the number of sports exchanges declined in the late 1960s and the budget for the broader cultural program was halved.

All the same, government endeavors to exploit the Olympics persisted.[27] One of the most enduring propaganda initiatives came from Radio Free Europe (RFE). During the 1970s and 1980s, the radio moved out of the covert shadows but continued to challenge the legitimacy of communist rule behind the Iron Curtain through its in-depth Olympic coverage. The presence of officially accredited RFE reporters in Olympic cities became a matter of immense frustration to the Soviet bloc, which almost relentlessly lobbied the

IOC to bar the "subversive" station from broadcasting at the Olympics.[28] One of the festivals from which RFE was shut out was the 1980 summer Olympics in Moscow, an event famous for being overshadowed by another dramatic act of U.S. psychological warfare. Responding to the Soviet Union's invasion of Afghanistan the previous year, the U.S. president, Jimmy Carter, concluded that undermining the Moscow Olympics was an effective way to punish the Kremlin's transgression. Believing that a boycott would be a "severe blow" to Soviet national prestige, the White House proceeded to cajole the USOC and a host of nations into canceling their plans to attend the 1980 summer Olympics. Not stopping there, Carter also tried to organize an alternative festival, sought to postpone, cancel, or move the Moscow Olympics to another site, and even attempted to permanently relocate the event to Greece. Refusing to be bullied on its own turf, the IOC ignored the U.S. president and the 1980 Olympics carried on as planned.[29]

Carter's decision was an exceptional act when put in the context of the past. For once, the president had told the USOC what to do and made sure that they did it. For once, the USOC had allowed itself to be governed by the state. But in other ways, the actions of the Carter administration and the value it placed upon the strategic importance of the Olympic Movement can be traced back to the Truman administration, when the government's interest in the festival really began to transform. It was during these early years of the Cold War that psychological warfare experts began concocting ways that would best utilize the Olympic Games to forward U.S. foreign policy objectives in the "free world" and the communist bloc. They never paused to wonder about whether these activities compromised the very sporting ideals they had hoped to promote. These contradictions were not relevant. It was the U.S. sporting philosophy that was "right," and communist sport that was "wrong." As Senator John Marshall Butler proclaimed in 1955, it was the Soviet Union that "polluted" the Olympics, not the United States. The moral dilemma, if indeed there was one, had to be brushed to one side. The same paradox sat at the heart of the state–private network. "The choice between innocence and power involves the most difficult of decisions," remarked a former CIA officer while the agency's covert web unraveled. "But when an adversary attacks with his weapons disguised as good works, to choose innocence is to choose defeat."[30]

Notes

Introduction

1. Butler was the Republican senator from Maryland. The full text of the speech is appended to a letter from John Marshall Butler to Avery Brundage, 25 July 1955, Avery Brundage Collection, 1908–75, Box 333, Reel 145, International Centre for Olympic Studies Archives, University of Western Ontario, London, Ontario, Canada.

2. Mario Del Pero, "The United States and 'Psychological Warfare' in Italy, 1948–1955," *Journal of American History* 87, no. 4 (2001): 1305–6; Kenneth Osgood, "Hearts and Minds: The Unconventional Cold War," *Journal of Cold War Studies* 4, no. 2 (2002): 85–86.

3. Kenneth Osgood, *Total Cold War: Eisenhower's Secret Propaganda Battle at Home and Abroad* (Lawrence: University Press of Kansas, 2006), 5.

4. See, for instance, Walter L. Hixson, *Parting the Curtain: Propaganda, Culture, and the Cold War* (New York: St. Martin's Press, 1997); Frances Stoner Saunders, *Who Paid the Piper? The CIA and the Cultural Cold War* (London: Granta Books, 1999); Laura A. Belmonte, *Selling the American Way: U.S. Propaganda and the Cold War* (Philadelphia: University of Pennsylvania Press, 2008); and Hans Krabbendam and Giles Scott-Smith, eds., *The Cultural Cold War in Western Europe, 1945–1960* (London: Frank Cass, 2003). For a fascinating essay on the historiography of culture and the Cold War, see Jessica C. E. Gienow-Hecht, "Shame on US? Academics, Cultural Transfer, and the Cold War—A Critical Review," *Diplomatic History* 24, no. 3 (2000): 465–94.

5. For instance, sport is given relatively little attention in David Caute's otherwise excellent *The Dancer Defects: The Struggle for Cultural Supremacy during the Cold War* (Oxford: Oxford University Press, 2003).

6. Stephen Wagg and David L. Andrews, "Introduction: War minus the Shooting," in *East Plays West: Sport and the Cold War*, ed. Stephen Wagg and David L. Andrews (New York: Routledge, 2007), 2, 4.

7. Peter J. Beck, "Britain and the Cold War's 'Cultural Olympics': Responding to the Political Drive of Soviet Sport, 1945–58," *Contemporary British History* 19, no. 2 (2005): 170.

8. For studies on Eastern European regimes, see, for instance, the special issue of *International Journal of the History of Sport* 26, no. 4 (March 2009).

9. See especially James Riordan, *Sport in Soviet Society* (London: Cambridge University Press, 1977); Jenifer Parks, "Red Sport, Red Tape: The Olympic Games, the Soviet Sports Bureaucracy, and the Cold War, 1952–1980," PhD diss., University of North Carolina at Chapel Hill, 2009; Robert Edelman, *Serious Fun: A History of Spectator Sports in the U.S.S.R.* (New York: Oxford University Press, 1993); and Henry Morton, *Soviet Sport, Mirror of Soviet Society* (London: Crowell-Collier, 1963).

10. Peter Beck, for instance, has produced several articles on the British government's sport policy. See Beck, "Britain and the 'Cultural Olympics,'" 169–85; and Beck, "The British Government and the Olympic Movement: The 1948 London Olympics," *International Journal of the History of Sport* 25, no. 5 (2008): 615–47.

11. Thomas M. Hunt, "American Sport Policy and the Cultural Cold War: The Lyndon B. Johnson Presidential Years," *Journal of Sport History* 33, no. 3 (2006): 273–97; Nicholas Evan Sarantakes, *Dropping the Torch: Jimmy Carter, the Olympic Boycott, and the Cold War* (New York: Cambridge University Press, 2011); Harold E. Wilson Jr., "The Golden Opportunity: Romania's Political Manipulation of the 1984 Los Angles Olympic Games," *Olympika* 3 (1994): 83–97; Nicholas Evan Sarantakes, "Moscow versus Los Angeles: The Nixon White House Wages Cold War in the Olympic Selection Process," *Cold War History* 9, no. 1 (2009): 135–57.

12. There are only a few exceptions. For instance, David Maraniss uncovers some CIA activities at the 1960 Rome Olympics in a revealing, though poorly documented, study. See David Maraniss, *Rome 1960: The Olympics That Changed the World* (New York: Simon and Schuster, 2008). Elsewhere, Roy Clumpner has surveyed the widest time span, covering the years from 1950 to 1973. He claims that the U.S. government unquestionably tried to deploy sport in foreign policy by encouraging athletic success and international cultural exchanges. He claims, however, that apart from a meager program of athletic goodwill tours started in 1948 and expanded in 1954, much of the bluster delivered by individuals in numerous speeches before Congress failed to inspire anything but superficial interference in sport, especially as a means for propaganda. Comparatively, argues Clumpner, "American federal involvement in sport to promote American interests and foreign policy objectives was miniscule when compared to the Soviet Union from 1950–1973." See Roy Clumpner, "Federal Involvement in Sport to Promote American Interest or Foreign Policy Objectives, 1950–1973," in *Sport and International Relations*, ed. B. Lowe, D. B. Kanin, A. Strenk (Champaign, IL: Stipes, 1978), 400–52. As well, there is a case to be made in claiming that athletic tours were the most sustained and productive of the U.S. government's sporting efforts to generate positive propaganda during the Cold War. Damian Thomas has composed the most detailed work on this area of cultural diplomacy and focused most specifically on the goodwill tours of African American athletes. See Damion Thomas, *Globetrotting: African American Athletes and Cold War Politics* (Urbana: University of Illinois Press, 2012). On this subject, also see Kevin B. Witherspoon, "'Fuzz Kids' and 'Musclemen': The U.S.–Soviet Basketball Rivalry, 1958–1975," in *Diplomatic Games: Sport, Statecraft, and International Relations since 1945*, ed. Heather L. Dichter and Andrew L. Johns (Lexington: University Press of Kentucky, 2014), 297–326; Witherspoon, "Going 'to the

Fountainhead': Black American Athletes as Cultural Ambassadors in Africa, 1970–1971," *International Journal of the History of Sport* 30, no. 13 (2013): 1508–22.

13. Thomas M. Domer, "Sport in Cold War America, 1953–1963: The Diplomatic and Political Use of Sport in the Eisenhower and Kennedy Administrations," PhD diss., Marquette University, 1976.

14. The Truman administration's interest in the Olympics for propaganda purposes is mentioned very briefly in Barbara Keys, "The Early Cold War Olympics, 1952–1960: Political, Economic and Human Rights Dimensions," in *The Palgrave Handbook of Olympic Studies*, ed. Helen Lenskyi and Stephen Wagg (Houndsmills, U.K.: Palgrave Macmillan, 2012), 76–78; and Nicholas J. Cull, "The Public Diplomacy of the Modern Olympic Games and China's Soft Power Strategy," in *Owning the Olympics: Narratives of the New China*, ed. Monroe E. Price and Daniel Dayan (Ann Arbor: University of Michigan Press, 2008), 127.

15. "Memorandum for the Cultural Presentation Committee" 30 November 1956, White House Office, National Security Council Staff: Papers, 1953–61, OCB Central File Series, Box 112, File 1, "OCB 353.8," Dwight D. Eisenhower Presidential Library, Abilene, Kansas.

16. I have borrowed this turn of phrase from Osgood, *Total Cold War*, 5.

17. [W.] Scott Lucas, *Freedom's War: The American Crusade against the Soviet Union* (New York: New York University Press, 1999), 1–3. The quotations are from these pages. For more on U.S. state–private operations, see, for instance, [W.] Scott Lucas, "Beyond Freedom, Beyond Control: Approaches to Culture and the State–Private Network in the Cold War," *Intelligence and National Security* 18, no. 2 (2003): 53–72; Stoner Saunders, *Who Paid the Piper?*; Hugh Wilford, *The Mighty Wurlitzer: How the CIA Played America* (Cambridge, MA: Harvard University Press, 2008); and Helen Laville and Hugh Wilford, eds., *The US Government, Citizen Groups and the Cold War: The State–Private Network* (New York: Routledge, 2006).

18. John Horne, "The Politics of Hosting the Olympic Games," in *The Politics of the Olympics: A Survey*, ed. Alan Bairner and Gyozo Molnar (London: Routledge, 2010), 27–40; Barbara Keys, *Globalizing Sport: National Rivalry and International Community in the 1930s* (Cambridge, MA: Harvard University Press, 2006).

19. John J. MacAloon, *This Great Symbol: Pierre de Coubertin and the Origins of the Modern Olympic Games* (Chicago: University of Chicago Press, 1981), 263.

20. John Hoberman, *The Olympic Crisis: Sport, Politics, and the Moral Order* (New Rochelle, NY: Caratzas, 1986), 57–64.

21. Mark Dyreson, *Making the America Team: Sport, Culture, and the Olympic Experience* (Urbana: University of Illinois Press, 1998).

22. Osgood, *Total Cold War*, 8; Belmonte, *Selling the American Way*, 7.

23. Both quotes appear in Stoner Saunders, *Who Paid the Piper?* 4, 430n. Another term used frequently is the "free world." I use "free world" only to denote how the United States referred to all noncommunist nations. I do not use this term out of any personal belief; the contradictions are obvious.

24. Osgood, *Total Cold War*, 93; U.S. Operations Coordinating Board, "Principles to Assure Coordination of Gray Activities," 14 May 1954, *United States Declassified Documents Reference System* (Woodbridge, CT, 1992), document 486.

25. G. M. Trevelyan, *Clio, A Muse and Other Essays* (London: Longmans, Green, 1949), 181.

Chapter 1. The Cold War, Propaganda, and the State–Private Network

1. "Organizational Developments and Delineation of Psychological Warfare Responsibilities since World War II," White House Report, no date, *United States Declassified Documents Reference System*—hereafter referred to as US DDRS (Woodbridge, CT, 1987)—document 3560.

2. Eric Hobsbawm, *Age of Extremes: The Short Twentieth Century, 1914–1991* (London: Abacus, 1994).

3. Philip M. Taylor, *Munitions of the Mind: A History of Propaganda from the Ancient World to the Present Day* (Manchester, U.K.: Manchester University Press, 2003), 173–75; Kenneth Osgood, *Total Cold War: Eisenhower's Secret Propaganda Battle at Home and Abroad* (Lawrence: University Press of Kansas, 2006), 15–22; Hobsbawm, *Age of Extremes*, 22–53, quote on 24.

4. George Creel, *How We Advertised America* (New York: Harper and Brothers, 1920), quotes on 3–4; Bruce Pinkleton, "The Campaign of the Committee on Public Information: Its Contributions to the History and Evolution of Public Relations," *Journal of Public Relations Research* 6, no. 4 (1994): 229–40; David F. Krugler, *The Voice of America and the Domestic Propaganda Battles, 1945–1953* (Columbia: University of Missouri Press, 2000), 18–23.

5. Frank Ninkovich, *U.S. Information Policy and Cultural Diplomacy* (New York: Foreign Policy Association, 1996), 9–11, Duggen quote on 10; Richard T. Arndt, *The First Resort of Kings: American Cultural Diplomacy in the Twentieth Century* (Washington, DC: Potomac, 2005), 22.

6. *History of the Office of the Coordinator of Inter-American Affairs* (Washington, DC: U.S. Government Printing Office, 1947), quote on 3.

7. Frank A. Ninkovich, *The Diplomacy of Ideas: U.S. Foreign Policy and Cultural Relations, 1938–1950* (Cambridge: Cambridge University Press, 1981), 26–45; Charles A. Thomson and Walter H. C. Laves, *Cultural Relations and U.S. Foreign Policy* (Bloomington: Indiana University Press, 1963), 31–40; Justin Hart, *Empire of Ideas: The Origins of Public Diplomacy and the Transformation of U.S. Foreign Policy* (New York: Oxford University Press, 2013), 15–30.

8. *History of the Office of the Coordinator*, 3–8, quote on 8; Ninkovich, *Diplomacy of Ideas*, 26–45.

9. Jennifer L. Campbell, "Creating Something Out of Nothing: The Office of Inter-American Affairs Music Committee (1940–1941) and the Inception of a Policy for Musical Diplomacy," *Diplomatic History* 36, no. 1 (2012): 29–39; Hart, *Empire of Ideas*, 30–40; Ninkovich, *U.S. Information Policy*, 13.

10. Clayton D. Laurie, *The Propaganda Warriors: America's Crusade against Nazi Germany* (Lawrence: University Press of Kansas, 1996), Donovan quote on 79.

11. Laurie, *Propaganda Warriors*, 112–27; Krugler, *Voice of America*, 29–31; Alan L. Heil, "The Voice of America: A Brief Cold War History," in *Cold War Broadcasting: Impact on the Soviet Union and Eastern Europe*, ed. A. Ross Johnson and R. Eugene Parta (New York: Central European University Press, 2010), quote on 25.

12. Alfred H. Paddock Jr. *U.S. Army Special Warfare: Its Origins* (Lawrence: University Press of Kansas, 2002), 28; Laurie, *Propaganda Warriors*, 128–42.

13. Paddock, *U.S. Army Special Warfare*, 11–14, Eisenhower quote on 20; Osgood, *Total Cold War*, 30; Blanche Wiesen Cook, *The Declassified Eisenhower: A Divided Legacy* (New York: Doubleday, 1981), Jackson quote on 14; Laurie, *Propaganda Warriors*, 143–65.

14. "Termination of O.W.I. and Disposition of Certain Functions of O.I.A.A.," *Department of State Bulletin*, 2 September 1945, 306; "Duties and Responsibilities of the Assistant Secretary in Charge of Public Affairs," *Department of State Bulletin*, 23 September 1945, 430.

15. Benton quote in "National Defense and National Reputation," *Department of State Bulletin*, 2 February 1947, 202; Hart, *Empire of Ideas*, 112–16, "capricious extravagance" quote on 113; Walter L. Hixson, *Parting the Curtain: Propaganda, Culture, and the Cold War, 1945–1961* (New York: St. Martin's Press, 1997), 5.

16. Melvyn P. Leffler, "The Emergence of an American Grand Strategy, 1945–1952," in *The Cambridge History of the Cold War*. Vol. 1, *Origins*, ed. Melvin P. Leffler and Odd Arne Westad (Cambridge: Cambridge University Press, 2010), 68–72, quote on 68.

17. Norman Naimark, "The Sovietization of Eastern Europe, 1944–1953," in *The Cambridge History of the Cold War*. Vol. 1, *Origins*, quotes on 177, 182, and 184; David Priestland, *The Red Flag: A History of Communism* (New York: Grove Press, 2009), 211–19; Vladislav Zubok and Constantine Pleshakov, *Inside the Kremlin's Cold War: From Stalin to Khrushchev* (Cambridge, MA: Harvard University Press, 1996), 27–35, 125–37.

18. Daniel Yergin, *Shattered Peace: The Origins of the Cold War and the National Security State* (Boston: Houghton Mifflin, 1977), 161.

19. "Special Message to the Congress on Greece and Turkey: The Truman Doctrine. March 12, 1947," *Public Papers of the Presidents of the United States: Harry S. Truman, 1947* (Washington, DC: U.S. Government Printing Office, 1963), 178.

20. Leffler, "Emergence," 77–79, Marshall quote on 77.

21. Edward P. Lilly, "The Development of American Psychological Operations, 1945–1951," 19 December 1951, US DDRS 1988: 1742, 15–16, 18, 26; Trevor Barnes, "The Secret Cold War: The CIA and American Foreign Policy in Europe, 1946–1956, Part 1," *Historical Journal* 24, no. 2 (1981): 404–5.

22. Rhodri Jeffreys-Jones, *The CIA and American Democracy* (New Haven, CT: Yale University Press, 1989), quote on 41; Wilson D. Miscamble, *George F. Kennan and the Making of American Foreign Policy, 1947–1950* (Princeton, NJ: Princeton University Press, 1992), 76.

23. Sarah-Jane Corke, "George Kennan and the Inauguration of Political Warfare," *Journal of Conflict Studies* 26, no. 1 (2006): 102–3, NSC quote on 103.

24. Mario Del Pero, "The United States and 'Psychological Warfare' in Italy, 1948–1955," *Journal of American History* 87, no. 4 (2001): quote on 1306; Corke, "George Kennan," 103–5; Christopher Simpson, *Science of Coercion: Communication Research and Psychological Warfare, 1945–1960* (New York: Oxford University Press, 1994), 38–39.

25. Kaeten Mistry, "The Case for Political Warfare: Strategy, Organization and US Involvement in the 1948 Italian Election," *Cold War History* 6, no. 3 (2006): 316–17; Del Pero, "United States and 'Psychological Warfare,'" 1306. The U.S. government also tried to prevent the communist infiltration of trade unions in France. The CIA, for instance, channeled funds to support the leading anticommunist trade union (Force Ouvrière) and the secretary of defense, James Forrestal, arranged for New York bankers to bribe

French labor leaders. See [W.] Scott Lucas, *Freedom's War: The American Crusade against the Soviet Union* (New York: New York University Press, 1999), 46.

26. "The Inauguration of Organized Political Warfare," Policy Planning Staff Memorandum, 4 May 1948, *Foreign Relations of the United States, 1945–1950* (hereafter referred to as *FRUS Intelligence*): *Emergence of the Intelligence Establishment* (Washington, DC: U.S. Government Printing Office, 1996), 668–72; Miscamble, *George F. Kennan*, 106–8.

27. Corke, "George Kennan," 108–13; OPC quote from "Office of Policy Coordination, 1948–1952," Central Intelligence Agency website, www.foia.cia.gov/ (hereafter referred to as CIA FOIA). The Marshall Plan dictated that for every dollar provided by the United States, Western European countries would match the amount, and 5 percent of that money was put aside in local currency for the use of the United States. These funds became a bottomless pit for the OPC. See Evan Thomas, *The Very Best Men: Four Who Dared; The Early Years of the CIA* (New York: Simon and Schuster, 1995), 40, 63.

28. Lucas, *Freedom's War*, 62–63, PPS quote on 62; Gregory Mitrovich, *Undermining the Kremlin: America's Strategy to Subvert the Soviet Bloc, 1947–1956* (Ithaca, NY: Cornell University Press, 2000), NSC 20/4 quote on 35.

29. Peter Grose, *Operation Rollback: America's Secret War behind the Iron Curtain* (New York: Houghton Mifflin, 2000), 154–89.

30. Kenneth Osgood, "Hearts and Minds: The Unconventional Cold War," *Journal of Cold War Studies* 4, no. 2 (2002): 89; Mitrovich, *Undermining the Kremlin*, 2, 35–36.

31. Sam Lebovic, "From War Junk to Educational Exchange: The World War II Origins of the Fulbright Program and the Foundations of American Cultural Globalism, 1945–1950," *Diplomatic History* 37, no. 2 (2013): 280–312.

32. Liam Kennedy and [W.] Scott Lucas, "Enduring Freedom: Public Diplomacy and U.S. Foreign Policy," *American Quarterly* 57, no. 2 (2005): 311–12; Simpson, *Science of Coercion*, NSC quote on 38.

33. Hixson, *Parting the Curtain*, 10–11; Ninkovich, *U.S. Information Policy*, 17–18; Wilson P. Dizard, *The Strategy of Truth: The Story of the U.S. Information Service* (Washington, DC: Public Affairs Press, 1961), 36–38; Krugler, *Voice of America*, 65–72, 214–15.

34. Acheson quote in "Support for an Expanded Information and Education Program," *Department of State Bulletin*, 17 July 1950, 101; Hixson, *Parting the Curtain*, 10–11, 34.

35. Barrett memorandum, 2 March 1950, *FRUS, 1950, IV, Central and Eastern Europe; The Soviet Union*, 272; Truman quote in "Address on Foreign Policy at a Luncheon of the American Society of Newspaper Editors," 20 April 1950, *Public Papers of the Presidents of the United States: Harry S. Truman, 1950* (Washington, DC: U.S. Government Printing Office, 1965), 264; Nicholas J. Cull, *The Cold War and the United States Information Agency: American Propaganda and Public Diplomacy, 1945–1989* (Cambridge: Cambridge University Press, 2008), 17–18, 51–55.

36. Melvyn P. Leffler, *A Preponderance of Power: National Security, the Truman Administration, and the Cold War* (Stanford, CA: Stanford University Press, 1992), 359.

37. [W.] Scott Lucas, "Campaigns of Truth: The Psychological Strategy Board and American Ideology, 1951–1953," *International History Review* 18, no. 2 (May 1996): 287–88, 296; quote in Lilly, "American Psychological Operations," 94.

38. Cull, *The Cold War*, 67–80.

39. "Princeton Meeting, 10–11 May 1952," US DDRS 1988: 1164; Lucas, *Freedom's War*, 152–54. For a discussion on the general incoherence of U.S. strategy, see [W.] Scott Lu-

cas and Kaeten Mistry, "Illusions of Coherence: George F. Kennan, U.S. Strategy and Political Warfare in the Early Cold War, 1946–1950," *Diplomatic History* 33, no.1 (2009): 39–66.

40. Osgood, *Total Cold War*, 45.

41. "Text of Gen. Eisenhower's Foreign Policy Speech in San Francisco," *New York Times*, 9 October 1952, 24; "Eisenhower Picks a 'Cold War' Chief," *New York Times*, 17 February 1953, 16. On Eisenhower and liberation, see Chris Tudda, "'Reenacting the Story of Tantalus': Eisenhower, Dulles, and the Failed Rhetoric of Liberation," *Journal of Cold War Studies* 7, no. 4 (Fall 2005): 3–35.

42. Blanche Wiesen Cook, "First Comes the Lie: C. D. Jackson and Political Warfare," *Radical History Review* 31 (December 1984): 43–70; Wiesen Cook, *The Declassified Eisenhower*, Jackson quote on 177–78; David Haight, "The Papers of C. D. Jackson: A Glimpse at President Eisenhower's Psychological Warfare Expert," *Manuscripts* 28 (Winter 1976): 27–37; Valur Ingimundarson, "Containing the Offensive: The 'Chief of the Cold War' and the Eisenhower Administration's German Policy," *Presidential Studies Quarterly* 27, no. 3 (1997): 480–95; H. W. Brands Jr., *Cold Warriors: Eisenhower's Generation and American Foreign Policy* (New York: Columbia University Press, 1988), 117–37.

43. "Jackson Committee Report," abridged version, no date, US DDRS: 1988 1163; Shawn J. Parry-Giles, "The Eisenhower Administration's Conception of the USIA: The Development of Overt and Covert Propaganda Strategies," *Presidential Studies Quarterly* 24, no. 2 (1994): 265–68, quote on 264; Osgood, *Total Cold War*, 76–98.

44. Alfred Dick Sander, *Eisenhower's Executive Office* (Westport, CT: Greenwood Press, 1999), 124–28; Osgood, *Total Cold War*, 86–88; Lucas, "Campaigns of Truth," 281.

45. Howland quote in "Helping the World to Know Us Better," *Department of State Bulletin*, 28 November 1948, 672; Nicholas J. Cull, "Public Diplomacy and the Private Sector: The United States Information Agency, Its Predecessors and the Private Sector," in *The U.S. Government, Citizen Groups and the Cold War: The State–Private Network*, ed. Helen Laville and Hugh Wilford (New York: Routledge, 2006), 210–15; Liping Bu, "Educational Exchange and Cultural Diplomacy in the Cold War," *Journal of American Studies* 33, no. 3 (December 1999): 393–415.

46. "Office of Policy Coordination."

47. Quote in "The Inauguration of Organized Political Warfare," 668–69; Hugh Wilford, *The Mighty Wurlitzer: How the CIA Played America* (Cambridge, MA: Harvard University Press, 2008), 6.

48. [W.] Scott Lucas, "Mobilizing Culture: The State–Private Network and the CIA in the Early Cold War," in *War and Cold War in American Foreign Policy 1942–62*, ed. Dale Carter and Robin Clifton (Houndsmills, U.K.: Palgrave, 2002), quote on 83.

49. Tom Braden, "I'm Glad the CIA Is 'Immoral,'" *Saturday Evening Post*, 20 May 1967; "Office of Policy Coordination"; Frances Stoner Saunders, *Who Paid the Piper? The CIA and the Cultural Cold War* (London: Granta Books, 1999), 96–97; Thomas, *The Very Best Men*, 62.

50. Lucas, "Mobilizing Culture," 91, 94.

51. A. Ross Johnson, *Radio Free Europe and Radio Liberty: The CIA Years and Beyond* (Stanford, CA: Stanford University Press, 2010), 8–12, quote on 10; Katalin Kádár Lynn, "At War while at Peace: United States Cold War Policy and the National Committee for a Free Europe, Inc.," in *The Inauguration of Organized Political Warfare: Cold War Organizations*

Sponsored by the National Committee for a Free Europe/Free Europe Committee, ed. Katalin Kádár Lynn (Saint Helena, CA: Helena History Press, 2013), 7–70; Miscamble, *George F. Kennan*, 182; Larry D. Collins, "The Free Europe Committee: An American Weapon of the Cold War" (PhD diss., Carleton University, Ottawa, 1973), 121; Arch Puddington, *Broadcasting Freedom: The Cold War Triumph of Radio Free Europe and Radio Liberty* (Lexington: University Press of Kentucky, 2000), 7–12.

52. "Memorandum on Organization and Operations," 25 July 1949, RFE/RL INC. Corporate Records (hereafter referred to as RFE/RL), Box 188, File 1, "Free Europe Committee, Inc. General, 1949–1957," Hoover Institution Archives (hereafter referred to as HA), Stanford University, Stanford, CA; "New Group Formed to Assist Refugees," *New York Times*, 2 June 1949, 29.

53. John Foster Leich, "Great Expectations: The National Councils in Exile, 1950–60," *Polish Review* 35, no. 3 (1990): 184; Miscamble, *George F. Kennan*, 204–5; Collins, "Free Europe Committee," 110.

54. Cited in Lucas, *Freedom's War*, 85.

55. "Radio Free Europe—Fact Sheet," no date (circa 1950), RFE/RL, Box 166, File 14, "Crusade for Freedom, General, July–Dec. 1950," HA, p. 1.

56. "Radio Free Europe Policy Handbook," 30 November 1951, US DDRS 1986: 1974, n.p.

57. Sig Mickelson, *America's Other Voice: The Story of Radio Free Europe and Radio Liberty* (New York: Praeger, 1983), 30–33, 48–50, quote on 41; "Thumbnail Sketches of Typical Radio Free Europe Programs," no date, Charles Hulten Papers (hereafter referred to as Hulten Papers), Box 22, File 2, "Radio Free Europe," Harry S. Truman Presidential Library (hereafter referred to as HSTL), Independence, Missouri; "Radio Free Europe—Fact Sheet"; "President's Report" for the NCFE, appended to a letter from Whitney H. Shepardson to Allen W. Dulles, 10 April 1953, CIA FOIA.

58. Mickelson, *America's Other Voice*, 51–58; Lucas, *Freedom's War*, 101–3; Johnson, *Radio Free Europe and Radio Liberty*, 14–15; Puddington, *Broadcasting Freedom*, 20–24; "Loop Freedom Rally to Hear Admiral Halsey," *Chicago Daily Tribune*, 11 September 1950, B10.

59. Kádár Lynn, "At War while at Peace," 29–41; "President's Report for the Year 1955," Hulten Papers, Box 22, File 3, "Radio Free Europe," HSTL; "President's Report" for the NCFE; Johnson, *Radio Free Europe and Radio Liberty*, 75–78. For work on many of the organizations funded by the NCFE, see Katalin Kádár Lynn, ed., *The Inauguration of Organized Political Warfare*.

60. "Reorientation of Exile Organizations," 1 April 1960, C. D. Jackson Papers, 1931–67, Series II Time INC. File, 1933–64, Subseries A. Alphabetical File, 1933–64, Box 53, File 2, "Free Europe Committee, 1960," Dwight D. Eisenhower Presidential Library, Abilene, Kansas.

61. Abbott Washburn to C. D. Jackson, 22 October 1951, RFE/RL, Box 355, File 13, "Alphabetical File, Washburn, Abbott, 1949–1963," HA.

Chapter 2. The United States, the Soviet Union, and the Olympic Games

1. "Opening of the International Olympic Committee Meeting in Vienna," *Olympic Review* 27 (June 1951): 27–29, first quote on 28, second quote on 29.

2. "What Does It Mean," *New York Times*, 8 January 1952, p. 32.

3. Jenifer Parks, "Verbal Gymnastics: Sports, Bureaucracy, and the Soviet Union's Entrance into the Olympic Games, 1946–1952," in *East Plays West: Sport and the Cold War*, ed. Stephen Wagg and David L. Andrews (New York: Routledge, 2007), 27–44.

4. Eric Hobsbawm, "Mass-Producing Traditions: Europe, 1870–1914," in *The Invention of Tradition*, ed. Eric Hobsbawm and Terence Ranger (Cambridge: Cambridge University Press, 1983): 263, 298.

5. David C. Young, *The Modern Olympics: A Struggle for Revival* (Baltimore: Johns Hopkins University Press, 1996), 92.

6. John J. MacAloon, *This Great Symbol: Pierre de Coubertin and the Origins of the Modern Olympic Games* (Chicago: University of Chicago Press, 1981), 51, 188–89, Coubertin quote on 51.

7. John Lucas, "The Influence of Anglo-American Sport on Pierre de Coubertin—Modern Olympic Games Founder," in *The Modern Olympics*, ed. Peter J. Graham and Horst Ueberhorst (Westpoint, NY: Leisure Press, 1976), 28.

8. Young, *Modern Olympics*, 8–12, 68–80. Although Coubertin controlled the movement, the first president of the IOC was a Greek named Demetrios Vikelas. After the Athens games, Coubertin assumed the presidency and held it until 1925.

9. MacAloon, *This Great Symbol*, 262–68.

10. Allen Guttmann, *The Olympics: A History of the Modern Games* (Urbana: University of Illinois Press, 2002), 2.

11. Norbert Müller, ed., *Pierre de Coubertin 1863–1937: Olympism; Selected Writings* (Lausanne, Switz.: International Olympic Committee, 2000), 360.

12. Guttmann, *The Olympics*, 2; Barrie Houlihan, "International Politics and Olympic Governance," in *Global Olympics: Historical and Sociological Studies of the Modern Games*, ed. Kevin Young and Kevin B. Wamsley (Amsterdam, Holland: Elsevier, 2005), 130.

13. Cited in Matthew P. Llewellyn, "The Battle of Shepherd's Bush," *International Journal of the History of Sport* 28, no. 5 (2011): 698.

14. "Olympic Games Doomed," *The Times*, 22 July 1924, p. 14.

15. Barbara Keys, *Globalizing Sport: National Rivalry and International Community in the 1930s* (Cambridge, MA: Harvard University Press, 2006), 136–37.

16. Richard Mandell, *The Nazi Olympics* (New York: Macmillan, 1971), xiv.

17. Matthew P. Llewellyn and John Gleaves, "A Universal Dilemma: The British *Sporting Life* and the Complex, Contested, and Contradictory State of Amateurism," *Journal of Sport History* 41, no. 1 (2014): 97–101.

18. David C. Young, *The Olympic Myth of Greek Amateur Athletics* (Chicago: Ares, 1984), 7, 15–22; Guttmann, *The Olympics*, 12–13; Matthew P. Llewellyn and John T. Gleaves, "The Rise of the 'Shamateur': The International Olympic Committee and the Preservation of the Amateur Ideal," in *Problems, Possibilities, and Promising Practices: Critical Dialogues on the Olympic and Paralympic Games*, ed. J. Forsyth and K. B. Wamsley (London, ON, Canada: International Centre for Olympic Studies, 2012), 23–28; Llewellyn and Gleaves, "Universal Dilemma," 101–11.

19. Steven Pope, *Patriotic Games: Sporting Traditions in the American Imagination, 1876–1926* (New York: Oxford University Press, 1997), 18–34; Joseph Turrini, *The End of Amateurism in American Track and Field* (Urbana: University of Illinois Press, 2010),

12–16; John Lucas and Ronald Smith, *The Saga of American Sport* (Philadelphia: Lea and Febiger, 1978), 156–58.

20. Robert E. Lehr, "The American Olympic Committee, 1896–1940: From Chaos to Order," PhD diss., Pennsylvania State University, 1985; Turrini, *The End of Amateurism*, 16; John Lucas, "Architects of the Modernized American Olympic Committee, 1921–1928: Gustavus Town Kirby, Roberts Means Thompson, and General Douglas MacArthur," *Journal of Sport History* 22, no. 1 (1995): 38–40.

21. Mark Dyreson, *Making the American Team: Sport, Culture, and the Olympic Experience* (Urbana: University of Illinois Press, 1998), 175.

22. "Americanism in the Olympic Games," by Clarence E. Bush, no date (circa 1934–35), Avery Brundage Collection, 1908–75 (hereafter referred to as ABC), Box 232, Reel 135, International Centre for Olympic Studies Archives (hereafter referred to as ICOSA), University of Western Ontario, London, Ontario, Canada.

23. Barbara Keys, "Spreading Peace, Democracy, and Coca-Cola: Sport and American Cultural Expansion in the 1930s," *Diplomatic History* 28, no. 2 (2004): 165–96, first quote on 168, second quote on 179.

24. "No Mollycoddles, Says Roosevelt," *New York Times*, 24 February 1907, p. 1; John S. Watterson, *The Games Presidents Play: Sports and the Presidency* (Baltimore: Johns Hopkins University Press, 2006).

25. Benjamin G. Radar, "The Quest for Subcommunities and the Rise of American Sport," *American Quarterly* 29, no. 4 (1977): 355–69; Turrini, *End of Amateurism*, 16–19.

26. Mark Dyreson, "Marketing National Identity: The Olympic Games of 1932 and American Culture," *Olympika* 4 (1995): 43.

27. John Lucas, *The Modern Olympic Games* (London: A. S. Barnes, 1980), Coubertin quotes on 137; Allen Guttmann, *The Games Must Go On: Avery Brundage and the Olympic Movement* (New York: Columbia University Press, 1984), 134–35.

28. Barbara Keys, "The Internationalization of Sport, 1890–1939," in *The Cultural Turn: Essays in the History of U.S. Foreign Relations*, ed. Frank A. Ninkovich and Liping Bu (Chicago: Imprint, 2001), 209; Roy Clumpner, "Pragmatic Coercion: The Role of Government in Sport in the United States," in *Sport and Politics*, ed. Gerald Redmond (Champaign, IL: Human Kinetics, 1984), 5–12. I refer only to U.S. government funding of and influence on international sport. Domestically, the government intervened in sporting matters of, among other things, law and commerce. For example, the Roosevelt administration promoted sport and outdoor recreation as part of its New Deal policies on improving social welfare. See John Wong, "FDR and the New Deal on Sport and Recreation," *Sport History Review* 29 (1998): 173–91.

29. Mark Dyreson, "Johnny Weissmuller and the Old Global Capitalism: The Origins of the Federal Blueprint for Selling American Culture to the World," *International Journal of the History of Sport* 25, no. 2 (2008): 268–83, quote on 270.

30. *History of the Office of the Coordinator of Inter-American Affairs* (Washington, DC: U.S. Government Printing Office, 1947), 97–98; "Bushnell Gets New Post," *New York Times*, 31 August 1941, S2; "Sports Seen as Boon to Hemisphere Unity," *New York Times*, 2 November 1941, S11; "Sports of the Times," *New York Times*, 7 November 1941, 30; Keys, *Globalizing Sport*, 70; "international accord" quote in Hoffman to Department of State, 10 September 1934, ABC, Box 1, Reel 1, ICOSA.

31. John Lucas, "American Preparations for the First Post World War Olympic Games, 1919–1920," *Journal of Sport History* 10, no. 2 (1983): 30–44, Kirby quote on 42.

32. George Eisen, "The Voices of Sanity: American Diplomatic Reports from the 1936 Berlin Olympiad," *Journal of Sport History* 11 no. 3 (1984): 56–78, Messersmith quote on 68; Stephen R. Wenn, "A Tale of Two Diplomats: George S. Messersmith and Charles H. Sherrill on Proposed American Participation in the 1936 Olympics," *Journal of Sport History* 16, no. 1 (1989): 27–43, Hull quote on 42; Stephen R. Wenn, "A Suitable Policy of Neutrality? FDR and the Question of American Participation in the 1936 Olympics," *International Journal of the History of Sport* 8, no. 3 (1991): 319–35.

33. Guttmann, *Games Must Go On*, 2–11, 28, 38–42, 47–49, first quote on 28, second quote on 254.

34. Avery Brundage to Miguel A. Moenck, 24 January 1955, ABC, Box 60, Reel 36, ICOSA.

35. The Olympic Charter operates as the constitution of the IOC and has had various names since Coubertin created it in 1908. Although it has been called the Olympic Charter only since 1978, for the sake of ease I will refer to it by this name.

36. Guttmann, *Games Must Go On*, 138; Robert K. Barney, "Avery Brundage," in *Encyclopedia of the Modern Olympic Movement*, ed. John E. Findling and Kimberly D. Pelle (Westport, CT: Greenwood Press, 2004), 471–82.

37. John D. Windhausen and Irina V. Tsypkina, "National Identity and the Emergence of the Sports Movement in Late Imperial Russia," *International Journal of the History of Sport* 12, no. 2 (1995):165–182; James Riordan, "The USSR and the Olympic Games," *Stadion* 6 (1980): 291–93; Victor Peppard and James Riordan, *Playing Politics: Soviet Sport Diplomacy to 1992* (Greenwich, CT: Jai Press, 1993), 22–24; Alexander Sunik, "Russia in the Olympic Movement around 1900," *Journal of Olympic History* 10, no. 3 (2002): 46–60.

38. Carolyn Marvin, "Avery Brundage and American Participation in the 1936 Olympic Games," *Journal of American Studies* 16, no. 1 (1982): 105.

39. Peter Singer, *Marx* (Oxford: Oxford University Press, 1980), 60.

40. James Riordan, "Marx, Lenin and Physical Culture," *Journal of Sport History* 3, no. 2 (1976): 152.

41. Barbara Keys, "Soviet Sport and Transnational Mass Culture in the 1930s," *Journal of Contemporary History* 38, no. 3 (2003): 417; Susan Grant, *Physical Culture and Sport in Soviet Society: Propaganda, Acculturation, and Transformation in the 1920s and 1930s* (New York: Routledge, 2013), 30–35.

42. Robert Edelman, *Serious Fun: A History of Spectator Sports in the U.S.S.R.* (New York: Oxford University Press, 1993), 44–56.

43. André Gounot, "Sport or Political Organization: Structures and Characteristics of the Red Sport International, 1921–1937," *Journal of Sport History* 28, no. 1 (Spring 2001): 23–39.

44. Keys, "Soviet Sport," 413–34; Edelman, *Serious Fun*, 49–51.

45. Keys, "Soviet Sport," 423–24, "reds" quote on 24; Henry Morton, *Soviet Sport, Mirror of Soviet Society* (London: Crowell-Collier, 1963), quote on 83.

46. Riordan, *Sport in Soviet Society*, 162–63, quotes on 162.

47. Cited in Jenifer Parks, "Red Sport, Red Tape: The Olympic Games, the Soviet Sports Bureaucracy, and the Cold War, 1952–1980" (PhD diss., University of North Carolina at Chapel Hill, 2009), 42.

48. Sigfrid Edström to Otto Mayer, 24 April 1951, Recognition Requests of the NOC of the USSR: Correspondence and Recognition, 1935–51, Box 238, International Olympic Committee Archives (hereafter referred to as IOC Archives), Lausanne, Switzerland.

49. Brundage to Edström, 15 November 1947, ABC, Box 149, Reel 84, ICOSA; Edström to Brundage, 25 October 1950, Recognition Requests of the NOC of the USSR: Correspondence and Recognition, 1935–51, Box 238, IOC Archives.

50. Edström to members of the IOC, no date (circa 1950), Recognition Requests of the NOC of the USSR: Correspondence and Recognition, 1935–51, Box 238, IOC Archives.

51. Guttmann, *Games Must Go On*, 72, 90–94; Marvin, "Avery Brundage and American Participation in the 1936 Olympic Games," 81–105.

52. Leif Yttergren, "J. Sigfrid Edström, Anti-Semitism, and the 1936 Berlin Olympics," *Olympika* 16 (2007): 77–91, quote on 78; Edward S. Goldstein, "Sigfrid Edström," in *Encyclopedia of the Modern Olympic Movement*, 468–71.

53. Edström to Friends and Family, 8 August 1950, Biography, Press Cuttings, Circulars, and Speeches of Sigfrid Edström, Box 4, IOC Archives.

54. Guttmann, *The Olympics*, 87.

55. Brundage to Edström, 7 December 1950, ABC, Box 149, Reel 84, ICOSA.

56. Guttmann, *Games Must Go On*, 133–38; "Private and Confidential," by Brundage, no date, ABC, Box 149, Reel 84, ICOSA.

57. Mayer to Nicolai Romanov, 25 May 1947, Recognition Requests of the NOC of the USSR: Correspondence and Recognition, 1935–51, Box 238, IOC Archives; Mayer to Romanov, 15 December 1947, Recognition Requests of the NOC of the USSR: Correspondence and Recognition, 1935–51, Box 238, IOC Archives; Parks, "Verbal Gymnastics," 30–33; Peter J. Beck, "The British Government and the Olympic Movement: The 1948 London Olympics," *International Journal of the History of Sport* 25, no. 5 (2008): 631–32, quote on 632.

58. Sobolev to Edström, 23 April 1951, Recognition Requests of the NOC of the USSR: Correspondence and Recognition, 1935–51, Box 238, IOC Archives; Edström to Mayer, 24 April 1951, Recognition Requests of the NOC of the USSR: Correspondence and Recognition, 1935–51, Box 238, IOC Archives; Edström to Mayer, 25 April 1951, Recognition Requests of the NOC of the USSR: Correspondence and Recognition, 1935–51, Box 238, IOC Archives; Guttmann, *Games Must Go On*, 138; Brundage, "Private and Confidential."

59. Quotes in Brundage, "Private and Confidential"; Guttmann, *Games Must Go On*, 139.

60. Quote in Edström to Mayer, 21 June 1951, Correspondence of Sigfrid Edström, April 1950–March 1952, Box 3, IOC Archives; Guttmann, *Games Must Go On*, 139–40.

61. Brundage to Douglas Roby, 15 November 1952, ABC, Box 62, Reel 37, ICOSA.

62. Brundage to Mayer, 3 November 1955, Correspondence of Avery Brundage, 1954–55, Box 4, IOC Archives.

63. Mayer to Andrianov, 16 January 1961, IOC Member Andrianov, Konstantin, 1951–, IOC Archives.

64. Quote in Brundage to Andrianov, 2 September 1954, ABC, Box 50, Reel 30, ICOSA; Guttmann, *Games Must Go On*, 140–41.

65. Brundage to Mayer, 9 December 1954, Correspondence of Brundage, 1954–55, Box 4, IOC Archives.

66. Brundage to George L. Rider, 11 April 1959, Correspondence of Avery Brundage, 1956–60, Box 5, IOC Archives.

67. Guttmann, *Games Must Go On*, 97.

68. "Brundage Pleas to Protect Olympics from Those with Ulterior Motives," *Hartford Courant*, 14 June 1955, p. 18A.

69. Barbara Keys, "The Early Cold War Olympics, 1952–1960: Political, Economic and Human Rights Dimensions," in *The Palgrave Handbook of Olympic Studies*, ed. Helen Lenskyi and Stephen Wagg (Houndsmills, U.K.: Palgrave Macmillan, 2012), 72–73.

70. Cited in Harold Lechenperg, ed., *Olympic Games 1960* (New York: A. S. Barnes, 1960), 5.

Chapter 3. A Campaign of Truth

1. W. Averell Harriman to Secretary of State, 12 December 1945, Record Group 59 (hereafter referred to as RG), Central Decimal File, 1945–49, Box 6659, 861.4063/12–1245, National Archives (hereafter referred to as NA), College Park, Maryland.

2. George Kennan to Secretary of State, 12 December 1945, RG59, Central Decimal File, 1945–49, Box 6659, 861.4063/12–1245, NA.

3. "Cultural Relations: U.S.–U.S.S.R.," *Department of State Bulletin*, 30 January 1949, 406; Harriman to Secretary of State, 15 November 1945, RG59, Central Decimal File, 1945–49, Box 6659, 861.40634/11–1545, NA; Peter J. Beck, "'War minus the Shooting': George Orwell on International Sport and the Olympics," *Sport in History* 33, no. 1 (2013): 72–94. For the tour of Dynamo Moscow, see, for example, Peter J. Beck, "Britain and the Cold War's 'Cultural Olympics': Responding to the Political Drive of Soviet Sport, 1945–58," *Contemporary British History* 19, no. 2 (2005): 169–85; and Ronnie Kowalski and Dilwyn Porter, "Cold War Football: British European Encounters in the 1940s and 1950s," in *East Plays West: Sport and the Cold War*, ed. Stephen Wagg and David L. Andrews (New York: Routledge, 2007), 64–81.

4. Barrett M. Reed, "Moscow Observations: Soviet Conduct of Tournaments as Indicated by Recent Women's World Chess Championship," 23 January 1950, RG59, Central Decimal File, 1950–54, Box 5167, 861.4536/I-2350, NA.

5. In 1940, the American Olympic Association was renamed the United States of America Sports Federation and then, in 1945, it was changed to the United States Olympic Association. Both these organizations administered the United States Olympic Committee (previously the American Olympic Committee), which was formed every four years to organize the Olympic team for each convocation of the games. For the sake of simplicity, I will use the United States Olympic Committee to refer to the organization of all Olympic matters in the United States during the Cold War. Apart from keeping things simple, there is a further justification. The correspondence from U.S. Olympic officials is nearly always with a USOC letterhead and they generally refer to this designation when discussing Olympic matters. For more on this, see Allen Guttmann, *The Games Must Go On: Avery Brundage and the Olympic Movement* (New York: Columbia University Press, 1984), 88; and Robert P. Watson and Larry Maloney, "The U.S. Olympic Committee," in *Encyclopedia of the Modern Olympic Movement*, ed. John E. Findling and Kimberly D. Pelle (Westport, CT: Greenwood Press, 2004), 500.

6. Both NSC quotes in Thomas H. Hertzold and John Lewis Gaddis, eds., *Containment: Documents on American Policy and Strategy, 1945–1950* (New York: Columbia University Press, 1978), 204, 391.

7. Shawn J. Parry-Giles, *The Rhetorical Presidency, Propaganda, and the Cold War, 1945–1955* (Westport, CT: Praeger, 2002), 49–50.

8. "The Soviet 'Peace' Offensive," 9 December 1949, *Foreign Relations of the United States* (hereafter referred to as *FRUS*) *1949, Volume V, Eastern Europe; The Soviet Union* (Washington, DC: U.S. Government Printing Office, 1976), 839–49.

9. Edward W. Barrett, *Truth Is Our Weapon* (New York: Funk and Wagnalls, 1953); Nicholas J. Cull, *The Cold War and the United States Information Agency: American Propaganda and Public Diplomacy, 1945–1989* (Cambridge: Cambridge University Press, 2008), 51–62.

10. "Address on Foreign Policy at a Luncheon of the American Society of Newspaper Editors," 20 April 1950, *Public Papers of the Presidents of the United States: Harry S. Truman, 1950* (Washington, DC: U.S. Government Printing Office, 1965), 260–64.

11. "Support for an Expanded Information and Education Program," *Department of State Bulletin*, 17 July 1950, 100–102.

12. "Forging a Free World with a Truth Campaign," *Department of State Bulletin*, 17 July 1950, 104.

13. Gary D. Rawnsley, "The Campaign of Truth: A Populist Propaganda," in *Cold War Propaganda in the 1950s*, ed. Gary D. Rawnsley (Houndsmills, U.K.: Macmillan, 1999), 36–37; Walter L. Hixson, *Parting the Curtain: Propaganda, Culture, and the Cold War, 1945–1961* (New York: St. Martin's Press, 1997), 16.

14. "The Overt International Information and Educational Exchange Programs of the United States," *Department of State Bulletin*, 31 March 1952, 483–89; Hixson, *Parting the Curtain*, 21, 35–55; [W.] Scott Lucas, "Campaigns of Truth: The Psychological Strategy Board and American Ideology, 1951–1953," *International History Review* 18, no. 2 (1996): 287–88.

15. Joseph A. Robinson to Department of State, 31 March 1950, RG59, Central Decimal File, 1950–54, Box 4937, 848.453/3–3150, NA.

16. Donald R. Heath to Secretary of State, 22 June 1948, RG59, Central Decimal File, 1945–49, Box 7101, 874.4063/6–2248, NA.

17. Jenifer Parks, "Verbal Gymnastics: Sports, Bureaucracy, and the Soviet Union's Entrance into the Olympic Games, 1946–1952," in *East Plays West: Sport and the Cold War*, ed. Stephen Wagg and David L. Andrews (New York: Routledge, 2007), 27–44.

18. "The Kremlin's Intensified Campaign in the Field of Cultural Affairs," *Department of State Bulletin*, 3 December 1951, 903–7.

19. John McSweeney to Department of State, 9 January 1952, RG59, Central Decimal File, 1950–54, Box 4371, 800.4531/1–952, NA.

20. McSweeney to Department of State, 15 February 1952, RG59, Central Decimal File, 1950–54, Box 4371, 800.4531/2–1552, NA; quotes in George Kennan to Secretary of State, 18 July 1952, RG59, Central Decimal File, 1950–54, Box 5167, 861.4531/7–1852, NA.

21. Frances E. Willis to Department of State, 10 August 1951, RG59, Central Decimal File, 1950–54, Box 4371, 800.4531/8–1051, NA. Jenifer Parks has noted that "Soviet sports

administrators exploited the rhetoric of peace, common to both Olympism and Soviet communist ideology, to justify the Soviet presence in the Olympic Movement" to both their government and the International Olympic Committee ("Red Sport, Red Tape: The Olympic Games, The Soviet Sports Bureaucracy, and the Cold War, 1952–1980," PhD diss.: University of North Carolina at Chapel Hill, 2009), 90.

22. "Stalin Trains His Olympic Teams," *New York Times*, 20 April 1952, SM19.

23. For more on the media reaction to the Soviet Union's entrance into the Olympics, see, for instance, Anthony Moretti, "*New York Times* Coverage of the Soviet Union's Entrance into the Olympic Games," *Sport History Review* 38 (2007): 55–72.

24. Stephen J. Whitfield, *The Culture of the Cold War* (Baltimore: Johns Hopkins University Press, 1991), 3–25, 37–42.

25. See T. L. Barnard to Dunning, Morris, Edwards, Kohler, LaBlonde, and Johnson, no date. The memorandum is appended to a report from Orville C. Anderson to Kirkpatrick and Kellerman, 3 October 1951, RG59, Central Decimal File, 1950–54, Box 4371, 800.4531/10–351, NA.

26. Truman quote in "Address on Foreign Policy," 264; see also Cull, *Cold War*, 56.

27. Barrett memorandum, 30 October 1951, RG306, Office of Administration, 1952–55, Box 4, "Private Enterprise Cooperation, 1952–53," NA.

28. For more on U.S. state–private connections see Scott Lucas, *Freedom's War: The American Crusade against the Soviet Union* (New York: New York University Press, 1999); and Hugh Wilford, *The Mighty Wurlitzer: How the CIA Played America* (Cambridge, MA: Harvard University Press, 2008).

29. Quote in Barrett, *Truth Is Our Weapon*, 94; Nicholas J. Cull, "Public Diplomacy and the Private Sector: The United States Information Agency, Its Predecessors and the Private Sector," in *The U.S. Government, Citizen Groups and the Cold War: The State–Private Network*, ed. Helen Laville and Hugh Wilford (New York: Routledge, 2006), 214–15; Cull, *Cold War*, 56–58; Kenneth Osgood, *Total Cold War: Eisenhower's Secret Propaganda Battle at Home and Abroad* (Lawrence: University Press of Kansas, 2006), 229–32; *USIE Newsletter* No. 2, 2 July 1951, Harry S. Truman Papers (hereafter referred to as Truman Papers), Staff Member and Office Files: Psychological Strategy Board Files, 1951–53, Box 29, "350 File 1, Department of State—USIE Program—July 27, 1951," Harry S. Truman Presidential Library (hereafter referred to as HSTL), Independence, Missouri.

30. Walsh to Barrett, 15 November 1951, RG306, Office of Administration, 1952–55, Box 4, "Private Enterprise Cooperation, 1952–53," NA.

31. Quote in Walsh to Barrett, "1952 Olympics—Progress Report No. 4," no date (circa December 1951), RG306, Office of Administration, 1952–55, Box 4, "Private Enterprise Cooperation, 1952–53," NA; Walsh to Avery Brundage, 22 January 1952, Avery Brundage Collection, 1908–75 (hereafter referred to as ABC), Box 158, Reel 90, International Centre for Olympic Studies Archives (hereafter referred to as ICOSA), University of Western Ontario, London, Canada.

32. Walsh to Ralph Block, 6 November 1951, RG306, Office of Administration, 1952–55, Box 4, "Private Enterprise Cooperation, 1952–53," NA; Walsh to John Begg and Wilson Compton, 10 April 1952, RG306, Office of Administration, 1952–55, Box 4, "Private Enterprise Cooperation, 1952–53," NA.

33. J. E. Saugsted to Joseph Mayber, 19 March 1952, RG59, Central Decimal File, 1950–54, Box 4371, 800.4531/3-1952, NA.

34. In 1951, the Psychological Strategy Board also listed the USOC as an organization that could be useful in psychological operations. See "Inventory of Instrumentalities," 28 November 1951, *United States Declassified Documents Reference System* (Woodbridge, CT, 1997), document 563.

35. The records of the AAU and USOC also reveal anticommunism in both organizations. In 1950, for example, the president of the AAU, Albert F. Wheltle, called attention to what he saw as the role of international sport in "combating communism." See "Minutes of the 62nd Annual Meeting of the AAU," December 1950, Archives of the Amateur Athletic Union of the United States (hereafter referred to as AAU Archives), Lake Buena Vista, Florida. For more on Avery Brundage's anticommunism, see, for instance, Guttmann, *Games Must Go On.*

36. Heather L. Dichter, "Sporting Democracy: The Western Allies' Reconstruction of Germany through Sport, 1944–1952," PhD diss.: University of Toronto, 2008, 236–309.

37. Elwood Williams to a Mr. Byroade, 30 August 1951, RG59, Central Decimal File, 1950–54, Box 4371, 800.4531/5-2851, NA; Donnelly [only last name on document] to Department of State, 4 May 1951, RG59, Central Decimal File, 1950–54, Box 4371, 800.4531/5-451, NA. Aside from representing the United States Olympic fencing team at the games of 1920 and 1924, Parker was an assistant secretary of War Risk Insurance for the Treasury Department from 1914 to 1916, and the assistant secretary of the American–Mexican Joint Commission on Arbitration for the State Department in 1916. During World War I, he served as an officer in army aviation and, in 1938, was the technical advisor to the U.S. delegation at a diplomatic conference on air law. See Dichter, "Sporting Democracy," 303–4; "J. Brooks Parker, Olympic Official," *New York Times*, 1 December 1951, 9.

38. James Webb to J. Brooks B. Parker, 11 September 1951, RG59, Central Decimal File, 1950–54, Box 4371, 800.4531/1357, NA; Parker to Dr. W. C. Johnstone, 2 October 1951, RG59, Central Decimal File, 1950–54, Box 4371, 800.4531/10-251, NA; E. M. Kraemer to Joseph Kolarek, 12 December 1951, RG59, Central Decimal File, 1950–54, Box 5116, 857.4531/12-1251, NA.

39. Barrett to Brundage, 16 October 1951, ABC, Box 332, Reel 145, ICOSA.

40. Arthur Daley, "Sports of the Times," *New York Times*, 10 June 1952, 32.

41. "1952 Olympics," *New York Times*, 13 June 1952, 22.

42. Brundage to Harry Truman, 27 October 1951, ABC, Box 332, Reel 145, ICOSA; Truman to Brundage, 7 November 1947, ABC, Box 332, Reel 145, ICOSA; quotes in Truman to Brundage, 10 November 1951, Truman Papers, Presidents Personal File, Box 485, "PPF 468-F Olympic Games," HSTL.

43. "Truman Proclamation for Olympic Week," 17 May 1952, RG59, Central Decimal File, 1950–54, Box 4371, 800.4531/5-1952, NA; "Congress Urges Olympic Fund," *Washington Post*, 16 May 1952, B7; "Olympic Week to Begin," *New York Times*, 17 May 1952, 24.; Thomas M. Domer, "Sport in Cold War America, 1953–1963: The Diplomatic and Political Use of Sport in the Eisenhower and Kennedy Administrations," PhD diss., Marquette University, 1976, 45–47; Brundage, "An Urgent Appeal to Newspaper Publishers of the United States," no date, ABC, Box 160, Reel 91, ICOSA.

44. For these and other advertisements, see ABC, Box 160, Reel 91, ICOSA.

45. Walsh to Barrett, "1952 Olympics—Progress Report No.4," no date (circa December 1951), RG306, Office of Administration, 1952–55, Box 4, "Private Enterprise Cooperation, 1952–53," NA.

46. "The Soviet Athlete in International Competition," *Department of State Bulletin*, 24 December 1951, 1007–10.

47. A rare deviation from this policy occurred in 1951, when the State Department organized an exhibition basketball game between the Harlem Globetrotters and the Boston Whirlwinds at the Olympic stadium in West Berlin. The contest, which attracted a massive crowd of 75,000 spectators, clearly left its mark on Dean Acheson, who admitted that the Globetrotters had provided a potential "answer to Communist charges of racial prejudice in the U.S.A." See Damion L. Thomas, *Globetrotting: African American Athletes and Cold War Politics* (Urbana: University of Illinois Press, 2012), 45–47; "75,000 in Berlin Hail Jesse Owens," *New York Times*, 23 August 1951, 37.

48. First quote in Walsh to Barrett, 30 October 1951, RG306, Office of Administration, 1952–55, Box 4, "Private Enterprise Cooperation, 1952–53," NA; Dean Acheson to Certain American Diplomatic Officers, 24 October 1951, RG59, Central Decimal File, 1950–54, Box 4371, 800.4531/10–2451, NA; second quote in Webb to Legation in Vienna, 24 November 1951, RG59, Central Decimal File, 1950–54, Box 4371, 800.4531/11–951, NA. The officers contacted, as the plan recommended, were mostly in Western Europe.

49. William R. Tyler to Department of State, 6 November 1951, RG59, Central Decimal File, 1950–54, Box 4371, 800.4531/11–651, NA.

50. Quote in Walsh to Compton and Begg, "Report on 1952 Winter Olympic Games at Oslo, Norway," 3 April 1952, RG306, Office of Administration, 1952–55, Box 4, "Private Enterprise Cooperation, 1952–53," NA; "Minutes of the 63rd Annual Meeting of the AAU," November–December 1951, AAU Archives; "Minutes of the 64th Annual Meeting of the AAU," December 1952, AAU Archives.

51. First quote in Walsh to Brundage, 22 January 1952, ABC, Box 158, Reel 90, ICOSA; John M. Cabot to Secretary of State, 10 July 1952, RG59, Central Decimal File, 1950–54, Box 4372, 800.4531/7–1052, NA; Brundage quote in "Olympic Team Cautioned," *Times of India*, 10 July 1952, 9; Walsh to Ralph Block, 6 November 1951, RG306, Office of Administration, 1952–55, Box 4, "Private Enterprise Cooperation, 1952–53," NA.

52. Walsh to Barrett, "1952 Olympics—Progress Report No.4," no date (circa December 1951), RG306, Office of Administration, 1952–55, Box 4, "Private Enterprise Cooperation, 1952–53," NA.

53. T. L. Barnard to Dunning, Morris, Edwards, Kohler, LaBlonde, and Johnson, no date, 3 October 1951, RG59, Central Decimal File, 1950–54, Box 4371, 800.4531/10–351, NA. For more on U.S. Olympic coverage in 1948, see Walsh to Barrett, 30 October 1951, RG306, Office of Administration, 1952–55, Box 4, "Private Enterprise Cooperation, 1952–53," NA.

54. Block to Walsh, 19 November 1951, RG306, Office of Administration, 1952–55, Box 4, "Private Enterprise Cooperation, 1952–53," NA. For the historical antecedents of these ideas, see Mark Dyreson, *Making the American Team: Sport, Culture, and the Olympic Experience* (Urbana: University of Illinois Press, 1998).

55. Johnstone to Parker, 30 November 1951, ABC, Box 158, Reel 90, ICOSA; Walsh to Barrett, 15 November 1951, RG306, Office of Administration, 1952–55, Box 4, "Private Enterprise Cooperation, 1952–53," NA; Walsh to Barrett, 22 January 1952, RG306, Office of Administration, 1952–55, Box 4, "Private Enterprise Cooperation, 1952–53," NA. The CIA front group, the National Committee for a Free Europe, also communicated with Walsh about the possibility of distributing brochures in Helsinki that would encourage the defection of Soviet bloc athletes. See H. B. Miller to Walsh, 18 April 1952, RFE/RL INC. Corporate Records, Box 245, File 4, "Olympic Games General, 1951–1959," Hoover Institution Archives, Stanford University, California.

56. Laura A. Belmonte, "Exporting America: The U.S. Propaganda Offensive, 1945–1959," in *The Arts of Democracy: Art, Public Culture, and the State,* ed. Casey Nelson Blake (Philadelphia: University of Pennsylvania Press, 2007), 123.

57. Reed Harris to Johnstone, 30 April 1952, RG59, Central Decimal File, 1950–54, Box 4371, 800.4531/4–3052, NA.

58. The term "sporting republic" is from Dyreson, *Making the American Team.*

59. Block to Walsh, 19 November 1951, RG306, Office of Administration, 1952–55, Box 4, "Private Enterprise Cooperation, 1952–53," NA. For an example of these themes, see "Sports World," 19 June 1952, *USIS Feature,* RG 306, USIS Feature via Airmail thru World Affairs Bulletin (hereafter referred to as USIS Feature), Box 3, File 2, "USIS Features via Airmail," NA.

60. "Sports World," 19 June 1952, *USIS Feature,* RG 306, USIS Feature, Box 3, File 2, "USIS Features via Airmail," NA.

61. "Sports World," 11 April 1952, *USIS Feature,* RG 306, USIS Feature, Box 3, File 1, "USIS Features via Airmail," NA.

62. T. L. Barnard to Dunning, Morris, Edwards, Kohler, LaBlonde, and Johnson, no date, RG59, Central Decimal File, 1950–54, Box 4371, 800.4531/10–351, NA.

63. "The United State Prepares for the 1952 Olympic Games," 5 December 1951, *U.S.A. Life Bulletin,* RG 306, USIS Feature, Box 2, File 2, "USA Life Bulletin," NA.

64. "U.S. Olympic Ski Team Ready for 1952 Winter Games in Oslo," 21 November 1951, *U.S.A. Life Bulletin,* RG 306, USIS Feature, Box 2, File 2, "USA Life Bulletin," NA.

65. "U.S. Equestrian Team Training for Olympics," 20 March 1952, *USIS Feature,* RG 306, USIS Feature, Box 3, File 1, "USIS Features via Airmail," NA.

66. See for instance, "Dick Button, U.S. Olympic and World Figure-Skating Champion," 9 January 1952, *U.S.A. Life Bulletin,* RG 306, USIS Feature, Box 2, File 2, "USA Life Bulletin," NA; and "The Reverend Robert E. Richards U.S. Pole-vaulter," 28 February 1952, *USIS Feature,* RG 306, USIS Feature, Box 3, File 2, "USIS Features via Airmail," NA.

67. "New York City Helping to Finance U.S. Olympic Team," 24 April 1952, *USIS Feature,* RG 306, USIS Feature, Box 3, File 1, "USIS Features via Airmail," NA.

68. "Harrison Dillard U.S. Hurdler and Sprinter," 8 May 1952, *USIS Feature,* RG 306, USIS Feature, Box 3, File 2, "USIS Features via Airmail," NA.

69. "16 U.S. Gymnasts Ready for Olympic Games," 5 June 1952, *USIS Feature,* RG 306, USIS Feature, Box 3, File 2, "USIS Features via Airmail," NA; Laura A. Belmonte, *Selling the America Way: U.S. Propaganda and the Cold War* (Philadelphia: University of Pennsylvania Press, 2008), 152.

70. Barrett to Walsh, 30 October 1951, RG306, Office of Administration, 1952–55, Box 4, "Private Enterprise Cooperation, 1952–53," NA. For more on the anticommunist rhetoric of the Campaign of Truth, see, for instance, Hixson, *Parting the Curtain*, 38.

71. "Olympic Torch Relay Symbol of International Good Will," 20 March 1952, *USIS Feature*, RG 306, USIS Feature, Box 3, File 1, "USIS Features via Airmail," NA.

72. Walsh to Compton and Begg, "Report on 1952 Winter Olympic Games at Oslo, Norway," 3 April 1952, RG306, Office of Administration, 1952–55, Box 4, "Private Enterprise Cooperation, 1952–53," NA.

73. Walsh to John Devine, 9 November 1951, RG306, Office of Administration, 1952–55, Box 4, "Private Enterprise Cooperation, 1952–53," NA; Walsh to Compton and Begg, "Report on 1952 Winter Olympic Games at Oslo, Norway," 3 April 1952, RG306, Office of Administration, 1952–55, Box 4, "Private Enterprise Cooperation, 1952–53," NA.

74. "Pep Talks by Soviet Press Urge Red Athletes to Annex Crowns," *New York Times*, 21 July 1952, 22; "Pravda Notes Finns' Aim," *New York Times*, 16 January 1951, 12; "Communists Defy Truce Tradition to Spread Propaganda at Classic," *New York Times*, 22 July 1952, 30.

75. Cabot to Secretary of State, 10 July 1952, RG59, Central Decimal File, 1950–54, Box 4372, 800.4531/7-1052, NA.

76. David G. Wilson to Department of State, 29 July 1952, RG59, Central Decimal File, 1950–54, Box 4372, 800.4531/7-2952, NA; Wilson to Department of State, 5 September 1952, RG59, Central Decimal File, 1950–54, Box 4372, 800.4531/9-552, NA.

77. Vesa Tikander, "Helsinki," in *Encyclopedia of the Modern Olympic Movement*, ed. John E. Findling and Kimberly D. Pelle (Westport, CT: Greenwood Press, 2004), 135–45; Allen Guttmann, *The Olympics: A History of the Modern Games* (Urbana: University of Illinois Press, 2002), 85–96.

78. Allison Danzig, "Russia Overtaken: U.S. Beats Soviet Five, 36 to 25, and Gains Five . . ." *New York Times*, 3 August 1952, S1.

79. Parks, "Verbal Gymnastics," 40.

80. For more on feedback on propaganda, see Maurice S. Rice to Department of State, 27 May 1952, RG59, Central Decimal File, 1950–54, Box 4371, 800.4531/5-2752, NA; Donald C. Dunham to Department of State, 5 June 1952, RG59, Central Decimal File, 1950–54, Box 4371, 800.4531/6-552, NA; Sidney Sober to Department of State, 13 June 1952, RG59, Central Decimal File, 1950–54, Box 4371, 800.4531/6-1352, NA.

81. Reed Harris to Johnstone, 30 April 1952, RG59, Central Decimal File, 1950–54, Box 4371, 800.4531/4-3052, NA.

82. Wilson to Department of State, 8 May 1952, RG59, Central Decimal File, 1950–54, Box 4371, 800.4531/5-852, NA.

83. Cabot to Secretary of State, 26 May 1952, RG59, Central Decimal File, 1950–54, Box 5155, 860E.4531/2-2652, NA; Cabot to Secretary of State, 29 April 1952, RG59, Central Decimal File, 1950–54, Box 5155, 860E.4531/4-2952, NA.

84. Brundage to Ketseas, 10 October 1952, Correspondence and Telegrams at the Olympic Games of Helsinki 1952, Box 3, IOC Archives; Brundage to Massard, Scharroo, Burghley, Prince Axel, Taher Pacha, and Mayer, 21 October 1952, Correspondence and Telegrams at the Olympic Games of Helsinki 1952, Box 3, IOC Archives.

85. "New Marathon for Zatopek," *San Francisco Chronicle*, 5 August 1952, Correspondence and Telegrams at the Olympic Games of Helsinki 1952, Box 3, IOC Archives.

86. Cabot to Department of State, 15 August 1952, RG59, Central Decimal File, 1950–54, Box 4372, 800.4531/8–1552, NA.

Chapter 4. *The Union of Free Eastern European Sportsmen*

1. Count Antal (Anthony) Szápáry to Avery Brundage, 17 January 1950, Avery Brundage Collection, 1908–75 (hereafter cited as ABC), Box 132, Reel 73, International Centre for Olympic Studies Archives (hereafter cited as ICOSA), University of Western Ontario, London, Ontario, Canada.

2. George Telegdy to John Matthews, no date, C. D. Jackson: Papers, 1931–67, Series 2, Time INC. File, 1933–64, Subseries A, Alphabetical File, 1933–64 (hereafter referred to as Jackson Papers), Box 53, File 3, "Free Europe Committee, 1960," Dwight D. Eisenhower Presidential Library (hereafter referred to as DDEL), Abilene, Kansas.

3. See, for example, Helen Laville, "The Committee of Correspondence: CIA Funding of Women's Groups, 1952–1967," *Intelligence and National Security* 12, no. 1 (1997): 112.

4. Shepardson memorandum, 25 March 1953, RFE/RL INC. Corporate Records (hereafter referred to as RFE/RL), Box 191, File 5, "Free Europe Committee, Inc. Policy General, 1949–1956," Hoover Institution Archives (hereafter referred to as HA), Stanford University, California.

5. Cited in Scott Lucas, *Freedom's War: The American Crusade against the Soviet Union* (New York: New York University Press, 1999), 100.

6. Wisner memorandum, 22 November 1950, Central Intelligence Agency website, www.foia.cia.gov/ (hereafter referred to as CIA FOIA).

7. "Radio Free Europe Policy Handbook," 30 November 1951, *United States Declassified Documents Reference System* (Woodbridge, CT, 1986), document 1974.

8. "Presidents Report" for the NCFE, appended to a letter from Whitney H. Sherpardson to Allen W. Dulles, 10 April 1953, CIA FOIA; Walter L. Hixson, *Parting the Curtain: Propaganda, Culture, and the Cold War, 1945–1961* (New York: St. Martin's Press, 1997), 60–63.

9. "Radio Free Europe Policy Handbook"; "Thumbnail Sketches of Typical Radio Free Europe Programs," no date, Charles Hulten Papers (hereafter referred to as Hulten Papers), Box 22, File 2, "Radio Free Europe," Harry S. Truman Presidential Library (hereafter referred to HSTL), Independence, Missouri.

10. Pavel Tigrid to William T. Rafael, 13 December 1950, RFE/RL, Box 275, File 4, "Czechoslovakian Desk, 1949–1950," HA.

11. "Special Report No. 16, Listener Suggestions for RFE Polish Programs," April 1957, RFE/RL, Box 278, File 3, "Polish Desk General, 1952–1958," HA.

12. Zbigniew Brzezinski to John L. Dunning, 14 October 1959, RFE/RL, Box 271, File 3, "Broadcasting Review, 1959," HA.

13. Lewis Galantiere memorandum, "Interview with Four Hungarian Refugees," 21 October 1953, RFE/RL, Box 211, File 4, "Hungary, 1949–1957," HA.

14. William Snow to Department of State, 2 February 1952, Record Group 59 (hereafter referred to as RG), Central Decimal File, 1950–54, Box 4371, 800.4531/1–3152, National

Archives (hereafter referred to as NA), College Park, Maryland; Snow to Department of State, 31 January 1952, RG59, Central Decimal File, 1950–54, Box 4371, 800.4531/1–3152, NA.

15. "Political Preparation for Sport," *News from behind the Iron Curtain* 1, no. 2 (February 1952): 37; "Presidents Report."

16. "Olympics Preview," *News from behind the Iron Curtain* 1, no. 7 (July 1952): 42.

17. C. K. Huston to Robert Minton, 29 September 1959, RFE/RL, Box 197, File 7, "Free Europe Organizations & Publications," HA; "FEOP Exile Organizations in Europe," 16 September 1960, RFE/RL, Box 199, File 1, "Free Europe Organizations & Publications, Exile Political Organizations Division, Exile Organizations in Europe, 1960," HA.

18. Szápáry to Brundage, 24 May 1950, ABC, Box 116, Reel 63, ICOSA. It appears that the Hungarian National Council did exercise—or, at least, tried to exercise—some control over the HNSF in return for supporting the HNSF's interests in the NCFE. This situation was indicative of the broader power struggles within the HNC, in which supporters of former Hungarian prime minister Ferenc Nagy collided with supporters of Tibor Eckhardt. In the case of the HNSF, it was Nagy's cohort that attempted to leverage influence on Szápáry and company by claiming that they would "sponsor the association [HNSF] at the NCFE providing that the association first elects individuals who follow their political line." Apparently Szápáry, Zerkowitz, Telegdy, and Geza Gyamarthy signed an agreement on this arrangement even though Telegdy and Zerkowitz were listed as undesirables. See the report by Paul Vajda, 15 February 1951, RFE/RL, Box 277, File 5, "Hungarian Desk," HA. For the power struggle in the HNC, see Katalin Kádár Lynn, *Tibor Eckhardt: His American Years, 1941–1972* (New York: Columbia University Press, 2007), 156–70.

19. "Anthony Szapary, Led Sports Group," *New York Times*, 26 December 1972, 27; "Sylvia Szechenyi Fiancee of Count," *New York Times*, 12 February 1949, 20; "Sylvia Szechenyi Married to Count," *New York Times*, 24 April 1949, 75.

20. Szápáry to Members of the IOC Executive Committee, 20 May 1952, ABC, Box 116, Reel 63, ICOSA.

21. Szápáry to Robert McKisson, 25 May 1950, RG59, Central Decimal File, 1950–54, Box 5296, 864.453/5–2550, NA. This information on the HNSF was drawn from a "Pro-Memoria" appended to the letter. For the HNSF's incorporation, see Stein to George Telegdy, 27 March 1959, Private Papers of Count Anthony Szápáry (hereafter referred to as Szápáry Papers), Box 2, "B," Pound Ridge, New York.

22. John Foster Leich, "Great Expectations: The National Councils in Exile, 1950–60," *Polish Review* 35, no. 3 (1990): 185.

23. "Reorientation of Exile Organizations," 1 April 1960, Jackson Papers, Box 53, File 2, "Free Europe Committee, 1960," DDEL.

24. International Olympic Committee, *Fundamental Principles Rules and Regulations* (Lausanne, Switz.: International Olympic Committee, 1958), 19.

25. Brundage to Szápáry, 25 January 1950, ABC, Box 132, Reel 73, ICOSA.

26. "Flight to Freedom," *New York Times*, 17 August 1948, 20.

27. A. Gellért to Robert Cutler, April 1951, RFE/RL, Box 245, File 4, "Olympic Games General, 1951–1959," HA.

28. Peter Zerkowitz to Wright, 23 May 1951, RFE/RL, Box 245, File 4, "Olympic Games General, 1951–1959," HA; Zerkowitz to Cutler, no date, RFE/RL, Box 245, File 4, "Olympic Games General, 1951–1959," HA.

29. "Excerpt from Budapest to Hungarian Desk," 9 May 1951, RFE/RL, Box 245, File 4, "Olympic Games General, 1951–1959," HA.

30. Frank C. Wright Jr. to Ferris, 5 June 1951, ABC, Box 24, Reel 14, ICOSA; Daniel Ferris to Brundage, 6 June 1951, ABC, Box 24, Reel 14, ICOSA.

31. Ferris to Wright, 6 June 1951, RFE/RL, Box 245, File 4, "Olympic Games General, 1951–1959," HA.

32. Wright to Jackson, 26 June 1951, RFE/RL, Box 245, File 4, "Olympic Games General, 1951–1959," HA; Jackson to Brundage, 26 June 1951, RFE/RL, Box 245, File 4, "Olympic Games General, 1951–1959," HA; Wright to John T. McGovern, 30 January 1952, RFE/RL, Box 245, File 4, "Olympic Games General, 1951–1959," HA. It is unclear how Wright knew of Brundage's opinion on this issue.

33. Jackson to Brundage, 30 January 1952, ABC, Box 116, Reel 63, ICOSA; International Olympic Committee, *Olympic Rules* (Lausanne, Switz.: International Olympic Committee, 1949), 5, 18.

34. Szápáry to Brundage, 13 November 1951, ABC, Box 116, Reel 63, ICOSA; George Santelli to Brundage, 20 November 1951, ABC, Box 116, Reel 63, ICOSA.

35. Brundage to Santelli, 27 December 1951, ABC, Box 116, Reel 63, ICOSA.

36. Brundage to Szápáry, 27 December 1951, ABC, Box 116, Reel 63, ICOSA.

37. Wright to Jackson, 4 February 1952, RFE/RL, Box 245, File 4, "Olympic Games General, 1951–1959," HA.

38. Rolf Peterson to Count István Révay, 21 December 1951, RFE/RL, Box 245, File 4, "Olympic Games General, 1951–1959," HA.

39. "Minutes of the International Olympic Committee 46th Session," Oslo, 12–13 February 1952, International Olympic Committee Archives (hereafter referred to as IOC Archives), Lausanne, Switzerland.

40. Sigfrid Edström to "Members of the IOC Executive Committee," 18 March 1952, ABC, Box 43, Reel 25, ICOSA.

41. Notably, Yugoslavia was included despite Tito's split with Stalin in 1948, and East Germany was avoided altogether. See Szápáry to Brundage, 14 May 1952, ABC, Box 116, Reel 63, ICOSA.

42. Wright to Augustine, 28 February 1952, RFE/RL, Box 245, File 4, "Olympic Games General, 1951–1959," HA; Miller to Zerkowitz, 4 March 1952, RFE/RL, Box 245, File 4, "Olympic Games General, 1951–1959," HA.

43. Draft of the Constitution of the Union of Free Eastern European Sportsmen, no date (circa 1952), RFE/RL, Box 245, File 4, "Olympic Games General, 1951–1959," HA.

44. The committee also had two vice chairmen. The first was a Yugoslav, Grga Zlatoper, and the second was a Latvian named Janis Dikmanis. Dikmanis had escaped to Germany after the Soviet Union annexed Latvia and eventually made his way to the United States. He later settled in the United States, wrote articles in an anticommunist Latvian newspaper in New York, and encouraged Latvian athletes in exile to "make sport propaganda" (Janis Dikmanis to Brundage, 23 September 1951, ABC, Box 22, Reel 13, ICOSA). See also Brundage to Dietrich Wortmann, 10 January 1951, ABC, Box 42, Reel 24, ICOSA.

45. Otto Mayer to Union of Free Eastern European Sportsmen, 19 May 1952, ABC, Box 116, Reel 63, ICOSA.

46. Szápáry to Brundage, 14 May 1952, ABC, Box 116, Reel 63, ICOSA; Szápáry to John T. McGovern, 9 May 1952, ABC, Box 116, Reel 63, ICOSA.

47. McGovern to Brundage, 12 May 1952, ABC, Box 116, Reel 63, ICOSA.

48. Brundage to McGovern, 15 May 1952, ABC, Box 116, Reel 63, ICOSA.

49. "Exiles of Satellites Ask Olympics Entry," *New York Times*, 25 May 1952, 63.

50. See, for example, "'Exiled Sportsmen' Appeal for Olympic Participation," *Albuquerque Tribune*, 21 May 1952, 16.

51. "Self-Exiled European Athletes Seek to Compete as a Unit in Olympics," *Portsmouth Times*, 20 June 1952, 24.

52. "Stella Walsh Still Hopes to Make Olympic Games as 'Union' Member," *Los Angeles Times*, 2 July 1952, C2.

53. "Russia Probably Will Skip Olympics, Refugees Avow," *Charleston Gazette*, 28 April 1952, 14.

54. See, for example, "Sports to Russians Are Completely Political," *Charleston Gazette*, 30 April 1952, 16; and Richard B. Walsh to Wilson Compton and John Begg, "Report on 1952 Winter Olympic Games at Oslo, Norway," 3 April 1952, RG 306, Office of Administration, 1952–55, Box 4, "Private Enterprise Cooperation, 1952–53," NA.

55. Paul Auer to Edström, 12 March 1952, ABC, Box 43, Reel 25, ICOSA.

56. Richard J. Aldrich, "OSS, CIA and European Unity: The American Committee on United Europe, 1949–60," *Diplomacy and Statecraft* 8, no. 1 (1997): 185, 189, 190–91. A conduit was thus created to filter the money to the European Movement, called the American Committee on United Europe, organized by Allen Dulles and William Donovan, both former OSS and leaders of the U.S. intelligence community.

57. Sigfrid Edström to Members of the IOC Executive Committee, 18 March 1952, ABC, Box 43, Reel 25, ICOSA.

58. Leich, "Great Expectations," 194; A. H. Robertson, "The Council of Europe, 1949–1953," *International and Comparative Law Quarterly* 3, no. 2 (1954): 286.

59. Auer to Leich, 9 April 1952, RFE/RL, Box 342, File 4, "Special Committee to Watch over Interests of European Nations, 1951–52," HA; Mayer quote in "Consultative Assembly of the Council of Europe: Fifth Ordinary Session, 31 March 1953. Report on the Participation of Exiles in the Olympic Games," ABC, Box 116, Reel 63, ICOSA.

60. Mayer to Union of Free Eastern European Sportsmen, 19 May 1952, ABC, Box 116, Reel 63, ICOSA.

61. Szápáry to Members of the Executive Committee, 20 May 1952, ABC, Box 116, Reel 63, ICOSA.

62. Zerkowitz to Wright, 1 July 1952, RFE/RL, Box 245, File 4, "Olympic Games General, 1951–1959," HA.

63. Wright to Miller, 3 July 1952, RFE/RL, Box 245, File 4, "Olympic Games General, 1951–1959," HA; Zerkowitz to Miller, 10 July 1952, RFE/RL, Box 245, File 4, "Olympic Games General, 1951–1959," HA.

64. Thomas de Márffy-Mantuano to Brundage, 14 June 1952, ABC, Box 116, Reel 63, ICOSA; Márffy to Boyle, 5 March 1952, MS 660/3043, Correspondence and Papers of the Rt Hon. Edward Charles Gurney Boyle, Special Collections, Brotherton Library, University

of Leeds, England; Márffy to Jackson, 11 May 1951, RFE/RL, Box 245, File 4, "Olympic Games General, 1951–1959," HA.

65. This information was drawn from a book written by Márffy's sister, the countess of Listowel. The book is a personal recollection of their upbringing and struggle under communist rule. It includes the story behind her efforts to get her brother's family out of Hungary after World War II: Judith Listowel, *The Golden Tree: The Story of Peter, Tomi, and Their Family Typifies the Enduring Spirit of Hungary* (London: Odhams Press, 1958), 53, 62, quote on communism on 147.

66. Listowel, *Golden Tree*, 22–25, 50; "Judith, Countess of Listowel," *Daily Telegraph*, 22 July 2003. http://www.telegraph.co.uk/news/obituaries/1436725/Judith-Countess-of-Listowel.html.

67. Peter Zerkowitz, "Activities of the Union in Connection with the IOC and the Olympic Games in Helsinki," 24 August 1952, RFE/RL, Box 245, File 4, "Olympic Games General, 1951–1959," HA.

68. Mayer to Brundage, 8 July 1960, Correspondence of Avery Brundage, 1956–60, Box 5, IOC Archives.

69. "IOC Executive Committee Minutes," Helsinki, 12, 22–24 July and 2 August 1952, in Wolf Lyberg, ed., *IOC Executive Committee Minutes*, vol. 2 (1948–1969), 111; "Extract of the Minutes of the Executive Committee of the I.O.C. with the Delegates of the International Federations," Helsinki, 14 July 1952, *Olympic Review* 34–35 (September 1952), 34.

70. "Minutes of the International Olympic Committee 47th Session," Helsinki, 16 July 1952, IOC Archives; Zerkowitz, "Activities of the Union."

71. "Olympic Ban Queried," *New York Times*, 20 July 1952, E8.

72. Zerkowitz, "Activities of the Union."

73. Wright to Sherpardson, 6 April 1953, RFE/RL, Box 245, File 4, "Olympic Games General, 1951–1959," HA.

74. Szápáry to Brundage, 10 April 1953, ABC, Box 116, Reel 63, ICOSA. See also the telegram from the UFEES to the IOC in Mexico, 20 April 1953, RFE/RL, Box 245, File 4, "Olympic Games General, 1951–1959," HA.

75. Brundage to Szápáry, 22 May 1953, ABC, Box 116, Reel 63, ICOSA.

76. Wright to Yarrow, 13 April 1954, RFE/RL, Box 245, File 4, "Olympic Games General, 1951–1959," HA; "UFEES Special Representative at the IOC Congress, Athens," no date, RFE/RL, Box 245, File 4, "Olympic Games General, 1951–1959," HA; Márffy to IOC, 8 May 1954, ABC, Box 116, Reel 63, ICOSA.

Chapter 5. A New Olympic Challenge

1. Vladislav Zubok and Constantine Pleshakov, *Inside the Kremlin's Cold War: From Stalin to Khrushchev* (Cambridge, MA: Harvard University Press, 1996), quote on 155; Vojtech Mastney, "The Elusive Détente: Stalin's Successors and the West," in *The Cold War after Stalin's Death*, ed. Klaus Larres and Kenneth Osgood (Lanham, MD: Rowman and Littlefield, 2006), 4.

2. Kenneth Osgood, *Total Cold War: Eisenhower's Secret Propaganda Battle at Home and Abroad* (Lawrence: University Press of Kansas, 2006), 47–48, 55–57, 67–68, quote on 48.

3. Osgood, *Total Cold War*, 46–48.

4. Quote in Frederick C. Barghoorn, *The Soviet Cultural Offensive: The Role of Cultural Diplomacy in Soviet Foreign Policy* (Princeton, NJ: Princeton University Press, 1960), 17–18; Abbott Washburn to C. D. Jackson, 11 January 1955, C. D. Jackson: Papers, 1931–67, Series 2 Time INC. File, 1933–64, Subseries A, Alphabetical File, 1933–64 (hereafter referred to as Jackson Papers), Box 62, "International Sports," Dwight D. Eisenhower Presidential Library (hereafter referred to as DDEL), Abilene, Kansas; Walter L. Hixson, *Parting the Curtain: Propaganda, Culture, and the Cold War, 1945–1961* (New York: St. Martin's Press, 1997), 136.

5. Dwight D. Eisenhower to President of the Senate, 27 July 1954, Bureau of Educational and Cultural Affairs Historical Collection (hereafter referred to as CU), Box 93, File 29, University of Arkansas, Fayetteville, Arkansas; Eisenhower to Streibert, 18 August 1954, CU, Box 93, File 29; Osgood, *Total Cold War*, 219, 224–29; "Groups Abroad under the President's Fund," January 1956, CU, Box 93, File 33; "President's Special International Program: First Semi-Annual Report," CU, Box 93, File 18.

6. "International Athletics—Cold War Battleground," 28 September 1954, Jackson Papers, Box 62, "International Sports," DDEL.

7. "The Communist Sports Offensive," no date, Jackson Papers, Box 62, "International Sports," DDEL.

8. "Communist Cultural and Sports Delegations to the Free World after 1953," 6 June 1955, Record Group (hereafter referred to as RG) 306, Office of Research and Intelligence (hereafter referred to as IRI), Box 5, "Intelligence Bulletins, Memorandums and Summaries, 1954–56," National Archives (hereafter referred to as NA), College Park, Maryland; "Sports Delegation Exchanges between Communist and Free World Countries in 1955," 3 May 1956, RG 306, IRI, Box 8, "Intelligence Bulletins, Memorandums and Summaries, 1954–56," NA; "Communist Propaganda Activities in Latin America, 1955," 29 February 1956, RG 306, IRI, Box 6, "Intelligence Bulletins, Memorandums and Summaries, 1954–56," NA.

9. Harold E. Howland to Daniel Ferris, 4 March 1955, Avery Brundage Collection, 1908–75 (hereafter referred to as ABC), Box 333, Reel 145, International Centre for Olympic Studies Archives (hereafter referred to as ICOSA), University of Western Ontario, London, Ontario, Canada; Damion L. Thomas, *Globetrotting: African American Athletes and Cold War Politics* (Urbana: University of Illinois Press, 2012). The Eisenhower administration immediately recognized that sports tours had considerable political potential. For example, the goodwill tour of the New York Giants baseball team in Japan in late 1953 was given enthusiastic support by C. D. Jackson and received the full approval of the Psychological Strategy Board. See C. D. Jackson to Ford Frick (commissioner of Major League Baseball), 8 July 1953, White House Office, National Security Council Staff: Papers, 1948–61 (hereafter referred to as WHO NSC Papers), Psychological Strategy Board, Central File Series (hereafter referred to as PSB), Box 25, "PSB 353.8," DDEL; "Agenda Item 3," 8 July 1953, WHO NSC Papers, PSB, Box 25, "PSB 353.8," DDEL.

10. "The Case for the State Department Athlete," *Sports Illustrated*, 16 July 1956, 67; "Area and Country Breakdown," no date, CU, Box 49, File 11.

11. Quote in USIS Belgrade to Department of State, 18 January 1955, CU, Box 93, File 8; "International Educational Exchange Digest," January 1955, CU, Box 24, File 10; Thomas, *Globetrotting*.

12. Jackson to Ralph Hills, 27 August 1953, Jackson, C. D.: Records, 1953–54, Series I: PSB-OCB Series, 1953–54, Box 3, "H," DDEL.

13. Washburn to Jackson, 28 October 1954, Jackson Papers, Box 62, "International Sports," DDEL.

14. Washburn to Jackson, 11 January 1955, Jackson Papers, Box 62, "International Sports," DDEL.

15. Sidney James to Harlan Logan, 14 May 1955, Jackson Papers, Box 62, "International Sports," DDEL; Jackson to Dorothy Goodgion, 4 February 1955, Jackson Papers, Box 62, "International Sports," DDEL.

16. They approached Bing Crosby and Colonel Edward P. Eagan, the chairman of the USOC fundraising drive for the 1956 games, but both men declined. See Goodgion to Jackson, 8 March 1955, Jackson Papers, Box 62, "International Sports," DDEL; Washburn to Jackson, 17 June 1955, Jackson Papers, Box 111, File 5, "Washburn, Abbott," DDEL; Jackson to Washburn, 21 June 1955, Jackson Papers, Box 111, File 5, "Washburn, Abbott," DDEL; Washburn to Jackson, no date, Jackson Papers, Box 62, "International Sports," DDEL; Washburn to Colonel Edward Eagan, 16 March 1956, Jackson Papers, Box 62, "International Sports," DDEL; Thomas M. Domer, "Sport in Cold War America, 1953–1963: The Diplomatic and Political Use of Sport in the Eisenhower and Kennedy Administrations," PhD diss., Marquette University, 1976, 79–84.

17. "Roby Calls for Olympic Preparation Now," *Amateur Athlete* 23, no. 10 (October 1952): 9.

18. "Mahoney Says 'We Must Beat Russia,'" *New York Times*, 27 January 1953, 29.

19. "Sports of the Times," *New York Times*, 10 September 1953, 34.

20. "We'll Lose the Next Olympics. . . ." *This Week Magazine*, 15 May 1954, 7, quotes on 16–17.

21. Nicholas McCausland to Charles Norberg, 21 June 1954, WHO NSC Papers, OCB Central File Series (hereafter referred to as OCB), Box 112, File 1, "OCB 353.8 (Amusements and Athletics) June 1954—April 1956" (hereafter referred to as "OCB 353.8"), File 1, DDEL.

22. Bourne to Berding, 30 September 1954, WHO NSC Papers, OCB, Box 112, File 1, "OCB 353.8," DDEL. The unnamed member from the USOC was probably John T. McGovern, the USOC counselor.

23. Bourne to Berding, 30 September 1954, WHO NSC Papers, OCB, Box 112, File 1, "OCB 353.8," DDEL; Act of 22 Apr. 1954, Pub. L. 83–342 ch. 171 (authorizing president to designate National Olympic Day), Dwight D. Eisenhower: Records as President, White House Central Files, 1953–61, Central File (hereafter referred to as Eisenhower Records), Box 734, "143-D Olympic Games," DDEL; Snyder to Stephens, 29 September 1954, Eisenhower Records, Box 734, "143-D Olympic Games," DDEL; "President Eisenhower Proclaims October 16 as National Olympic Day," *Amateur Athlete* 25, no. 6 (June 1954): 12–13.

24. Bourne to Berding, 30 September 1954, WHO NSC Papers, OCB, Box 112, File 1, "OCB 353.8," DDEL; "National Olympic Day—October 16," *Amateur Athlete* 25, no. 10 (October 1954): 5, 30; "President Eisenhower Asks Support for Olympic Team," *Amateur Athlete* 25, no. 11 (November 1954): 4; "Nationwide Olympic Day Activities," *Amateur Athlete* 25, no. 11 (November 1954): 6; "National Olympic Day Celebrations," *Amateur Athlete* 25, no. 12 (December 1954): 6; "'Olympic Day' to be observed in the United States,"

RG306, Feature Packets with Recurring Subjects, 1953–59, Box 25, "No. 3: USIS Sports Packet, August 1954," NA.

25. "A.A.U. Plans 'Olympic Development Meets,'" *Amateur Athlete* 26, no. 6 (June 1955): quotes on 8–9.

26. "A.A.U. Olympic Development Program in Full Swing," *Amateur Athlete* 26, no. 7 (July 1955): 10; quote in "A.A.U. Olympic Development Program Continues," *Amateur Athlete* 26, no. 10 (October 1955): 9.

27. The full text of the speech is appended to a letter from John Marshall Butler to Avery Brundage, 25 July 1955, ABC, Box 333, Reel 145, ICOSA, p. 2.

28. Roy Clumpner, "Federal Involvement in Sport to Promote American Interest or Foreign Policy Objectives, 1950—1973," in *Sport and International Relations*, ed. B. Lowe, D. B. Kanin, and A. Strenk (Champaign, IL: Stipes, 1978) 402–3, quote on 403; Domer, "Sport in Cold War America," 157–60.

29. "Olympic Fund Benefits from Capital Luncheon," *Amateur Athlete* 27, no. 5 (May 1956): 27.

30. Robert C. Hill to Butler, 31 May 1956, RG59, Central Decimal File, 1955–59, Box 4062, 800.453/2–1058, NA.

31. Clumpner, "Federal Involvement in Sport," 402–3; Domer, "Sport in Cold War America," 160–61; quote is from "Vice President Nixon Hails A.A.U. and Its Olympic Fund Drive," *Amateur Athlete* 27, no. 1 (January 1956): 11.

32. "If the Russians Win . . . So What?" *San Francisco Chronicle*, 23 May 1955; Correspondence of Avery Brundage, 1954–55, Box 4, International Olympic Committee Archives (hereafter referred to as IOC Archives), Lausanne, Switzerland. Quote is in the *Chronicle* clipping.

33. Jimmy Jemail, "Hotbox," *Sports Illustrated*, 15 October 1956, 8, 10.

34. See, for example, Douglas Roby's comments on federal funding for the U.S. team in "Reject Offer of Government Olympics Aid," *Chicago Daily Tribune*, 28 November 1954, A3.

35. McGovern to Vanderhoef, 3 November 1955, WHO NSC Papers, OCB, Box 112, File 1, "OCB 353.8," DDEL; Domer, "Sport in Cold War America, 1953–1963," 164–66.

36. "Army Stars to Head U.S. Olympic Team, Says Wilson," *Chicago Daily Tribune*, 20 March 1955, A2; quote appears in Peter J. Beck, "Britain and the Cold War's 'Cultural Olympics': Responding to the Political Drive of Soviet Sport, 1945–58," *Contemporary British History* 19, no. 2 (2005): 170.

37. Domer, "Sport in Cold War America, 1953–1963," 164–66.

38. McGovern to Vanderhoef, 24 June 1955, WHO NSC Papers, OCB, Box 112, File 1, "OCB 353.8," DDEL.

39. McGovern to Vanderhoef, 11 July 1955, WHO NSC Papers, OCB, Box 112, File 1, "OCB 353.8," DDEL.

40. McGovern to Vanderhoef, 11 July 1955, WHO NSC Papers, OCB, Box 112, File 1, "OCB 353.8," DDEL.

41. McGovern to Vanderhoef, 14 July 1955, WHO NSC Papers, OCB, Box 112, File 1, "OCB 353.8," DDEL.

42. "Extract of the 49th Session of the International Olympic Committee," Athens, 11–14 May 1954, *Olympic Review* 46 (June–July, 1954), 53.

43. Brundage to Konstantin Andrianov, 28 July 1955, ABC, Box 50, Reel 30, ICOSA.

44. "Brundage Blasts U.S. Hysteria," *Chicago Daily Tribune*, 8 April 1956, B1.

45. Brundage to Wilson, 23 February 1955, ABC, Box 41, Reel 24, ICOSA; Brundage to Wilson, 28 March 1955, ABC, Box 41, Reel 24, ICOSA; Brundage to McGovern, 3 August 1955, ABC, Box 32, Reel 19, ICOSA; quote in "Brundage Blasts U.S. Hysteria," B1.

46. "Of Greeks—and Russians," *Sports Illustrated*, 6 February 1956, 30–32, 56; "Army Stars to Head U.S. Olympic Team, Says Wilson," *Chicago Daily Tribune*, 20 March 1955, A2; Brundage to Ferris, 14 June 1954, ABC, Box 24, Reel 15, ICOSA.

47. Leslie S. Brady to Staats, 13 January 1956, WHO NSC Papers, OCB, Box 112, File 2, "OCB 353.8," DDEL.

48. Brady to Washburn, 13 January 1956, WHO NSC Papers, OCB, Box 112, File 2, "OCB 353.8," DDEL.

49. "Terms of Reference for OCB Working Group on 1956 Olympics," 25 January 1956, WHO NSC Papers, OCB, Box 112, File 2, "OCB 353.8," DDEL.

50. "Terms of Reference for OCB Working Group on 1956 Olympics," 8 February 1956, WHO NSC Papers, OCB, Box 112, File 2, "OCB 353.8," DDEL.

51. "Memorandum for the Cultural Presentation Committee," 30 November 1955, WHO NSC Papers, OCB, Box 112, File 1, "OCB 353.8," DDEL.

52. "Interim Report: Consideration of U.S. Position in Connection with 1956 Olympic Games," 17 April 1956, WHO NSC Papers, OCB, Box 112, File 3, "OCB 353.8," DDEL; "Consideration of U.S. Position in Connection with 1956 Olympic Games," 21 February 1956, WHO NSC Papers, OCB, Box 112, File 2, "OCB 353.8," DDEL; "Courses of Action," 8 February 1956, WHO NSC Papers, OCB, Box 112, File 2, "OCB 353.8," DDEL.

53. "Interim Report: Consideration of U.S. Position in Connection with 1956 Olympic Games," 17 April 1956, WHO NSC Papers, OCB, Box 112, File 3, "OCB 353.8," DDEL.

54. Osgood, *Total Cold War*, 92–93. The USIA retained the title of the United States Information Service overseas and USIS posts also produced their own propaganda material. For more on the themes of feature packets and USIA propaganda, see also Laura A. Belmonte, *Selling the American Way: U.S. Propaganda and the Cold War* (Philadelphia: University of Pennsylvania Press, 2008), and Hixson, *Parting the Curtain*.

55. "Note to Public Affairs Officer," 19 July 1954, RG306, Feature Packets with Recurring Subjects, 1953–59, Box 25, "No. 2: USIS Sports Packet, July 1954," NA.

56. "Olympic Head Gives Warning," and "Communist Sports Hit," RG306, Feature Packets with Recurring Subjects, 1953–59, Box 25, "No. 17: USIS Sports Packet, November 1955," NA.

57. "President Dwight Eisenhower Sends Best Wishes to U.S. Olympians," RG306, Feature Packets with Recurring Subjects, 1953–59, Box 26, "No. 28: USIS Sports Packet, October 1956," NA.

58. "U.S. Track Coach Bill Bowerman Lauds Pakistani Athletes," RG306, Feature Packets with Recurring Subjects, 1953–59, Box 25, "No. 24: USIS Sports Packet, June 1956," NA.

59. "U.S. Businessmen Help Japanese Olympic Team," RG306, Feature Packets with Recurring Subjects, 1953–59, Box 25, "No. 20: USIS Sports Packet, February 1956," NA.

60. "Jim Bradford, One of the World's Top Weightlifters," RG306, Feature Packets with Recurring Subjects, 1953–59, Box 25, "No. 25: USIS Sports Packet, July 1956," NA.

61. "Harold Connolly, Outstanding U.S. Olympic Prospect," RG306, Feature Packets with Recurring Subjects, 1953–59, Box 26, "No. 25: USIS Sports Packet, June 1956," NA.

62. For the Karl Schwenzfeier cartoon, see RG306, Feature Packets with Recurring Subjects, 1953–59, Box 25, "No. 24: USIS Sports Packet, June 1956," NA.

63. "Andrea Mead Lawrence—America's Top Woman Skier," RG306, Feature Packets with Recurring Subjects, 1953–59, Box 25, "No. 19: USIS Sports Packet, January 1956," NA.

64. For the Wanda Werner cartoon, see RG306, Feature Packets with Recurring Subjects, 1953–59, Box 26, "No. 24: USIS Sports Packet, June 1956," NA.

65. Judy Howe in RG306, Feature Packets with Recurring Subjects, 1953–59, Box 26, "No. 27: USIS Sports Packet, September 1956," NA; and Carin Cone in RG306, Feature Packets with Recurring Subjects, 1953–59, Box 26, "No. 28: USIS Sports Packet, September 1956," NA.

66. For the Ruben Mendoza cartoon, see RG306, Feature Packets with Recurring Subjects, 1953–59, Box 26, "No. 26: USIS Sports Packet, August 1956," NA.

67. For Bill Russell, see RG306, Feature Packets with Recurring Subjects, 1953–59, Box 26, "No. 28: USIS Sports Packet, October 1956," NA.

68. For the Gregory Bell cartoon, see RG306, Feature Packets with Recurring Subjects, 1953–59, Box 26, "No. 27: USIS Sports Packet, September 1956," NA.

69. "Hungarian Athlete Tells of Treatment behind Iron Curtain," RG306, Feature Packets with Recurring Subjects, 1953–59, Box 25, "No. 17: USIS Sports Packet, November 1955," NA.

70. "Stella Walsh Will Not Run for Poland," RG306, Feature Packets with Recurring Subjects, 1953–59, Box 25, "No. 17: USIS Sports Packet, November 1955," NA.

71. "Interim Report: Consideration of U.S. Position in Connection with 1956 Olympic Games," 17 April 1956, WHO NSC Papers, OCB, Box 112, File 3, "OCB 353.8," DDEL.

72. Dennis to Brundage, 27 February 1956, ABC, Box 333, Reel 145, ICOSA; "Courses of Action," 8 February 1956, WHO NSC Papers, OCB, Box 112, File 2, "OCB 353.8," DDEL; Brundage to Dennis, 28 February 1956, ABC, Box 114, Reel 62, ICOSA.

73. Dennis to Brundage, 15 March 1956, ABC, Box 333, Reel 145, ICOSA. It is likely that the article Dennis referred to was written by C. L. Sulzberger. See "State and Sport—What Makes Sandor Run?" *New York Times*, 14 March 1956, 32.

74. Brundage to Dennis, 23 April 1956, ABC, Box 333, Reel 145, ICOSA.

75. "Committee on the 1956 Olympic Games," 14 February 1956, WHO NSC Papers, OCB, Box 112, File 2, "OCB 353.8," DDEL.

76. Brundage to Department of State, 28 February 1956, ABC, Box 333, Reel 145, ICOSA.

77. Howland to Brundage, 30 July 1956, ABC, Box 333, Reel 145, ICOSA. The response from Harold Howland in the State Department read, "After receiving your letter I went into it very carefully again with the Heraldic Branch of the Department of Defense and found that Public Law 829 of the 77th Congress, December 22, 1942, Section 4, specifically forbids civilian groups from dipping the flag 'to any person or thing.' This, of course, even includes the president of our own United States."

78. Mark Dyreson, *Crafting Patriotism for Global Dominance: America at the Olympics* (Abingdon, U.K.: Routledge, 2009), 33.

79. Quote in Orray Taft to Department of State, 21 December 1956, Eisenhower Records, Box 734, "143-D Olympic Games," DDEL; Eisenhower to Ferris, 15 October 1956,

Eisenhower Records, Box 734, "143-D Olympic Games," DDEL; Barbara Keys, "The 1956 Melbourne Olympic Games and the Postwar International Order," in *1956: European and Global Perspectives*, ed. C. Fink, F. Hadler, and T. Schramm (Leipzig, Ger.: Leipziger Universitätsverlag, 2006), 296–97; Eisenhower to Ferris, 26 March 1957, published in *Amateur Athlete* 28, no. 5 (May 1957): 23; "Secretary Dan Ferris Recovers from Illness," *Amateur Athlete* 28, no. 1 (January 1957): 19.

80. Brundage to Mayer, 19 March 1959, Correspondence of Avery Brundage, 1956–60, Box 5, IOC Archives.

81. "Must Accent Minor Sports, Says Wilson," *Chicago Daily Tribune*, 9 December 1956, B7; Keys, "The 1956 Melbourne Olympic Games," 293–94.

Chapter 6. Sports Illustrated *and the Melbourne Defection*

1. Chris Tudda, "'Reenacting the Story of Tantalus': Eisenhower, Dulles, and the Failed Rhetoric of Liberation," *Journal of Cold War Studies* 7, no. 4 (2005): 3–35.

2. "Down a Road Called Liberty," *Sports Illustrated*, 17 December 1956, first quote on 14, second quote on 16.

3. Thomas M. Domer, "Sport in Cold War America, 1953–1963: The Diplomatic and Political Use of Sport in the Eisenhower and Kennedy Administrations," PhD diss., Marquette University, 1976, 90–95. *Sports Illustrated* published another article on the defection in 2012, but it still did not acknowledge the HNSF and FEC connection. See "Revolution Games," *Sports Illustrated*, 18 June 2012, 66–73. The defection also is mentioned, albeit very briefly, in Michael MacCambridge, *The Franchise: A History of Sports Illustrated Magazine* (New York: Hyperion, 1997), 92—93. For the FEC's change of name, see "Notice of Change of Name," *New York Times*, 10 March 1954, 43.

4. Tudda, "Reenacting the Story of Tantalus," 3–11; Valur Ingimundarson, "Containing the Offensive: The 'Chief of the Cold War' and the Eisenhower Administration's German Policy," *Presidential Studies Quarterly* 27, no. 3 (1997): 480–95.

5. Tudda, "Reenacting the Story of Tantalus," 16–19; Ingimundarson, "Containing the Offensive," 484–85; Csaba Békés, "East Central Europe, 1953–1956," in *The Cambridge History of the Cold War*, ed. Melvin P. Leffler and Odd Arne Westad. Vol. 1, *Origins*, 337 (Cambridge: Cambridge University Press, 2010).

6. [W.] Scott Lucas, *Freedom's War: The American Crusade against the Soviet Union* (New York: New York University Press, 1999), 184–85, 189; Robert J. McMahon, "US National Security Policy from Eisenhower to Kennedy," in *Cambridge History of the Cold War*, ed. Leffler and Westad, 1: 292–95; Tudda, "Reenacting the Story of Tantalus," 19–20; Kenneth Osgood, *Total Cold War: Eisenhower's Secret Propaganda Battle at Home and Abroad* (Lawrence: University Press of Kansas, 2006), 71–75.

7. Walter L. Hixson, *Parting the Curtain: Propaganda, Culture, and the Cold War, 1945–1961* (New York: St. Martin's Press, 1997), quote on 101; Lucas, *Freedom's War*, 220–31; Evan Thomas, *The Very Best Men: Four Who Dared; The Early Years of the CIA* (New York: Simon and Schuster, 1995), 107–26.

8. Kenneth Osgood, "Hearts and Minds: The Unconventional Cold War," *Journal of Cold War Studies* 4, no. 2 (2002): 98.

9. Csaba Békés, "East Central Europe, 1953–1956," 334–47; Ben Fowkes, *The Rise and Fall of Communism in Eastern Europe* (New York: St. Martin's Press, 1993), 76–77.

10. Charles Gati, *Hungary and the Soviet Bloc* (Durham, NC: Duke University Press, 1986), 134–35; Csaba Békés, "East Central Europe, 1953–1956," 340–47; Fowkes, *Communism in Eastern Europe*, 76–77.

11. Both quotes cited in Hixson, *Parting the Curtain*, Dulles on 81, and Eisenhower on 82; Tudda, "Reenacting the Story of Tantalus"; Gati, *Hungary and the Soviet Bloc*, 135–55; Fowkes, *Communism in Eastern Europe*, 78–91.

12. Gregory Mitrovich, *Undermining the Kremlin: America's Strategy to Subvert the Soviet Bloc, 1947–1956* (Ithaca, NY: Cornell University Press, 2000), 175.

13. A. Ross Johnson, *Radio Free Europe and Radio Liberty: The CIA Years and Beyond* (Stanford, CA: Stanford University Press, 2010), 79–118, quote on 117; Hixson, *Parting the Curtain*, 82–83.

14. John Lewis Gaddis, *The Cold War: A New History* (New York: Penguin, 2005), 126–28; David S. Painter, *The Cold War: An International History* (London: Routledge, 1999), 46–48; T. E. Vadney, *The World since 1945* (London: Penguin, 1992), 220–25.

15. Ian Jobling, "Strained Beginnings and Friendly Farewells: The Games of the XVI Olympiad Melbourne 1956," *Stadion* 21–22 (1995–96): 258; Eric Monnin and Renaud David, "The Melbourne Games in the Context of the International Tensions of 1956," *Journal of Olympic History* 17, no. 3 (2009): 36–39; Avery Brundage to Otto Mayer, 9 November 1956, Correspondence of Avery Brundage, 1956–60, Box 5, International Olympic Committee Archives (hereafter referred to as IOC Archives), Lausanne, Switzerland; Mayer to Brundage, 8 November 1956, Correspondence of Avery Brundage, 1956–60, Box 5, IOC Archives.

16. Otto Mayer to W. S. Kent Hughes, 7 November 1956, Telegrams about the Olympic Games of Melbourne, 1956, 1952–57, IOC Archives; Mayer cable to IOC headquarters in Lausanne, 14 November 1956, Telegrams about the Olympic Games of Melbourne, 1956, 1952–57, IOC Archives.

17. Cited in Richard Espy, *The Politics of the Olympic Games* (Berkeley: University of California Press, 1979), 54.

18. "Olympic Head Appeals for Nations to Stay," *Harford Courant*, 8 November 1956, 21A.

19. "Minutes of the International Olympic Committee 53rd Session," Melbourne, 19–21 November, 4 December 1956, in Wolf Lyberg, ed., *IOC General Session Minutes*, vol. 4 (1956–1988), 11.

20. "Notes on the 44th Meeting of Special Committee on Soviet and Related Problems," 6 November 1956, *Foreign Relations of the United States* (hereafter referred to as *FRUS*), *1955–57*. Vol. 25, *Eastern Europe* (Washington, DC: U.S. Government Printing Office, 1990), 400–404.

21. Russell L. Riley to Carl McCardle, 9 November 1956, Record Group 59 (hereafter referred to as RG), Central Decimal File, 1955–59, Box 4062, 800.4531/11–956, National Archives (hereafter referred to as NA), College Park, Maryland; Fisher Howe to Macomber, 9 November 1956, RG59, Central Decimal File, 1955–59, Box 4062, 800.4531/11–956, NA.

22. "Hungary Out of Melbourne Olympics," *Daily Mail*, 29 October 1956, 11; "Hungary's Heroes in Their Hour of Staggering Strain," *Sports Illustrated*, 3 December 1956, 22–23.

23. "Hungary Not to Miss Olympics," *Daily Mail*, 30 October 1956, 10; "I Listen to the Radio, Hear I'm Dead!" *Daily Mail*, 21 March 1957, 8.

24. "Olympic Newsletter No. 19," Olympic Games Organizing Committee of Melbourne, 1956: Circulars, Communications, Organizing Program and Press Releases, 1954–56, IOC Archives.

25. Mayer to Brundage, 30 October 1956, Correspondence of Avery Brundage, 1956–60, Box 5, IOC Archives; Mayer to Brundage, 28 October 1956, Correspondence of Avery Brundage, 1956–60, Box 5, IOC Archives; Espy, *Politics of the Olympic Games*, 54–55; "Hungary Will Send Team to Olympics," *New York Times*, 30 October 1956, 49; "Hungary's Team Is on the Way," *Argus* (Melbourne), 31 October 1956, 26.

26. "Hungary's Heroes in Their Hour of Staggering Strain," *Sports Illustrated*, 3 December 1956, 22–23.

27. "Hungarians Demand Removal of Red Flag," *The Washington Post and Times Herald*, 11 November 1956, C1; "Hungarian Team Stunned by News," *New York Times*, 11 November 1956, 35; "Hungarian Athletes Show Little Interest for Olympic Competition," *Los Angeles Times*, 11 November 1956, D8.

28. "Hungarian Olympic Athletes Greeted by 2,000 upon Arrival at Melbourne," *New York Times*, 13 November 1956, 62.

29. "Pan American World Airways Airlifts Soviet Olympic Team," 11 October 1956, RG59, Central Decimal File, 1955–59, Box 4062, 800.453/2–1058, NA.

30. "Tea Drinking Russian Athletes Spurn Vodka," *Hartford Courant*, 6 November 1956, 17.

31. Frances Stoner Saunders, *Who Paid the Piper? The CIA and the Cultural Cold War* (London: Granta Books, 1999), 281.

32. Hugh Wilford, *The Mighty Wurlitzer: How the CIA Played America* (Cambridge, MA: Harvard University Press, 2008), 225–32, quote on 227; Stuart Loory, "The CIA's Use of the Press: A 'Mighty Wurlitzer,'" *Columbia Journalism Review* 13 (September–October 1974): 9–18; Thomas, *Very Best Men*, 63, 117; Carl Bernstein, "The CIA and the Media," *Rolling Stone*, 20 October 1977, 55–63; Osgood, *Total Cold War*, 82; Blanche Wiesen Cook, "First Comes the Lie: C. D. Jackson and Political Warfare," *Radical History Review* 31 (1984), 58.

33. MacCambridge, *The Franchise*, 12–16, 63.

34. John Massaro, "Press Box Propaganda? The Cold War and *Sports Illustrated*, 1956," *Journal of American Culture* 26, no. 3 (2003): 361–70.

35. Whitney Tower to Sid James, "Documentary Chronology" (hereafter referred to as DC), 15 November 1956, C. D. Jackson Papers, 1931–67, Series 2, Time Inc. File, 1933–64, Subseries A, Alphabetical File, 1933–64 (hereafter referred to as Jackson Papers), Box 104, "Sports Illustrated—Hungarian Olympic Team Defectors," Dwight D. Eisenhower Presidential Library (hereafter referred to as DDEL), Abilene, Kansas.

36. All quotes in Tower to Szápáry, 15 November 1956, The Private Papers of Count Anthony Szápáry (hereafter referred to as Szápáry Papers), Box 2, "HNSF, 1956," Pound Ridge, New York; Szápáry to James, 18 June 1957, Szápáry Papers, Box 2, "HNSF, 1956."

37. Tower to Szápáry, 19 November 1956, Szápáry Papers, Box 2, "HNSF, Sports Illustrated, 1956–57."

38. For more on Laguerre's career, see MacCambridge, *The Franchise*, 77–87.

39. Tower to Sid James, DC, 15 November 1956, Jackson Papers, Box 104, "Sports Illustrated—Hungarian Olympic Team Defectors," DDEL; Phinizy memorandum, DC, no date, Jackson Papers, Box 104, "Sports Illustrated—Hungarian Olympic Team Defectors," DDEL; M. Schmidt to Yarrow, 27 November 1956, RFE/RL, Box 245, File 4, "Olympic Games General, 1951–1959," HA; Alexander Hahn to John F. Leich, 9 November 1956, RFE/RL, Box 245, File 4, "Olympic Games General, 1951–1959," HA.

40. Quote in John Matthews to R. W. Minton, 21 July 1960, RFE/RL, Box 245, File 5, "Olympic Games General, 1960," HA; "Curriculum" of Telegdy, no date, RFE/RL, Box 343, File 20, "Telegdy, George," HA; "Biography of George Telegdy, no date, Szápáry Papers, Box 2, "misc"; Tibor Szy, *Hungarians in America* (New York: Kossuth Foundation, 1966), 428.

41. Szápáry to John Richardson, 30 April 1962, RFE/RL, Box 343, File 20, "Telegdy, George," HA; Tower to Szápáry, 10 January 1957, Szápáry Papers, Box 2, "HNSF, Sports Illustrated, 1956–57."

42. "Operation Griffin," by George Telegdy, no date, Szápáry Papers, Box 2, "Melbourne." Telegdy explained that the griffin is a "bird of battle in ancient Hungarian mythology." The griffin was also on his family crest.

43. All quotes in "Operation Griffin," 1, by Telegdy, no date, Szápáry Papers, Box 2, "Confidential Reports—Operation Eagle." This report is Telegdy's personal account of Operation Griffin and is the version referred to throughout this chapter. For more on the fencing and water polo contests, see Hilary Kent and John Merritt, "The Cold War and the Melbourne Olympic Games," in *Better Dead Than Red: Australia's First Cold War, 1945–1959,* ed. Ann Curthoys and John Merritt (Sydney, Australia: Allen and Unwin, 1986), vol. 2, 170–85. The Hungarians defeated the Soviet Union 4–0.

44. Laguerre cable, DC, 23 November 1956, Jackson Papers, Box 104, "Sports Illustrated—Hungarian Olympic Team Defectors," DDEL.

45. Telegdy to Szápáry, DC, 24 November 1956, Jackson Papers, Box 104, "Sports Illustrated—Hungarian Olympic Team Defectors," DDEL.

46. Telegdy cable, 29 November 1956, Szápáry Papers, Box 2, "HNSF, Sports Illustrated, 1956–57."

47. Laguerre cable, DC, 29 November 1956, Jackson Papers, Box 104, "Sports Illustrated—Hungarian Olympic Team Defectors," DDEL; James cable, DC, 30 November 1956, Jackson Papers, Box 104, "Sports Illustrated—Hungarian Olympic Team Defectors," DDEL; James cable, DC, 1 December 1956, Jackson Papers, Box 104, "Sports Illustrated—Hungarian Olympic Team Defectors," DDEL.

48. "Notes on the 46th Meeting of the Special Committee on Soviet Related Problems," 13 November 1956, *FRUS, 1955–57,* 25:436–40.

49. "5 Hungarian Athletes Ask Australian Asylum," *New York Times,* 4 December 1956, 18.

50. "Hungarians Decide to 'Choose Freedom,'" *Los Angeles Times,* 6 December 1956, C5; "Hungarian Athletes Set Freedom Dash," *Christian Science Monitor,* 6 December 1956, 25.

51. "Hungarians Free to Stay in Australia," *Canberra Times* (Australia), 6 December 1956, 3.

52. "Hungarian Athletes Cutting Ties," *New York Times,* 6 December 1956, 5.

53. "Operation Griffin," 9.

54. "Down a Road Called Liberty," *Sports Illustrated,* 17 December 1956, 14–15.

55. "Now 11 athletes have vanished at Village," *Argus,* 7 December 1956, 3.

56. "Operation Griffin," 10. Gyarmathy won gold in the long jump in 1948.

57. Laguerre cable, DC, 6 December 1956, Jackson Papers, Box 104, "Sports Illustrated—Hungarian Olympic Team Defectors," DDEL.

58. Quotes in James cable, DC, 6 December 1956, Jackson Papers, Box 104, "Sports Illustrated—Hungarian Olympic Team Defectors," DDEL; Laguerre cable, DC, 5 December 1956, Jackson Papers, Box 104, "Sports Illustrated—Hungarian Olympic Team Defectors," DDEL; Telegdy cable, 4 December 1956, Szápáry Papers, Box 2, "HNSF, Sports Illustrated, 1956–57."

59. Laguerre cable, DC, 5 December 1956, Jackson Papers, Box 104, "Sports Illustrated—Hungarian Olympic Team Defectors," DDEL; Laguerre cable, DC, 6 December 1956, Jackson Papers, Box 104, "Sports Illustrated—Hungarian Olympic Team Defectors," DDEL; quotes in James cable, DC, 6 December 1956, Jackson Papers, Box 104, "Sports Illustrated—Hungarian Olympic Team Defectors," DDEL.

60. Terrell cable, DC, 8 December 1956, Jackson Papers, Box 104, "Sports Illustrated—Hungarian Olympic Team Defectors," DDEL.

61. For more on Brody, see the Documentary Chronology in the Jackson Papers.

62. Terrell cable, DC, 9 December 1956, Jackson Papers, Box 104, "Sports Illustrated—Hungarian Olympic Team Defectors," DDEL; quotes in "Operation Griffin," 13. On the International Rescue Committee, see Wilford, *Mighty Wurlitzer*, 175–76.

63. Quote in Terrell cable, DC, 10 December 1956, Jackson Papers, Box 104, "Sports Illustrated—Hungarian Olympic Team Defectors," DDEL; Burton cable, DC, 10 December 1956, Jackson Papers, Box 104, "Sports Illustrated—Hungarian Olympic Team Defectors," DDEL; Laguerre cable, DC, 13 December 1956, Jackson Papers, Box 104, "Sports Illustrated—Hungarian Olympic Team Defectors," DDEL; "Operation Griffin"; "Hungarians Given Aussie Police Shield," *Chicago Daily Tribune*, 10 December 1956, C5.

64. Carl J. Bon Tempo, *Americans at the Gate: The United States and Refugees during the Cold War* (Princeton, NJ: Princeton University Press, 2008), 45, 65–66, 70; Michael Gill Davis, "The Cold War, Refugees, and U.S. Immigration Policy, 1952–1965," PhD diss., Vanderbilt University, 1996), 128–33.

65. Quotes in telephone conversation between Jackson and Tracy Voorhees, 7 December 1956, Jackson Papers, Box 69, File 4, "Log—1956," DDEL; "President Names Aide to Expedite Refugees' Entry," *New York Times*, 30 November 1956, 1; "Refugee Expediter: Tracy Stebbins Voorhees," *New York Times*, 30 November 1956, 14.

66. James cable, DC, 15 December 1956, Jackson Papers, Box 104, "Sports Illustrated—Hungarian Olympic Team Defectors," DDEL.

67. "Interdepartmental Escapee Committee," 14 December 1956, US DDRS: 1996 2860.

68. Quote in Laguerre cable, DC, 18 December 1956, Jackson Papers, Box 104, "Sports Illustrated—Hungarian Olympic Team Defectors," DDEL; Laguerre cable, DC, 19 December 1956, Jackson Papers, Box 104, "Sports Illustrated—Hungarian Olympic Team Defectors," DDEL; Telegdy to Yarrow, 22 December 1956, RFE/RL, Box 245, File 4, "Olympic Games General, 1951–1959," HA; "Haven in U.S. for Tabori and Coach," *Argus*, 20 December 1956, 19.

69. Pollard cable, DC, 20 December 1956, Jackson Papers, Box 104, "Sports Illustrated—Hungarian Olympic Team Defectors," DDEL; James cable, DC, 20 December 1956, Jackson Papers, Box 104, "Sports Illustrated—Hungarian Olympic Team Defectors," DDEL; Neale cable, DC, 22 December 1956, Jackson Papers, Box 104, "Sports Illustrated—Hungarian Olympic Team Defectors," DDEL.

70. This information was drawn from a special supplement of *Sports Illustrated* called the *Hungarian Athletes Freedom Tour*.

71. "Operation Griffin," 25.

72. "Red Orator Takes Fling at Olympics," *Chicago Daily Tribune*, 19 December 1956, C4.

73. Emese Ivan and Dezső Iván, "The 1956 Revolution and the Melbourne Olympics: The Changing Perceptions of a Dramatic Story," *Hungarian Studies Review* 35, nos. 1–2 (2008): 16–17, quote on 17.

74. "Hungarian Athletes in San Francisco," *Los Angeles Times*, 25 December 1956, C1.

75. The *Gazette* article was translated in a cable from Moscow, 10 April 1957, Allen W. Dulles Papers, Series 5, Subject Files, Box 106, Folder 12, "Olympic Games—Melbourne, Australia, 1957," Seeley G. Mudd Manuscript Library, Princeton University, New Jersey.

76. J. Lawton Collins memorandum, 22 December 1956, U.S. President's Committee for Hungarian Refugee Relief: Records, Box 19, "Hungarian Athletes," DDEL.

77. H. W. Brands Jr., *Cold Warriors: Eisenhower's Generation and American Foreign Policy* (New York: Columbia University Press, 1988), 132–33, quote on 133.

78. Jackson to Cord Meyer, 12 January 1960, US DDRS: 1995 1394.

79. Jackson to Larsen, 4 April 1957, Jackson Papers, Box 104, "Sports Illustrated—Hungarian Olympic Team Defectors," DDEL.

Chapter 7. Symbols of Freedom

1. "Reunion," *Reno Evening Gazette*, 10 December 1957, 7.

2. Hungarian National Olympic Team to C. D. Jackson, 8 December 1957, C. D. Jackson: Papers, 1931–67, Series 2, Time Inc. File, 1933–64, Subseries A, Alphabetical File, 1933–64 (hereafter referred to as Jackson Papers), Box 104, "Sports Illustrated—Hungarian Olympic Team Defectors," Dwight D. Eisenhower Presidential Library (hereafter referred to as DDEL), Abilene, Kansas.

3. Jackson to Piller, 10 December 1957, Jackson Papers, Box 104, "Sports Illustrated—Hungarian Olympic Team Defectors," DDEL.

4. "Operation Griffin," by George Telegdy, no date, The Private Papers of Count Anthony Szápáry (hereafter referred to as Szápáry Papers), Box 2, "Confidential Reports—Operation Eagle," Pound Ridge, New York; "Lag Is Reported in Refugee Help," *New York Times*, 22 December 1956, 6; "Exiled Athletes Hailed," *New York Times*, 28 December 1956, 34. The team arrived in the United States under the sponsorship of *Sports Illustrated*, the National Catholic Welfare Conference, and First Aid for Hungary. The National Catholic Welfare Conference was a refugee resettlement agency that oversaw other Catholic sponsors, and First Aid for Hungary was a highly successful relief initiative founded by Tibor Eckhardt. For more on First Aid for Hungary, see Katalin Kádár Lynn, *Tibor Eckhardt: His American Years, 1941–1972* (New York: Columbia University Press, 2007), 181–87. For more on the screening process for Hungarians arriving in the United States after the revolution, see Carl J. Bon Tempo, *Americans at the Gate: The United States and Refugees during the Cold War* (Princeton, NJ: Princeton University Press, 2008), 66–70; Michael Gill Davis, "The Cold War, Refugees, and U.S. Immigration Policy, 1952–1965," PhD diss., Vanderbilt University, 1996, 128–33. The HNSF also set up an office at Camp Kilmer to aid additional exiled Hungarian athletes. See Toby C. Rider, "The Cold War Activities of the Hungarian National Sports Federation," in *The Inauguration of Organized Political Warfare: Cold War Organizations Sponsored by the National Committee for a Free Europe/*

Free Europe Committee, ed. Katalin Kádár Lynn (Saint Helena, CA: Helena History Press, 2013), 531–32.

5. Jackson to General Joseph M. Swing, 2 January 1957, Jackson Papers, Box 69, File 1, "Log—1957," DDEL; "Hungarian Olympic Athletes Schedule, December 31–January 8," no date, Szápáry Papers, Box 2, "HNSF, Sports Illustrated 1956–1957."

6. Jackson to General Willis D. Crittenberger, 2 January 1957, Jackson Papers, Box 69, File 1, "Log—1957," DDEL.

7. "Other Editors," *Charleston Gazette*, 9 April 1952, 6.

8. "Czech Skater Tells Why She Fled Reds," *Chicago Daily News*, 23 February 1955, Avery Brundage Collection, 1908–75 (hereafter referred to as ABC), Box 125, Reel 69, International Centre for Olympic Studies Archives (hereafter referred to as ICOSA), University of Western Ontario, London, Canada.

9. "Hungarians Serve Freedom's Cause Thursday," *The Washington Post and Times Herald*, 29 January 1957, A20; Neale letter, no date, Szápáry Papers, Box 2, "HNSF, Sports Illustrated 1956–1957."

10. *Sports Illustrated* press release, no date, Szápáry Papers, Box 2, "HNSF, Sports Illustrated 1956–1957"; "Across a Free Land," *Sports Illustrated*, 8 April 1957, 37; "American Welcome," *Sports Illustrated*, 7 January 1957, 18–19; "Hungarian Water Polo—Swimmers Tour," 26 January 1957, Szápáry Papers, Box 2, "HNSF, Sports Illustrated 1956–1957."

11. "Spirit of Hungary," *Mason City Globe-Gazette*, 10 January 1957.

12. "Hungarians Take Water Polo Test," *New York Times*, 16 January 1957, 37.

13. "Hungarians Call U.S. 'Wonderful,'" *The Washington Post and Times Herald*, 31 January 1957, D1.

14. "Across a Free Land," *Sports Illustrated*, 8 April 1957, 37.

15. Bon Tempo, *Americans at the Gate*, 75–82, quote on 77; Davis, "Cold War, Refugees, and U.S. Immigration Policy," 133–39.

16. Richard Neale to staff, 19 February 1957, Szápáry Papers, Box 2, "HNSF, Sports Illustrated 1956–1957."

17. Neale memorandum, no date, Szápáry Papers, Box 2, "HNSF, Sports Illustrated 1956–1957"; Neale to staff, 19 February 1957, Szápáry Papers, Box 2, "HNSF, Sports Illustrated 1956–1957."

18. "Across a Free Land," *Sports Illustrated*, 8 April 1957, 37.

19. Tracy Voorhees to Neale, 23 April 1957, Jackson Papers, Box 90, "Rerrick, Bela," DDEL.

20. Davis, "Cold War, Refugees, and U.S. Immigration Policy," 136, n. 79.

21. "Hungarian Runner Tabori Wants to Stay in the United States," Record Group 306 (hereafter referred to as RG), Feature Packets with Recurring Subjects, 1953–59, Box 27, "No. 31: USIS Sports Packet, January 1957," National Archives (hereafter referred to as NA), College Park, Maryland.

22. "Refugee Athletes Make Friends in the United States," RG306, Feature Packets with Recurring Subjects, 1953–59, Box 27, "No. 33: USIS Sports Packet, March 1957," NA; "Hungarian Refugee Athletes Plan U.S. Tours," RG306, Feature Packets with Recurring Subjects, 1953–59, Box 27, "No. 31: USIS Sports Packet, January 1957," NA.

23. Jackson to Larsen, 4 April 1957, Jackson Papers, Box 104, "Sports Illustrated—Hungarian Olympic Team Defectors," DDEL.

24. Whitney Tower to Count Anthony Szápáry, 10 January 1957, Szápáry Papers, Box 2, "HNSF, Sports Illustrated 1956–1957."

25. Neale to Count and Countess Szápáry, 3 April 1957, Szápáry Papers, Box 2, "HNSF, Sports Illustrated 1956–1957"; Telegdy to Neale, 28 February 1957, Szápáry Papers, Box 2, "HNSF, Sports Illustrated 1956–1957"; "Operation Eagle—Summary Report on three months' activities," 15 April 1957, Szápáry Papers, Box 2, "Confidential Reports—Operation Eagle."

26. Neale to Team Members, 14 May 1957, Szápáry Papers, Box 2, "HNSF, Sports Illustrated 1956–1957"; Neale to Szápáry, 15 May 1957, Szápáry Papers, Box 2, "HNSF, Sports Illustrated 1956–1957."

27. Jackson to Voorhees, 11 January 1957, Jackson Papers, Box 110, "Voorhees, Tracy," DDEL.

28. Jackson to Voorhees, 29 January 1957, Jackson Papers, Box 110, "Voorhees, Tracy," DDEL; Voorhees to Swing, 19 January 1957, Jackson Papers, Box 110, "Voorhees, Tracy," DDEL

29. Voorhees to Jackson, 18 January 1957, Jackson Papers, Box 110, "Voorhees, Tracy," DDEL; Jackson to Signe Bolander, 4 December 1957, Jackson Papers, Box 90, "Rerrick, Bela," DDEL.

30. Szápáry to Sidney James, 18 June 1957, Szápáry Papers, Box 2, "HNSF 1956"; Neale to Team Members, 14 May 1957, Szápáry Papers, Box 2, "HNSF, Sports Illustrated 1956–1957"; "Across a Free Land," *Sports Illustrated*, 8 April 1957, 37; "2 Hungarian Athletes Change Minds, Go Home," *Hartford Courant*, 5 February 1957, 3 ; "Operation Eagle—Summary Report on three months' activities," 15 April 1957, Szápáry Papers, Box 2, "Confidential Reports—Operation Eagle"; "Operation Eagle—Summary Report on six months' activities," 10 July 1957, Szápáry Papers, Box 2, "Confidential Reports—Operation Eagle."

31. Szápáry to Jackson, 8 July 1957, Szápáry Papers, Box 2, "Misc"; Jackson to Tibor Eckhardt, 9 July 1957, Jackson Papers, Box 52, "First Aid for Hungary," DDEL; "Operation Eagle—Summary Report on six months' activities," 10 July 1957, Szápáry Papers, Box 2, "Confidential Reports—Operation Eagle."

32. Neale to Hamori, 16 June 1958, Jackson Papers, Box 104, "Sports Illustrated—Hungarian Olympic Team Defectors," DDEL; Neale to Rod O'Connor, 16 June 1958, Jackson Papers, Box 104, "Sports Illustrated—Hungarian Olympic Team Defectors," DDEL; Neale to José de Capriles, 20 June 1958, Jackson Papers, Box 104, "Sports Illustrated—Hungarian Olympic Team Defectors," DDEL; Neale to Jackson, 20 June 1958, Jackson Papers, Box 104, "Sports Illustrated—Hungarian Olympic Team Defectors," DDEL; Jackson to O'Connor, 10 July 1958, Jackson Papers, Box 104, "Sports Illustrated—Hungarian Olympic Team Defectors," DDEL.

33. Jackson to O'Connor, 10 July 1958, Jackson Papers, Box 104, "Sports Illustrated—Hungarian Olympic Team Defectors," DDEL.

34. Bon Tempo, *Americans at the Gate*, 84.

35. Jackson to Neale, 17 April 1958, Jackson Papers, Box 93, File 3, "Santa Clara Youth Village," DDEL.

36. Mihály Iglói to Neale, 2 April 1957, Jackson Papers, Box 90, "Rerrick, Bela," DDEL; Iglói to George Telegdy, 6 July 1957, Szápáry Papers, Box 2, "Mihaly Igloi"; "Meeting of the Hungarian National Olympic Team," 8 December 1958, Szápáry Papers, Box 2, "HNSF";

"Miler to Return to Red Hungary," *New York Times*, 24 November 1957, 5; "Across a Free Land," *Sports Illustrated*, 8 April 1957, 37; Alexander Brody to Sigurd Larmon, 16 December 1957, Jackson Papers, Box 93, File 3, "Santa Clara Youth Village," DDEL.

37. Richard Pollard to Jackson, 4 December 1957, Jackson Papers, Box 93, File 3, "Santa Clara Youth Village," DDEL; Jackson to Douglas J. Brown, 4 December 1957, Jackson Papers, Box 104, "Sports Illustrated—Hungarian Olympic Team Defectors," DDEL; Kenneth Fairman to Jackson, 17 December 1957, Jackson Papers, Box 93, File 3, "Santa Clara Youth Village," DDEL.

38. Jack Tibby to Pollard, 20 December 1957, Walter E. Schmidt, S.J., Papers, 1944–1988 (hereafter referred to as Schmidt Papers), Santa Clara Youth Village Files, Box 12, "Time, Inc. Track & Field Campaign, 1957–1959," Department of Archives and Special Collections, Santa Clara University Library (hereafter referred to as SCUA), Santa Clara, California. Brody, who worked for the marketing firm Young and Rubicam, was also involved in the Melbourne defection. The president of Young and Rubicam, Sigurd Larmon, was good friends with Jackson and appears to have allowed Brody to help out in San Francisco. Not only was Brody highly capable, but he was also born in Hungary and fluent in the language.

39. Pollard and Brody to Jackson, 9 December 1957, Jackson Papers, Box 93, File 3, "Santa Clara Youth Village," DDEL; Brody to Larmon, 16 December 1957, Jackson Papers, Box 93, File 3, "Santa Clara Youth Village," DDEL.

40. "Walter E. Schmidt, S.J.," 2 December 1969, Schmidt Papers, Santa Clara Youth Village Files, Box 12, "Bequest Brochures," SCUA; Marion R. Royle to Robert O'Brian, 5 May 1959, Schmidt Papers, Santa Clara Youth Village Files, Box 12, "Coach Mihaly Igloi Press Release," SCUA; Father Schmidt to All Members of the SCVYV Track Team, 8 January 1960, Schmidt Papers, Santa Clara Youth Village Files, Box 12, "The Track Team/Igloi, Letters of Application, 1960," SCUA.

41. Father Schmidt to Jackson, 16 December 1957, Jackson Papers, Box 93, File 3, "Santa Clara Youth Village," DDEL.

42. Jackson to Father Schmidt, 20 December 1957, Schmidt Papers, Santa Clara Youth Village Files, Box 12, "Time, Inc. Track & Field Campaign, 1957–1959," SCUA.

43. Jackson to Fairman, 20 December 1957, Jackson Papers, Box 93, File 3, "Santa Clara Youth Village," DDEL.

44. Tibby to Pollard, 20 December 1957, Schmidt Papers, Santa Clara Youth Village Files, Box 12, "Time, Inc. Track & Field Campaign, 1957–1959," SCUA; "The Readers Take Over," *Sports Illustrated*, 13 January 1957, 61.

45. Larmon to Jackson, 23 January 1958, Jackson Papers, Box 93, File 3, "Santa Clara Youth Village," DDEL.

46. Father Schmidt to Time Inc., 19 February 1958, Schmidt Papers, Santa Clara Youth Village Files, Box 12, "Time, Inc. Track & Field Campaign, 1957–1959," SCUA.

47. Jackson to Clifford Roberts, 6 February 1958, Jackson Papers, Box 93, File 3, "Santa Clara Youth Village," DDEL.

48. Jackson to Neale, 17 April 1958, Jackson Papers, Box 93, File 3, "Santa Clara Youth Village," DDEL.

49. Father Schmidt to Pollard, 16 April 1958, Schmidt Papers, Santa Clara Youth Village Files, Box 12, "Coach Mihaly Igloi Press Release," SCUA.

50. Jackson to Father Schmidt, 22 April 1958, Jackson Papers, Box 93, File 3, "Santa Clara Youth Village," DDEL.

51. Jackson to Allen Dulles, 16 June 1958, Jackson Papers, Box 93, File 2, "Santa Clara Youth Village," DDEL.

52. Dulles to Jackson, 25 June 1958, Jackson Papers, Box 93, File 2, "Santa Clara Youth Village," DDEL.

53. Father Schmidt to Jackson, 29 August 1958, Jackson Papers, Box 93, File 2, "Santa Clara Youth Village," DDEL; Yarrow to Jackson, 19 March 1959, Jackson Papers, Box 93, File 2, "Santa Clara Youth Village," DDEL; Jackson to Father Schmidt, 20 March 1959, Jackson Papers, Box 93, File 2, "Santa Clara Youth Village," DDEL; Yarrow to Jackson, 22 June 1959, Jackson Papers, Box 93, File 2, "Santa Clara Youth Village," DDEL; Jackson to Father Schmidt, 24 June 1959, Schmidt Papers, Santa Clara Youth Village Files, Box 12, "Time, Inc. Track & Field Campaign, 1957–1959," SCUA; Father Schmidt to Jackson, 30 October 1959, Schmidt Papers, Santa Clara Youth Village Files, Box 12, "Time, Inc. Track & Field Campaign, 1957–1959," SCUA; Jackson to Archibald Alexander, 21 January 1960, Jackson Papers, Box 93, File 2, "Santa Clara Youth Village," DDEL; Theodore Augustine to Jackson, 22 January 1960, Jackson Papers, Box 93, File 2, "Santa Clara Youth Village," DDEL; Jackson to Father Schmidt, 22 January 1960, Schmidt Papers, Santa Clara Youth Village Files, Box 12, "Misc," SCUA.

54. "History on the Boards," *Sports Illustrated*, 19 February 1962, 14–18. Beatty's comment is in "The Magic of the Great Igloi," *Life*, 1 March 1963, 57.

55. Jackson to Father Schmidt, 4 October 1960, Jackson Papers, Box 93, File 1, "Santa Clara Youth Village," DDEL.

56. Father Schmidt to Jackson, 20 October 1960, Jackson Papers, Box 93, File 1, "Santa Clara Youth Village," DDEL.

57. Marie McCrum to Father Schmidt, 16 February 1961, Jackson Papers, Box 93, File 1, "Santa Clara Youth Village," DDEL. Iglói later moved on to coach at the Los Angeles Track Club. See "Sport: Ready for Anything," *Time*, 31 August 1962, http://content.time.com/time/magazine/article/0,9171,938923,00.html; "Magic of the Great Igloi."

58. Brundage to Ferenc Mező, 18 February 1957, ABC, Box 60, Reel 36, ICOSA.

59. Telegdy to Mayer, 29 April 1957, Correspondence of the NOC of Hungary, 1907–1969, Box 166, International Olympic Committee Archives (hereafter referred to as IOC Archives), Lausanne, Switzerland.

60. Brundage to Mayer, 11 May 1957, Correspondence of Avery Brundage, 1956–60, Box 5, IOC Archives.

61. Mayer to Telegdy, 15 May 1957, Correspondence of the NOC of Hungary, 1907–1969, Box 166, IOC Archives.

62. Telegdy to Mayer, 3 June 1957, Correspondence of the NOC of Hungary, 1907–1969, Box 166, IOC Archives.

63. Brundage to Mayer, 12 August 1957, Correspondence of Avery Brundage, 1956–60, Box 5, IOC Archives.

64. Szápáry to Avery Brundage, 1 August 1960, ABC, Box 132, Reel 73, ICOSA.

65. Brundage to Szápáry, 6 August 1960, ABC, Box 132, Reel 73, ICOSA.

66. Mayer to Brundage, 8 July 1960, Correspondence of Avery Brundage, 1956–60, Box 5, IOC Archives.

67. Mayer to Thomas de Márffy-Mantuano, 28 July 1960, ABC, Box 116, Reel 63, ICOSA.

68. Brundage to Roger Langley, 21 October 1952, ABC, Box 116, Reel 63, ICOSA.

69. Jackson to Jack Dowd, 8 June 1959, Jackson Papers, Box 60, "Hungarian Olympic Team," DDEL; Dowd to Jackson, 10 June 1959, Jackson Papers, Box 60, "Hungarian Olympic Team," DDEL.

70. Matthews to Jackson, 21 January 1960, Jackson Papers, Box 53, File 3, "Free Europe Committee, 1960," DDEL; Matthews to Jackson, 2 February 1960, Jackson Papers, Box 53, File 3, "Free Europe Committee, 1960," DDEL; Telegdy to Edward Rosenblum, 16 December 1959, Szápáry Papers, Box 2, "Roma."

71. "How to Try Too Hard," *Sports Illustrated*, 15 February 1960, 55.

72. Quoted from a copy of the *Congressional Record* sent to Father Schmidt by Congressman Charles S. Gubser. See Gubser to Father Schmidt, 6 April 1960, Schmidt Papers, Santa Clara Youth Village Files, Box 12, "Olympic Track Team—Biographies/Correspondence, 1960–61," SCUA; Father Schmidt to Gubser, 14 April 1960, Schmidt Papers, Santa Clara Youth Village Files, Box 12, "Olympic Track Team—Biographies/Correspondence, 1960–61," SCUA.

73. "How to Try Too Hard," *Sports Illustrated*, 15 February 1960, 55.

74. Brody to Larmon, 16 December 1957, Jackson Papers, Box 93, File 3, "Santa Clara Youth Village," DDEL.

Chapter 8. Operation Rome

1. Kenneth Osgood, *Total Cold War: Eisenhower's Secret Propaganda Battle at Home and Abroad* (Lawrence: University Press of Kansas, 2006), quote on 336.

2. Roy Clumpner, "Federal Involvement in Sport to Promote American Interest or Foreign Policy Objectives, 1950—1973," in *Sport and International Relations*, ed. B. Lowe, D. B. Kanin, and A. Strenk (Champaign, IL: Stipes, 1978), quote on 404; David Caute, *The Dancer Defects: The Struggle for Cultural Supremacy during the Cold War* (Oxford: Oxford University Press, 2003), 38–39.

3. Walter L. Hixson, *Parting the Curtain: Propaganda, Culture, and the Cold War, 1945–1961* (New York: St. Martin's Press, 1997), 101.

4. J. D. Parks, *Culture, Conflict and Coexistence: American–Soviet Cultural Relations, 1917–1958* (Jefferson, NC: McFarland, 1983), 116–33.

5. Nigel Gould-Davies, "The Logic of Soviet Cultural Diplomacy," *Diplomatic History* 27, no. 2 (2003): 200–205, quote on 213.

6. Frank Ninkovich, *U.S. Information Policy and Cultural Diplomacy* (New York: Foreign Policy Association, 1996), 23–25; Parks, *Culture, Conflict and Coexistence*, 134–55.

7. Hixson, *Parting the Curtain*, quotes on 110, 154; Ninkovich, *U.S. Information Policy and Cultural Diplomacy*, Dulles quote on 25–26; Parks, *Culture, Conflict and Coexistence*, 156–71; Yale Richmond, *Cultural Exchange and the Cold War: Raising the Iron Curtain* (University Park: Pennsylvania State University Press, 2003), 15.

8. Joseph M. Turrini, "'It Was Communism versus the Free World': The USA–USSR Dual Track Meet Series and the Development of Track and Field in the United States, 1958–1985," *Journal of Sport History* 28, no. 3 (2001): 428–29, quotes on 428; "Minutes of the 71st Annual Convention of the AAU," 4–7 December 1958, Archives of the Amateur Athletic Union of the United States (hereafter referred to as AAU Archives), Lake Buena Vista, Florida.

9. Konstantin Andrianov to Otto Mayer, 28 March 1957, IOC Member Andrianov, Konstantin, 1951–, International Olympic Committee Archives (hereafter referred to as IOC Archives), Lausanne, Switzerland.

10. "Minutes of the Joint AAU Executive and Foreign Relations Meeting," 20–21 June 1958, AAU Archives; "Minutes of the 71st Annual Convention of the AAU," 4–7 December 1958, AAU Archives; "Minutes of the 69th Annual Convention of the AAU," October–November 1956, AAU Archives.

11. Turrini, "'Communism versus the Free World,'" 429–30, quote on 430; Victor Peppard and James Riordan, *Playing Politics: Soviet Sport Diplomacy to 1992* (Greenwich, CT: Jai Press, 1993), 75–80.

12. Hixson, *Parting the Curtain*, 110.

13. Robert Thayer to Department of State, 18 September 1956, Record Group 59 (hereafter referred to as RG), Central Decimal File, 1955–59, Box 4835, 866.453/9–1856, National Archives (hereafter referred to as NA), College Park, Maryland.

14. Beam to Department of State, 14 August 1958, RG59, Central Decimal File, 1955–59, Box 4549, 848.453/8–1458, NA.

15. Osgood, *Total Cold War*, 230–36; "Remarks at the People-to-People Conference, September 11, 1956," *Public Papers of the Presidents of the United States: Dwight D. Eisenhower, 1956* (Washington, DC: U.S. Government Printing Office, 1958), 749–52.

16. "Report to the Nation: The First Seven Years," People-to-People Sports Committee pamphlet, Avery Brundage Collection, 1908–75 (hereafter referred to as ABC), Box 228, Reel 132, International Centre for Olympic Studies Archives (hereafter referred to as ICOSA), University of Western Ontario, London, Canada.

17. Edward Eagan to Fellow Americans, 20 August 1957, RG306, Subject Files, 1953–67, Box 24, "Sports Committee General," NA.

18. "Minutes of the Executive Body—People-to-People Sports Committee," 16 May 1957, RG306, Subject Files, 1953–67, Box 24, "Sports Committee Administration—Meetings—Minutes," NA; "Report to the Nation."

19. Avery Brundage to Manuel González Guerra, 16 November 1964, Correspondence of the NOC of Cuba, 1964–79, Box 98, IOC Archives; Brundage to Eagan, 12 November 1964, ABC, Box 228, Reel 132, ICOSA. Brundage was asked to become a member of the Sports Committee but had to decline because of his position as IOC president. See Brundage to Eagan, 9 February 1957, ABC, Box 333, Reel 145, ICOSA.

20. Richard C. Salvatierra to Department of State, 30 January 1959, RG59, Central Decimal File, 1955–59, Box 4062, 800.453/1–3059, NA; "Loss to Russia Costs U.S. Basketball Prestige," *New York Times*, 30 January 1959, 23.

21. Howson Ryan to Department of State, 3 February 1959, RG59, Central Decimal File, 1955–59, Box 4062, 800.453/2–359, NA.

22. See, for instance, Harold Zimman, "Memo from the Publisher," *Amateur Athlete* 29, no. 12 (June 1958): 5.

23. For more on this "dwindling," see Stephen J. Whitfield, *The Culture of the Cold War* (Baltimore: Johns Hopkins University Press, 1991), 205.

24. "1960 U.S. Olympic Committee Seeks $1,500,000 for Games Bid," *Amateur Athlete* 29, no. 7 (1958): quote on 8; "A.A.U. Olympic Development Sweeps Forward," *Amateur Athlete,* 29, no. 12 (1958): 7; "The New President Speaks," *Amateur Athlete* 31, no. 1 (1960): 8; "A.A.U. Aids Olympics," *New York Times*, 10 January 1958, 31; Thomas M. Domer,

"Sport in Cold War America, 1953–1963: The Diplomatic and Political Use of Sport in the Eisenhower and Kennedy Administrations," PhD diss., Marquette University, 1976, 179–81.

25. Henry P. McNulty to Bernard Yarrow, 6 June 1960, RFE/RL INC. Corporate Records (hereafter referred to as RFE/RL), Box 245, File 5, "Olympic Games General, 1960," Hoover Institution Archives (hereafter referred to as HA), Stanford University, California; Count Anthony Szápáry to Yarrow, 10 June 1960, RFE/RL, Box 245, File 5, "Olympic Games General, 1960," HA; "Olympic Evening Festival Program," no date (circa 1960), The Private Papers of Count Anthony Szápáry, Box 2, "Misc," Pound Ridge, New York; FEC press release, 8 July 1960, RFE/RL, Box 245, File 5, "Olympic Games General, 1960," HA; "Olympic Drive Opened," *New York Times*, 12 July 1960, 43.

26. "President Proclaims U.S. Olympic Week," *Amateur Athlete* 29, no. 10 (1958): 17.

27. "Transcript of Eisenhower's News Conference on Domestic and Foreign Matters," *New York Times*, 4 February 1960, 12.

28. Robert Ball, "The Big 'Little Olympics,'" *Sports Illustrated*, 8 September 1958, 53.

29. Tex Maule, "Is America a Second-Class Track Power?" *Sports Illustrated*, 2 February 1959, 34.

30. For more on the President's Council on Youth Fitness, see, for instance, Matthew T. Bowers and Thomas M. Hunt, "The President's Council on Physical Fitness and the Systematisation of Children's Play in America," *International Journal of the History Sport* 28, no. 11 (2011): 1496–1511.

31. Brundage to Rod O'Connor, 24 July 1957, ABC, Box 333, Reel 145, ICOSA.

32. Robert Cartwright to Christian Herter, 13 August 1957, Herter, Christian A.: Papers, 1957–61, Box 2, File 2, "Chronological File, August 1957," Dwight D. Eisenhower Presidential Library (hereafter referred to as DDEL), Abilene, Kansas.

33. "U.S. Relaxes 7-Year Ban on Travel Into Bulgaria," *New York Times*, 6 September 1957, 1.

34. Richard Espy, *The Politics of the Olympic Games* (Berkeley: University of California Press, 1979), 62; "U.S. Agrees to Admit Red China's Athletes," *New York Times*, 18 September 1957, 1.

35. Andrianov to Mayer, 28 March 1957, IOC Member Andrianov, Konstantin, 1951–, IOC Archives.

36. Mayer to Brundage, 2 April 1957, Correspondence of Avery Brundage, 1956–60, Box 5, IOC Archives.

37. "Red Issue May Bar '60 Olympics in U.S.," *New York Times*, 2 July 1957, 29.

38. Butler to Dulles, 9 September 1957, RG59, Central Decimal File, 1955–59, Box 4063, 800.4531/7–1257, NA.

39. "Visa Requirements for foreign athletes participating in the 1960 Winter Olympics, Squaw Valley, California," no date, RG59, Central Decimal File, 1955–59, Box 4063, 800.4531/7–1257, NA.

40. "Record of Dulles News Conference on Middle East Crisis and Other World Affairs," *New York Times*, 11 September 1957, 10; quote in Robert Cartwright to William Macomber, 9 August 1957, Dulles, John Foster: Papers, 1951–59, General Correspondence and Memoranda Series, Box 5, "Miscellaneous Correspondence May 16, 1957—August, 9, 1957," DDEL.

41. Espy, *Politics of the Olympic Games*, 61–62; "U.S. Agrees to Admit Red China's Athletes," *New York Times*, 18 September 1957, 1.

42. "Olympics View Decried," *New York Times*, 20 February 1960, 4.

43. "55th Session of the International Olympic Committee," Munich, 25–28 May 1959, IOC Archives. For more on China and the Olympics. see Susan Brownell, "'Sport and Politics Don't Mix': China's Relationship with the IOC during the Cold War," in *East Plays West: Sport and the Cold War*, ed. Stephen Wagg and David L. Andrews (New York: Routledge, 2007), 253–71.

44. "Olympic Body Ousts Chinese Nationalists," *New York Times*, 29 May 1959, 1.

45. Kenneth Wilson and Asa Bushnell to IOC, 31 July 1959, Correspondence of the NOC of the United States of America, 1955–66, Box 118, IOC Archives; Daniel Ferris to IOC, 23 June 1959, Correspondence of the NOC of the United States of America, 1955–66, Box 118, IOC Archives.

46. Page to Secretary of State, 28 May 1959, White House Office, Office of the Special Assistant for National Security Affairs: Records, 1952–61, OCB Series, Subject Series, Box 5, "Olympics," DDEL; "International Olympic Committee Resolution on Chinese Participation," 12 June 1959, RG59, Central Decimal File 1955–59, Box 4063, 800.4531/6–1259, NA.

47. Quote in "Censure by State Department," *New York Times*, 29 May 1959, 16; "U.S. Scores Ban on Taiwan Team," *New York Times*, 3 June 1959, 9.

48. Brundage to Albert Mayer, 15 August 1959, Correspondence of Avery Brundage, 1956–60, Box 5, IOC Archives.

49. "Brundage Denies Pressure by Reds," *New York Times*, 4 June 1959, 15.

50. Brundage to IOC Members, 23 June 1959, Douglas F. Roby Papers, Box 4, "People's Republic of China, 1965–1981," Bentley Historical Library, University of Michigan, Ann Arbor.

51. Karl Harr memorandum, 5 June 1959, White House Office, Office of the Special Assistant for National Security Affairs: Records, 1952–61, OCB Series, Subject Series, Box 5, "Olympics," DDEL.

52. "Statement on Olympic Situation," by Walter Robertson, 16 June 1959, White House Office, Office of the Special Assistant for National Security Affairs: Records, 1952–61, OCB Series, Subject Series, Box 5, "Olympics," DDEL.

53. "President Sees Politics in Olympics' China Step," *New York Times*, 18 June 1959, 14.

54. "Item for OCB Luncheon Discussion," 1 June 1959, White House Office, Office of the Special Assistant for National Security Affairs: Records, 1952–61, OCB Series, Subject Series, Box 5, "Olympics," DDEL.

55. "House Votes on Issue," *New York Times*, 4 June 1959, 15; Domer, "Sport in Cold War America, 1953–1963," 193.

56. "OCB Activity Report," 22 June 1959, White House Office, National Security Council Staff: Papers, 1948–1961, OCB Secretariat Series, Box 10, File 4, "OCB319.1 Activity Report," DDEL.

57. David Maraniss, *Rome 1960: The Olympics That Changed the World* (New York: Simon and Schuster, 2008), 58.

58. Whitney to Department of State, 25 June 1959, RG59, Central Decimal File 1955–59, Box 4063, 800.4531/6–2559, NA; Espy, *Politics of the Olympic Games*, 65–66.

59. Harold Zimman, "Best Winter Olympics—Ever!" *Amateur Athlete* 31, no. 3 (1960):

8; "The Winter Olympics Are On!" *Amateur Athlete* 31, no. 2 (1960): 8–9; Tim Ashwell, "Squaw Valley 1960," in *Encyclopedia of the Modern Olympic Movement*, ed. John E. Findling and Kimberly D. Pelle (Westport, CT: Greenwood Press, 2004)," 337–43; John Lucas, *The Modern Olympic Games* (London: A. S. Barnes, 1980): 174; Allen Guttmann, *The Olympics: A History of the Modern Games* (Urbana: University of Illinois Press, 2002), 104.

60. "Soviet Hails Olympics," *New York Times*, 2 March 1960, 45.

61. "The Haunted Valley," *New York Times*, 27 February 1960, 14.

62. "RFE's Coverage of the Winter Olympics, 1960," 11 March 1960, RFE/RL, Box 271, File 6, "Broadcasting Review Special Reports, 1958–1960," HA.

63. Quote in Clumpner, "Federal Involvement," 404; Ashwell, "Squaw Valley 1960," 341.

64. George Telegdy to John Matthews, no date (circa January–February 1960), C. D. Jackson: Papers, 1931–67, Series 2, Time INC. File, 1933–64, Subseries A, Alphabetical File, 1933–64 (hereafter referred to as Jackson Papers), Box 53, File 3, "Free Europe Committee, 1960," DDEL.

65. Jackson to Alexander Brody, 17 February 1960, Jackson Papers, Box 93, File 1, "Santa Clara Youth Village," DDEL.

66. André Laguerre to Jackson, 11 February 1960, Jackson Papers, Box 53, File 3, "Free Europe Committee, 1960," DDEL.

67. "HNSF Secretary General and Delegation's Trip to Europe and Attendance at XVII Olympic Games in Rome," no date, RFE/RL, Box 245, File 5, "Olympic Games General, 1960," HA.

68. A. Ross Johnson, *Radio Free Europe and Radio Liberty: The CIA Years and Beyond* (Stanford, CA: Stanford University Press, 2010), 51–55, 62, 118–29.

69. Quotes in "Evaluation of Current FEC Mission," 18 February 1960, Jackson Papers, Box 53, File 2, "Free Europe Committee, 1960," DDEL; "Plan of FEOP Operation in Europe," December 1959, RFE/RL, Box 197, File 7, "Free Europe Organizations and Publications," HA.

70. "Free Europe Committee and East–West Contacts," 10 June 1959, Jackson Papers, Box 53, File 2, "Free Europe Committee, 1959," DDEL.

71. "Round-up of FEOP Projects for the Rome Olympic Games," 22 July 1960, RFE/RL, Box 245, File 5, "Olympic Games General, 1960," HA.

72. "Round-up of FEOP Projects for the Rome Olympic Games," 22 July 1960, RFE/RL, Box 245, File 5, "Olympic Games General, 1960," HA.

73. Maraniss, *Rome 1960*, quote on 80; Corey Brennan, "The 1960 Rome Olympics: Spaces and Spectacle," in *Rethinking Matters Olympic: Investigations into the Socio-Cultural Study of the Modern Olympic Movement*, 10th International Symposium for Olympic Research, ed. R. K. Barney, J. Forsyth, and M. K. Heine (London, ON, Canada: International Centre for Olympic Studies, 2010), 18; Charles Thayer, "A Question of the Soul," Sports Illustrated, 15 August 1960, 73.

74. Barbara Keys comprehensively challenges Maraniss in Keys, "The 1960 Rome Summer Olympics: Birth of a New World?" in *Myths and Milestones in the History of Sport*, ed. Stephen Wagg (London: Palgrave Macmillan, 2011), 287–303. See also Guttmann, *Olympics*, 104–5.

75. Maraniss, *Rome 1960*, quote on 80; Guttmann, *Olympics*, 104–5; Keys, "1960 Rome Summer Olympics," 291–92.

76. Martin Kane, "Ready to Go in Rome," *Sports Illustrated*, 29 August 1960, first quote on 10; "The Olympic Torch," *New York Times*, 12 September 1960, second quote on 28.

77. Alfred V. Boerner to Department of State, 30 September 1960, RG59, Central Decimal File, 1960–63, Box 2698, 865.4531/9–3060, NA; Eagan to Brundage, 29 July 1960, ABC, Box 168, Reel 96, ICOSA; "Report to the Nation."

78. USIA official's quotes in Alfred V. Boerner to Department of State, 30 September 1960, RG59, Central Decimal File, 1960–63, Box 2698, 865.4531/9–3060, NA; "Czechoslovak Press Survey, No.746," no date, RFE/RL, Box 245, File 5, "Olympic Games General, 1960," HA; Stanislaus B. Milus to Department of State, 23 August 1960, RG59, Central Decimal File, 1960–63, Box 2239, 800.4531/1–460, NA; *Trud* quote in "Preliminary Account of the Olympic Games Operation," RFE/RL, Box 245, File 5, "Olympic Games General, 1960," HA.

79. Minton to Keith Turner, 16 July 1960, RFE/RL, Box 245, File 5, "Olympic Games General, 1960," HA.

80. Matthews to Minton, 21 July 1960, RFE/RL, Box 245, File 5, "Olympic Games General, 1960," HA.

81. Minton to John F. Leich, 27 July 1960, RFE/RL, Box 245, File 5, "Olympic Games General, 1960," HA.

82. Matthews to Minton, 21 July 1960, RFE/RL, Box 245, File 5, "Olympic Games General, 1960," HA.

83. "HNSF Secretary General and Delegation's Trip to Europe and Attendance at XVII Olympic Games in Rome," no date, RFE/RL, Box 245, File 5, "Olympic Games General, 1960," HA.

84. Campanaro to Leich, 28 August 1960, RFE/RL, Box 245, File 5, "Olympic Games General, 1960," HA; Campanaro to Leich, 5 September 1960, RFE/RL, Box 245, File 5, "Olympic Games General, 1960," HA; "Round-up of FEOP Projects for the Rome Olympic Games," 22 July 1960, RFE/RL, Box 245, File 5, "Olympic Games General, 1960," HA.

85. Campanaro to Leich, 8 September 1960, RFE/RL, Box 245, File 5, "Olympic Games General, 1960," HA. There also is evidence that the CIA approached a U.S. athlete, David Sime, for assistance in Rome. The CIA was under the impression that a Soviet long-jumper, Igor Ter-Ovanesyan, was ready to defect. Sime was asked to speak with Ter-Ovanesyan and arrange a meeting for the athlete with a CIA agent who operated under the fictitious name of Mr. Wolf. Sime accepted the mission and communicated with Ter-Ovanesyan during practice. Eventually a meeting was arranged where the Soviet could talk with Mr. Wolf at a restaurant. When the critical moment arrived, however, Ter-Ovanesyan panicked. He was unsure whether the man was a double agent. Rather than find out, he left the restaurant and abandoned any plans to defect. See Maraniss, *Rome 1960*, 26–28, 30, 114, 258.

86. "No Discrimination," *The Times* [London], 21 July 1960, 13; Minton to Leich, 27 July 1960, RFE/RL, Box 245, File 5, "Olympic Games General, 1960," HA.

87. Lord Birdwood, Chataway, and McWhirter to Mayer, 1960, ABC, Box 116, Reel 63, ICOSA; "Stateless Athletes and the Future," *The Times* [London], 10 September 1960, 3; "To Aid of Stateless Athletes," *The Times* [London], 9 August 1960, 3.

88. "New Olympic Appeal," *The Times* [London], 18 August 1960, 4.

89. "FEOP-Sponsored Activities in Connection with the Rome Olympics," no date, RFE/RL, Box 245, File 5, "Olympic Games General, 1960," HA. Before the Olympics, Tábori and Iglói were in the middle of a European tour paid for by the British Amateur Athletic Board. The FEC extended the tour by flying the pair to Rome.

90. "FEOP-Sponsored Activities in Connection with the Rome Olympics," no date, RFE/RL, Box 245, File 5, "Olympic Games General, 1960," HA; Campanaro to Leich, 2 September 1960, RFE/RL, Box 245, File 5, "Olympic Games General, 1960," HA; "Rome Olympics Report," 17 October 1960, RFE/RL, Box 245, File 5, "Olympic Games General, 1960," HA; "Hungarian Waterball Team to Participate in Olympic Games in Rome," 2 May 1960, RFE/RL, Box 245, File 5, "Olympic Games General, 1960," HA; "Preparatory Training for Olympic Water Ball Match," 5 July 1960, RFE/RL, Box 245, File 5, "Olympic Games General, 1960," HA.

91. Quotes in "Preliminary Account of the Olympic Games Operation," no date, RFE/RL, Box 245, File 5, "Olympic Games General, 1960," HA; "A general characteristic of persons who came from Poland for the 1960 Olympic Games in Rome as compared with the Youth Festival in Vienna in 1959," October 1960, RFE/RL, Box 245, File 5, "Olympic Games General, 1960," HA; "Rome Olympics Report," 17 October 1960, RFE/RL, Box 245, File 5, "Olympic Games General, 1960," HA; "FEOP-Sponsored Activities in Connection with the Rome Olympics," no date, RFE/RL, Box 245, File 5, "Olympic Games General, 1960," HA.

92. "Rome Olympics Report," 17 October 1960, RFE/RL, Box 245, File 5, "Olympic Games General, 1960," HA; "Olympic Games—Student Contact Program," 29 April 1960, RFE/RL, Box 245, File 5, "Olympic Games General, 1960," HA.

93. W. Zahorski, I. Barev, and R. Frasheri to Peter Zenki, 27 June 1960, RFE/RL, Box 245, File 5, "Olympic Games General, 1960," HA; Campanaro to Leich, 2 September 1960, RFE/RL, Box 245, File 5, "Olympic Games General, 1960," HA. For more on the Assembly of Captive European Nations, see Anna Mazurkiewicz, "'The Voice of the Silenced Peoples': The Assembly of Captive European Nations," in *Anti-Communist Minorities in the U.S.: Political Activism of Ethnic Refugees*, ed. Ieva Zake (New York: Palgrave Macmillan, 2009), 167–85.

94. "Rome Olympics Report," 17 October 1960, RFE/RL, Box 245, File 5, "Olympic Games General, 1960," HA; quote in "Round-up of FEOP Projects for the Rome Olympic Games," 22 July 1960, RFE/RL, Box 245, File 5, "Olympic Games General, 1960," HA.

95. Quotes in "Rome Olympics Report," 17 October 1960, RFE/RL, Box 245, File 5, "Olympic Games General, 1960," HA; "Round-up of FEOP Projects for the Rome Olympic Games," 22 July 1960, RFE/RL, Box 245, File 5, "Olympic Games General, 1960," HA; Campanaro to Leich, 2 September 1960, RFE/RL, Box 245, File 5, "Olympic Games General, 1960," HA.

96. "Rome Olympics Report," 17 October 1960, RFE/RL, Box 245, File 5, "Olympic Games General, 1960," HA.

97. "Olympians Rated Best U.S. Has Had," *New York Times*, 13 August 1960, 19.

98. "Somber Second Thoughts," *New York Times*, 13 September 1960, 42.

99. "Conclusions and Recommendations of the President's Committee on Information Activities Abroad—Chapter VI," December 1960, *United States Declassified Documents Reference System* (Woodbridge, CT, 1990), document number 2216, 55.

Conclusion

1. A. Ross Johnson, *Radio Free Europe and Radio Liberty: The CIA Years and Beyond* (Stanford, CA: Stanford University Press, 2010), 131–32.

2. Sig Mickelson, *America's Other Voice: The Story of Radio Free Europe and Radio Liberty* (New York: Praeger, 1983), 121–28, Case quote on 130; Johnson, *Radio Free Europe and Radio Liberty*, 202–5, 215–17; Hugh Wilford, *The Mighty Wurlitzer: How the CIA Played America* (Cambridge, MA: Harvard University Press, 2008), 233–48, "harebrained" quote on 234.

3. John Richardson to Count Anthony Szápáry, 3 January 1962, Private Papers of Count Anthony Szápáry (hereafter referred to as Szápáry Papers), Box 2, "Antal Szapary," Pound Ridge, New York; Szápáry to Richardson, 5 December 1961, Szápáry Papers, Box 2, "R."

4. Szápáry to C. D. Jackson, 2 February 1962, C. D. Jackson: Papers, 1931–67, Series 2, Time Inc. File, 1933–64, Subseries A, Alphabetical File, 1933–64 (hereafter referred to as Jackson Papers), Box 53, "Free Europe Committee, 1962," Dwight D. Eisenhower Presidential Library (hereafter referred to as DDEL), Abilene, Kansas.

5. Jackson to Bernard Yarrow, 16 March 1962, Jackson Papers, Box 53, "Free Europe Committee, 1962," DDEL.

6. Yarrow to Jackson, 27 March 1962, Jackson Papers, Box 53, "Free Europe Committee, 1962," DDEL.

7. "Minutes of the International Olympic Committee 60th Session," Annex 4, Baden-Baden, 16–20 October 1963, International Olympic Committee Archives (hereafter referred to as IOC Archives), Lausanne, Switzerland.

8. "IOC Executive Board Meeting," Lausanne, 26–27 June 1964, IOC Archives; "Minutes of the International Olympic Committee 62nd Session," Annex 10, Tokyo, 6–8 October 1964, IOC Archives.

9. Asa Bushnell, ed., *The United States Olympic Book* (Providence, RI: Riverhouse, 1964), 38, 39, 50.

10. "List of Amendments to the Olympic Charter, 1964," Szápáry Papers, Box 2, "International Olympic Committee."

11. J. W. Brinkley to Christopher Emmet, 3 September 1963, RFE/RL Inc. Corporate Records (hereafter referred to as RFE/RL), Box 343, File 20, "Telegdy, George," Hoover Institute Archives (hereafter referred to as HA), Stanford University, California.

12. "Hungary's Professional Sportsmen," *East Europe* 12, no. 2 (1963): quotes on 11, 12, and 14; "George Telegdy, Aided Defectors at Olympics," *New York Times*, 15 February 1984, A25. Telegdy also sent his article to Avery Brundage. See Telegdy to Brundage, 22 March 1963, Avery Brundage Collection, 1908–75 (hereafter referred to as ABC), Box 132, Reel 73, International Centre for Olympic Studies Archives (hereafter referred to as ICOSA), University of Western Ontario, London, Ontario, Canada.

13. "Operation Griffin," by George Telegdy, no date, Szápáry Papers, Box 2, "Confidential Reports—Operation Eagle."

14. "Jackson Committee Report," abridged version, no date, US DDRS, document number 1163; [W.] Scott Lucas, "Mobilizing Culture: The State–Private Network and the CIA in the Early Cold War," in *War and Cold War in American Foreign Policy 1942–62*, ed. Dale Carter and Robin Clifton (Houndsmills, U.K.: Palgrave, 2002), 98–99.

15. Wilford, *Mighty Wurlitzer*, 5–10, quote on 10.

16. For more on the degree of CIA control, see [W.] Scott Lucas, "Beyond Freedom, Beyond Control: Approaches to Culture and the State–Private Network in the Cold War," *Intelligence and National Security* 18, no. 2 (2003): 58–61.

17. See pamphlet in IOC file, World Federation of Democratic Youth, Correspondence, 1955–59, IOC Archives.

18. Another example is the Committee for a Free Asia. See Harry Edward to Brundage, 7 January 1953, ABC, Box 223, Reel 130, ICOSA.

19. Philip M. Taylor, "Through a Glass Darkly? The Psychological Climate and Psychological Warfare of the Cold War," in *Cold War Propaganda in the 1950's*, ed. Gary D. Rawnsley (Houndsmills, U.K.: Macmillan, 1999), 225; Laura A. Belmonte, *Selling the American Way: U.S. Propaganda and the Cold War* (Philadelphia: University of Pennsylvania Press, 2008), 178–79.

20. Jessica C. E. Gienow-Hecht, "Culture and the Cold War in Europe," in *The Cambridge History of the Cold War*, ed. Melvin P. Leffler and Odd Arne Westad. Vol. 1, *Origins*, (Cambridge: Cambridge University Press, 2010), 406–11.

21. Thomas M. Domer, "Sport in Cold War America, 1953–1963: The Diplomatic and Political Use of Sport in the Eisenhower and Kennedy Administrations," PhD diss., Marquette University, 1976, 33.

22. For a survey of the rivalry, see David B. Kanin, "Superpower Sport in Cold War and 'Détente,'" in *Sport and International Relations*, ed. B. Lowe, D. B. Kanin, and A. Strenk (Champaign, IL: Stipes, 1978), 249–62.

23. Robert F. Kennedy, "A Bold Proposal for America Sport," *Sports Illustrated*, 27 July 1964, 13.

24. Gerald R. Ford, "In Defense of the Competitive Urge," *Sports Illustrated*, 8 July 1974, 17.

25. Thomas M. Hunt, "Countering the Soviet Threat in the Olympic Medals Race," *International Journal of the History of Sport* 24, no. 6 (2007): 796–818; James A. R. Nafziger, "The Amateur Sports Act of 1978," *BYU Law Review* no. 1 (1983): 47–99; Robert K. Barney, Stephen R. Wenn, and Scott G. Martyn, *Selling the Five Rings: The International Olympic Committee and the Rise of Olympic Commercialism* (Salt Lake City: University of Utah Press, 2004.

26. Thomas M. Hunt, "American Sport Policy and the Cultural Cold War: The Lyndon B. Johnson Presidential Years," *Journal of Sport History* 33, no. 3 (2006): 277–78; "Administrative History of the Department of State during the Johnson Administration," vol. 1, ch. 2, US DDRS: 1990 3412.

27. The Richard Nixon White House, for instance, sanctioned bribes for IOC officials to bring the 1976 Olympics to the United States. See Nicholas Evan Sarantakes, "Moscow versus Los Angeles: The Nixon White House Wages Cold War in the Olympic Selection Process," *Cold War History* 9, no. 1 (2009): 135–57. The Ronald Reagan administration also used a persuasive propaganda campaign to urge African and Asian national Olympic committees to send teams to the 1984 Los Angeles Olympics after the Soviet Union had anonymously sent the committees fake Ku Klux Klan leaflets. See Nicholas J. Cull, *The Cold War and the United States Information Agency: American Propaganda and Public Diplomacy, 1945–1989* (Cambridge: Cambridge University Press, 2008), 438–39.

28. Toby C. Rider, "Filling the Information Gap: Radio Free Europe–Radio Liberty and the Politics of Accreditation at the 1984 Los Angeles Olympic Games," *International Journal of the History of Sport* 32, no. 1 (2015): 37–52.

29. Nicholas Evan Sarantakes, *Dropping the Torch: Jimmy Carter, the Olympic Boycott, and the Cold War* (New York: Cambridge University Press, 2011).

30. Tom Braden, "I'm Glad the CIA Is 'Immoral,'" *Saturday Evening Post*, 20 May 1967, 14.

Bibliography

Aldrich, Richard J. "OSS, CIA and European Unity: The American Committee on United Europe, 1949–60." *Diplomacy and Statecraft* 8, no.1 (1997): 184–227.

Arndt, Richard T. *The First Resort of Kings: American Cultural Diplomacy in the Twentieth Century*. Washington, DC: Potomac, 2005.

Ashwell, Tim. "Squaw Valley 1960." In *Encyclopedia of the Modern Olympic Movement*, edited by John E. Findling and Kimberly D. Pelle, 337–43. Westport, CT: Greenwood Press, 2004.

Barghoorn, Frederick C. *The Soviet Cultural Offensive: The Role of Cultural Diplomacy in Soviet Foreign Policy*. Princeton, NJ: Princeton University Press, 1960.

———. *Soviet Foreign Propaganda*. Princeton, NJ: Princeton University Press, 1964.

Barnes, Trevor. "The Secret Cold War: The CIA and American Foreign Policy in Europe, 1946–1956, Part I." *Historical Journal* 24, no. 2 (1981): 399–415.

Barney, Robert K. "Avery Brundage." In *Encyclopedia of the Modern Olympic Movement*, edited by John E. Findling and Kimberly D. Pelle, 471–82. Westport, CT: Greenwood Press, 2004.

Barney, Robert K., Stephen R. Wenn, and Scott G. Martyn. *Selling the Five Rings: The International Olympic Committee and the Rise of Olympic Commercialism*. Salt Lake City: University of Utah Press, 2004.

Barrett, Edward W. *Truth Is Our Weapon*. New York: Funk and Wagnalls, 1953.

Beck, Peter J. "Britain and the Cold War's 'Cultural Olympics': Responding to the Political Drive of Soviet Sport, 1945–58." *Contemporary British History* 19, no. 2 (2005): 169–85.

———. "The British Government and the Olympic Movement: The 1948 London Olympics." *International Journal of the History of Sport* 25, no. 5 (2008): 615–47.

———. "'War minus the Shooting': George Orwell on International Sport and the Olympics." *Sport in History* 33, no. 1 (2013): 72–94.

Békés, Csaba. "East Central Europe, 1953–1956." In *The Cambridge History of the Cold War*. edited by Melvin P. Leffler and Odd Arne Westad, Vol. 1, *Origins*, 334–52. Cambridge, U.K.: Cambridge University Press, 2010.

Belmonte, Laura A. "Exporting America: The U.S. Propaganda Offensive, 1945–1959." In *The Arts of Democracy: Art, Public Culture, and the State*, edited by Casey Nelson Blake, 123–50. Philadelphia: University of Pennsylvania Press, 2007.

———. *Selling the American Way: U.S. Propaganda and the Cold War*. Philadelphia: University of Pennsylvania Press, 2008.

Bon Tempo, Carl J. *Americans at the Gate: The United States and Refugees during the Cold War*. Princeton, NJ: Princeton University Press, 2008.

Bowers, Matthew T., and Thomas M. Hunt. "The President's Council on Physical Fitness and the Systematisation of Children's Play in America." *International Journal of the History Sport* 28, no. 11 (2011): 1496–1511.

Brands, H. W. Jr. *Cold Warriors: Eisenhower's Generation and American Foreign Policy*. New York: Columbia University Press, 1988.

Brennan, Corey. "The 1960 Rome Olympics: Spaces and Spectacle." In *Rethinking Matters Olympic: Investigations into the Socio-Cultural Study of the Modern Olympic Movement, 10th International Symposium for Olympic Research*, edited by R. K. Barney, J. Forsyth and M. K. Heine, 17–29. London, ON, Canada: International Centre for Olympic Studies, 2010.

Brownell, Susan. "Sport and Politics Don't Mix: China's Relationship with the IOC during the Cold War." In *East Plays West: Sport and the Cold War*, edited by Stephen Wagg and David L. Andrews, 253–71. New York: Routledge, 2007.

Bu, Liping. "Educational Exchange and Cultural Diplomacy in the Cold War." *Journal of American Studies* 33, no. 3 (1999): 393–415.

Bushnell, Asa, editor. *The United States Olympic Book*. Providence, RI: Riverhouse, 1964.

Campbell, Jennifer L. "Creating Something Out of Nothing: The Office of Inter-American Affairs Music Committee (1940–1941) and the Inception of a Policy for Musical Diplomacy." *Diplomatic History* 36, no. 1 (2012): 29–39.

Caute, David. *The Dancer Defects: The Struggle for Cultural Supremacy during the Cold War*. Oxford: Oxford University Press, 2003.

Clumpner, Roy. "Federal Involvement in Sport to Promote American Interest or Foreign Policy Objectives, 1950–1973." In *Sport and International Relations*, edited by B. Lowe, D. B. Kanin, and A. Strenk, 400–52. Champaign, IL: Stipes, 1978.

———. "Pragmatic Coercion: The Role of Government in Sport in the United States." In *Sport and Politics*, edited by Gerald Redmond, 5–12. Champaign, IL: Human Kinetics, 1984.

Collins, Larry D. "The Free Europe Committee: An American Weapon of the Cold War." PhD diss., Carleton University, 1973.

Corke, Sarah-Jane. "George Kennan and the Inauguration of Political Warfare." *Journal of Conflict Studies* 26, no. 1 (2006): 101–19.

Creel, George. *How We Advertised America*. New York: Harper and Brothers, 1920.

Cull, Nicholas J. *The Cold War and the United States Information Agency: American Propaganda and Public Diplomacy, 1945–1989*. Cambridge, U.K.: Cambridge University Press, 2008.

———. "Public Diplomacy and the Private Sector: The United States Information Agency, Its Predecessors and the Private Sector." In *The U.S. Government, Citizen Groups and the Cold War: The State–Private Network*, edited by Helen Laville and Hugh Wilford, 210–26. New York: Routledge, 2006.

———. "The Public Diplomacy of the Modern Olympic Games and China's Soft Power Strategy." In *Owning the Olympics: Narratives of the New China*, edited by Monroe E. Price and Daniel Dayan. 117–44. Ann Arbor: University of Michigan Press, 2008.

Davis, Michael Gill. "The Cold War, Refugees, and U.S. Immigration Policy, 1952–1965." PhD diss., Vanderbilt University, 1996.

Del Pero, Mario. "The United States and 'Psychological Warfare' in Italy, 1948–1955." *Journal of American History* 87, no. 4 (2001): 1304–34.

Dichter, Heather L. "Sporting Democracy: The Western Allies' Reconstruction of Germany through Sport, 1944–1952." PhD diss., University of Toronto, 2008.

Dizard, Wilson P. *The Strategy of Truth: The Story of the U.S. Information Service*. Washington, DC: Public Affairs Press, 1961.

Domer, Thomas M. "Sport in Cold War America, 1953–1963: The Diplomatic and Political Use of Sport in the Eisenhower and Kennedy Administrations." PhD diss., Marquette University, 1976.

Dyreson, Mark. *Crafting Patriotism for Global Dominance: America at the Olympics*. New York: Routledge, 2009.

———. "Johnny Weissmuller and the Old Global Capitalism: The Origins of the Federal Blueprint for Selling American Culture to the World." *International Journal of the History of Sport* 25, no. 2 (2008): 268–83.

———. *Making the American Team: Sport, Culture, and the Olympic Experience*. Urbana: University of Illinois Press, 1998.

———. "Marketing National Identity: The Olympic Games of 1932 and American Culture." *Olympika* 4 (1995): 23–48.

Edelman, Robert. *Serious Fun: A History of Spectator Sports in the U.S.S.R.* New York: Oxford University Press, 1993.

Eisen, George. "The Voices of Sanity: American Diplomatic Reports from the 1936 Berlin Olympiad." *Journal of Sport History* 11 no. 3 (1984): 56–78.

Espy, Richard. *The Politics of the Olympic Games*. Berkeley: University of California Press, 1979.

Fowkes, Ben. *The Rise and Fall of Communism in Eastern Europe*. New York: St. Martin's Press, 1993.

Gaddis, John Lewis. *The Cold War: A New History*. New York: Penguin, 2005.

Gati, Charles. *Hungary and the Soviet Bloc*. Durham, NC: Duke University Press, 1986.

Gienow-Hecht, Jessica C. E. "Culture and the Cold War in Europe." In *The Cambridge History of the Cold War: Volume 1: Origins*, edited by Melvin P. Leffler and Odd Arne Westad, 398–419. Cambridge, U.K.: Cambridge University Press, 2010.

———. "Shame on US? Academics, Cultural Transfer, and the Cold War—A Critical Review." *Diplomatic History* 24, no. 3 (2000): 465–94.

Goldstein, Edward S. "Sigfrid Edström." In *Encyclopedia of the Modern Olympic Movement*, edited by John E. Findling and Kimberly D. Pelle, 468–70. Westport, CT: Greenwood Press, 2004.

Gounot, André. "Sport or Political Organization: Structures and Characteristics of the Red Sport International, 1921–1937." *Journal of Sport History* 28, no. 1 (2001): 23–39.

Grant, Susan. *Physical Culture and Sport in Soviet Society: Propaganda, Acculturation, and Transformation in the 1920s and 1930s*. New York: Routledge, 2013.

Grose, Peter. *Operation Rollback: America's Secret War behind the Iron Curtain*. New York: Houghton Mifflin, 2000.

Guttmann, Allen. *The Games Must Go On: Avery Brundage and the Olympic Movement*. New York: Columbia University Press, 1984.

———. *The Olympics: A History of the Modern Games*. Urbana: University of Illinois Press, 2002.

Haight, David. "The Papers of C. D. Jackson: A Glimpse at President Eisenhower's Psychological Warfare Expert." *Manuscripts* 28 (Winter 1976): 27–37.

Hart, Justin. *Empire of Ideas: The Origins of Public Diplomacy and the Transformation of U.S. Foreign Policy*. New York: Oxford University Press, 2013.

Heil, Alan L. "The Voice of America: A Brief Cold War History." In *Cold War Broadcasting: Impact on the Soviet Union and Eastern Europe*, edited by A. Ross Johnson and R. Eugene Parta, 25–48. New York: Central European University Press, 2010.

History of the Office of the Coordinator of Inter-American Affairs. Washington, DC: United States Government Printing Office, 1947.

Hixon, Walter L. *Parting the Curtain: Propaganda, Culture, and the Cold War, 1945–1961*. New York: St. Martin's Press, 1997.

Hoberman, John. *The Olympic Crisis: Sport, Politics and the Moral Order*. New Rochelle, NY: Aristide D. Caratzas, 1986.

Hobsbawm, Eric. *Age of Extremes: The Short Twentieth Century, 1914–1991*. London: Abacus, 1994.

———. "Mass-Producing Traditions: Europe, 1870–1914." In *The Invention of Tradition*, edited by Eric Hobsbawm and Terence Ranger. Cambridge, U.K.: Cambridge University Press, 1983.

Horne, John. "The Politics of Hosting the Olympic Games." In *The Politics of the Olympics: A Survey*, edited by Alan Bairner and Gyozo Molnar, 27–40. London: Routledge, 2010.

Houlihan, Barrie. "International Politics and Olympic Governance." In *Global Olympics: Historical and Sociological Studies of the Modern Games*, edited by Kevin Young and Kevin B. Wamsley, 127–42. Amsterdam, Holland: Elsevier, 2005.

Hunt, Thomas M. "American Sport Policy and the Cultural Cold War: The Lyndon B. Johnson Presidential Years." *Journal of Sport History* 33, no. 3 (2006): 273–97.

———. "Countering the Soviet Threat in the Olympic Medals Race." *International Journal of the History of Sport* 24, no. 6 (2007): 796–818.

Ingimundarson, Valur. "Containing the Offensive: The 'Chief of the Cold War' and the Eisenhower Administration's German Policy." *Presidential Studies Quarterly* 27, no. 3 (1997): 480–95.

Ivan, Emese, and Dezső Iván. "The 1956 Revolution and the Melbourne Olympics: The Changing Perceptions of a Dramatic Story." *Hungarian Studies Review* 35, nos. 1–2 (2008): 9–23.

Jeffreys-Jones, Rhodri. *The CIA and American Democracy*. New Haven, CT: Yale University Press, 1989.

Johnson, A. Ross. *Radio Free Europe and Radio Liberty: The CIA Years and Beyond*. Stanford, CA: Stanford University Press, 2010.

Kádár Lynn, Katalin. "At War while at Peace: United States Cold War Policy and the National Committee for a Free Europe, Inc." In *The Inauguration of Organized Politi-*

cal Warfare: Cold War Organizations Sponsored by the National Committee for a Free Europe/Free Europe Committee*, edited by Katalin Kádár Lynn, 7–70. Saint Helena, CA: Helena History Press, 2013.

———. *Tibor Eckhardt: His American Years, 1941–1972*. New York: Columbia University Press, 2007.

Kanin, David B. "Superpower Sport in Cold War and 'Détente.'" In *Sport and International Relations*, edited by B. Lowe, D. B. Kanin, and A. Strenk, 249–62. Champaign, IL: Stipes, 1978.

Kennedy, Liam, and [W.] Scott Lucas. "Enduring Freedom: Public Diplomacy and U.S. Foreign Policy." *American Quarterly* 57, no. 2 (2005): 309–33.

Kent, Hilary, and John Merritt. "The Cold War and the Melbourne Olympic Games." In *Better Dead Than Red: Australia's First Cold War, 1945–1959*, vol. 2, edited by Ann Curthoys and John Merritt, 170–210. Sydney, Australia: Allen and Unwin, 1986.

Keys, Barbara. "The Early Cold War Olympics, 1952–1960: Political, Economic and Human Rights Dimensions." In *The Palgrave Handbook of Olympic Studies*, edited by Helen Lenskyi and Stephen Wagg, 72–87. Houndsmills, U.K.: Palgrave Macmillan, 2012.

———. *Globalizing Sport: National Rivalry and International Community in the 1930s*. Cambridge, MA: Harvard University Press, 2006.

———. "The Internationalization of Sport, 1890–1939." In *The Cultural Turn: Essays in the History of U.S. Foreign Relations*, ed. Frank A. Ninkovich and Liping Bu (Chicago: Imprint, 2001), 201–19.

———. "The 1956 Melbourne Olympic Games and the Postwar International Order." In *1956: European and Global Perspectives*, edited by C. Fink, F. Hadler, and T. Schramm, 283–307. Leipzig, Germany: Leipziger Universitätsverlag, 2006.

———. "The 1960 Rome Summer Olympics: Birth of a New World?" In *Myths and Milestones in the History of Sport*, edited by Stephen Wagg, 287–303. London: Palgrave Macmillan, 2011.

———. "Soviet Sport and Transnational Mass Culture in the 1930s." *Journal of Contemporary History* 38, no. 3 (2003): 413–34.

———. "Spreading Peace, Democracy, and Coca-Cola: Sport and American Cultural Expansion in the 1930s." *Diplomatic History* 28, no. 2 (2004): 165–96.

Kowalski, Ronnie, and Dilwyn Porter. "Cold War Football: British European Encounters in the 1940s and 1950s." In *East Plays West: Sport and the Cold War*, edited by Stephen Wagg and David L. Andrews, 64–81. New York: Routledge, 2007.

Krabbendam, Hans, and Giles Scott-Smith, editors. *The Cultural Cold War in Western Europe, 1945–1960*. London: Frank Cass, 2003.

Krugler, David F. *The Voice of America and the Domestic Propaganda Battles, 1945–1953*. Columbia: University of Missouri Press, 2000.

Laurie, Clayton D. *The Propaganda Warriors: America's Crusade against Nazi Germany*. Lawrence: University Press of Kansas, 1996.

Laville, Helen. *Cold War Women: The International Activities of American Women's Organizations*. Manchester, U.K.: Manchester University Press, 2002.

———. "The Committee of Correspondence: CIA Funding of Women's Groups, 1952–1967." *Intelligence and National Security* 12, no. 1 (1997): 104–21.

Laville, Helen, and Hugh Wilford, editors. *The US Government, Citizen Groups and the Cold War: The State–Private Network.* New York: Routledge, 2006.

Lebovic, Sam. "From War Junk to Educational Exchange: The World War II Origins of the Fulbright Program and the Foundations of American Cultural Globalism, 1945–1950." *Diplomatic History* 37, no. 2 (2013): 280–312.

Lechenperg, Harold, editor. *Olympic Games 1960.* New York: A. S. Barnes, 1960.

Leffler, Melvyn P. "The Emergence of an American Grand Strategy, 1945–1952." In *The Cambridge History of the Cold War.* Vol. 1, *Origins,* edited by Melvin P. Leffler and Odd Arne Westad, 67–89. Cambridge, U.K.: Cambridge University Press, 2010.

———. *A Preponderance of Power: National Security, the Truman Administration, and the Cold War.* Stanford, CA: Stanford University Press, 1992.

Lehr, Robert E. "The American Olympic Committee, 1896–1940: From Chaos to Order." PhD diss., Pennsylvania State University, 1985.

Leich, John Foster. "Great Expectations: The National Councils in Exile, 1950–60." *Polish Review* 35, no. 3 (1990): 183–96.

Listowel, Judith. *The Golden Tree: The Story of Peter, Tomi and Their Family Typifies the Enduring Spirit of Hungary.* London: Odhams Press, 1958.

Llewellyn, Matthew P. "The Battle of Shepherd's Bush." *International Journal of the History of Sport* 28, no. 5 (2011): 688–710.

Llewellyn, Matthew P., and John T. Gleaves. "The Rise of the 'Shamateur': The International Olympic Committee and the Preservation of the Amateur Ideal." In *Problems, Possibilities, and Promising Practices: Critical Dialogues on the Olympic and Paralympic Games,* edited by J. Forsyth and K. B. Wamsley, 23–28. London, ON, Canada: International Centre for Olympic Studies, 2012.

———. "A Universal Dilemma: The British *Sporting Life* and the Complex, Contested, and Contradictory State of Amateurism." *Journal of Sport History* 41, no. 1 (2014): 95–116.

Loory, Stuart. "The CIA's Use of the Press: A 'Mighty Wurlitzer.'" *Columbia Journalism Review* 13 (1974): 9–18.

Lucas, John A. "American Preparations for the First Post World War Olympic Games, 1919–1920." *Journal of Sport History* 10, no. 2 (1983): 30–44.

———. "Architects of the Modernized American Olympic Committee, 1921–1928: Gustavus Town Kirby, Roberts Means Thompson, and General Douglas MacArthur." *Journal of Sport History* 22, no. 1 (1995): 38–45.

———. "The Influence of Anglo-American Sport on Pierre de Coubertin—Modern Olympic Games Founder." In *The Modern Olympics,* edited by Peter J. Graham and Horst Ueberhorst, 27–36. Westpoint, NY: Leisure Press, 1976.

———. *The Modern Olympic Games.* London: A. S. Barnes, 1980.

Lucas, John A., and Smith, Ronald. *The Saga of American Sport.* Philadelphia: Lea and Febiger, 1978.

Lucas, [W.] Scott. "Beyond Freedom, Beyond Control: Approaches to Culture and the State–Private Network in the Cold War." *Intelligence and National Security* 18, no. 2 (2003): 53–72.

———. "Campaigns of Truth: The Psychological Strategy Board and American Ideology, 1951–1953." *International History Review* 18, no. 2 (1996): 253–504.

———. *Freedom's War: The American Crusade against the Soviet Union*. New York: New York University Press, 1999.

———. "Mobilizing Culture: The State-Private Network and the CIA in the Early Cold War." In *War and Cold War in American Foreign Policy 1942-62*, edited by Dale Carter and Robin Clifton, 83–107. Houndsmills, U.K.: Palgrave, 2002.

Lucas, [W.] Scott, and Kaeten Mistry. "Illusions of Coherence: George F. Kennan, U.S. Strategy and Political Warfare in the Early Cold War, 1946–1950." *Diplomatic History* 33, no. 1 (2009): 39–66.

MacAloon, John J. *This Great Symbol: Pierre de Coubertin and the Origins of the Modern Olympic Games*. Chicago: University of Chicago Press, 1981.

MacCambridge, Michael. *The Franchise: A History of Sports Illustrated Magazine*. New York: Hyperion, 1997.

Mandell, Richard. *The Nazi Olympics*. New York: Macmillan, 1971.

Maraniss, David. *Rome 1960: The Olympics That Changed the World*. New York: Simon and Schuster, 2008.

Marrus, Michael R. *The Unwanted: European Refugees in the Twentieth Century*. New York: Oxford University Press, 1985.

Marvin, Carolyn. "Avery Brundage and American Participation in the 1936 Olympic Games." *Journal of American Studies* 16, no. 1 (1982): 81–105.

Massaro, John. "Press Box Propaganda? The Cold War and *Sports Illustrated*, 1956." *Journal of American Culture* 26, no. 3 (2003): 361–70.

Mastney, Vojtech. "The Elusive Détente: Stalin's Successors and the West." In *The Cold War after Stalin's Death*, edited by Klaus Larres and Kenneth Osgood, 3–26. Lanham, MD: Rowman and Littlefield, 2006.

Mazurkiewicz, Anna. "The Voice of the Silenced Peoples: The Assembly of Captive European Nations." In *Anti-Communist Minorities in the U.S.: Political Activism of Ethnic Refugees*, edited by Ieva Zake, 167–85. New York: Palgrave Macmillan, 2009.

McMahon, Robert J. "US National Security Policy from Eisenhower to Kennedy." In *The Cambridge History of the Cold War*. Vol. 1, *Origins*, edited by Melvin P. Leffler and Odd Arne Westad, 288–311. Cambridge, U.K.: Cambridge University Press, 2010.

Mickelson, Sig. *America's Other Voice: The Story of Radio Free Europe and Radio Liberty*. New York: Praeger, 1983.

Miller, James E. "Taking Off the Gloves: The United States and the Italian Elections of 1948." *Diplomatic History* 7, no. 1 (1983): 35–55.

Miscamble, Wilson D. *George F. Kennan and the Making of American Foreign Policy, 1947–1950*. Princeton, NJ: Princeton University Press, 1992.

Mistry, Kaeten. "The Case for Political Warfare: Strategy, Organization and US Involvement in the 1948 Italian Election." *Cold War History* 6, no. 3 (2006): 301–29.

Mitrovich, Gregory. *Undermining the Kremlin: America's Strategy to Subvert the Soviet Bloc, 1947–1956*. Ithaca, NY: Cornell University Press, 2000.

Monnin, Eric, and Renaud David. "The Melbourne Games in the Context of the International Tensions of 1956." *Journal of Olympic History* 17, no. 3 (2009): 34–40.

Moretti, Anthony. "*New York Times* Coverage of the Soviet Union's Entrance into the Olympic Games." *Sport History Review* 38 (2007): 55–72.

Morton, Henry. *Soviet Sport, Mirror of Soviet Society*. London: Crowell-Collier, 1963.

Müller, Norbert, editor. *Pierre de Coubertin 1863–1937: Olympism; Selected Writings*. Lausanne, Switzerland: International Olympic Committee, 2000.

Nafziger, James A. R. "The Amateur Sports Act of 1978." *BYU Law Review* no. 1 (1983): 47–99.

Naimark, Norman. "The Sovietization of Eastern Europe, 1944–1953." In *The Cambridge History of the Cold War*. Vol. 1, *Origins*, edited by Melvyn P. Leffler and Odd Arne Westad, 175–97. Cambridge, U.K.: Cambridge University Press, 2010.

Ninkovich, Frank A. *The Diplomacy of Ideas: U.S. Foreign Policy and Cultural Relations, 1938–1950*. Cambridge, U.K.: Cambridge University Press, 1981.

——. *U.S. Information Policy and Cultural Diplomacy*. New York: Foreign Policy Association, 1996.

Osgood, Kenneth. "Hearts and Minds: The Unconventional Cold War." *Journal of Cold War Studies* 4, no. 2 (2002): 85–107.

——. *Total Cold War: Eisenhower's Secret Propaganda Battle at Home and Abroad*. Lawrence: University Press of Kansas, 2006.

Paddock, Alfred H. Jr. *U.S. Army Special Warfare: Its Origins*. Lawrence: University Press of Kansas, 2002.

Painter, David S. *The Cold War: An International History*. London: Routledge, 1999.

Parks, J. D. *Culture, Conflict and Coexistence: American-Soviet Cultural Relations, 1917–1958*. Jefferson, NC: McFarland, 1983.

Parks, Jenifer. "Red Sport, Red Tape: The Olympic Games, the Soviet Sports Bureaucracy, and the Cold War, 1952–1980." PhD diss., University of North Carolina at Chapel Hill, 2009.

——. "Verbal Gymnastics: Sports, Bureaucracy, and the Soviet Union's Entrance into the Olympic Games, 1946–1952." In *East Plays West: Sport and the Cold War*, edited by Stephen Wagg and David L. Andrews, 27–44. New York: Routledge, 2007.

Parry-Giles, Shawn J. "The Eisenhower Administration's Conception of the USIA: The Development of Overt and Covert Propaganda Strategies." *Presidential Studies Quarterly* 24, no. 2 (1994): 263–76.

——. *The Rhetorical Presidency, Propaganda, and the Cold War, 1945–1955*. Westport, CT: Praeger, 2002.

Peppard, Victor, and James Riordan. *Playing Politics: Soviet Sport Diplomacy to 1992*. Greenwich, CT: Jai Press, 1993.

Pinkleton, Bruce. "The Campaign of the Committee on Public Information: Its Contributions to the History and Evolution of Public Relations." *Journal of Public Relations Research* 6, no. 4 (1994): 229–40.

Pope, Steven. *Patriotic Games: Sporting Traditions in the American Imagination, 1876–1926*. New York: Oxford University Press, 1997.

Priestland, David. *The Red Flag: A History of Communism*. New York: Grove Press, 2009.

Puddington, Arch. *Broadcasting Freedom: The Cold War Triumph of Radio Free Europe and Radio Liberty*. Lexington: University Press of Kentucky, 2000.

Radar, Benjamin G. "The Quest for Subcommunities and the Rise of American Sport." *American Quarterly* 29, no. 4 (1977): 355–69.

Rawnsley, Gary D. "The Campaign of Truth: A Populist Propaganda." In *Cold War Propaganda in the 1950s*, edited by Gary D. Rawnsley, 31–46. Houndsmills, U.K.: Macmillan, 1999.

Richmond, Yale. *Cultural Exchange and the Cold War: Raising the Iron Curtain*. University Park: Pennsylvania State University Press, 2003.

Rider, Toby C. "The Cold War Activities of the Hungarian National Sports Federation." In *The Inauguration of Organized Political Warfare: Cold War Organizations Sponsored by the National Committee for a Free Europe/Free Europe Committee*, edited by Katalin Kádár Lynn, 515–46. Saint Helena, CA: Helena History Press, 2013.

———. "Filling the Information Gap: Radio Free Europe-Radio Liberty and the Politics of Accreditation at the 1984 Los Angeles Olympic Games." *International Journal of the History of Sport* 32, no. 1 (2015): 37–52.

Riordan, James. "Marx, Lenin and Physical Culture." *Journal of Sport History* 3, no. 2 (1976): 152–61.

———. *Sport in Soviet Society*. Cambridge, U.K.: Cambridge University Press, 1977.

———. "The USSR and the Olympic Games." *Stadion* 6 (1980): 291–313.

Robertson, A. H. "The Council of Europe, 1949–1953." *International and Comparative Law Quarterly* 3, no.2 (1954): 235–55.

Sander, Alfred Dick. *Eisenhower's Executive Office*. Westport, CT: Greenwood Press, 1999.

Sarantakes, Nicolas Evan. *Dropping the Torch: Jimmy Carter, the Olympic Boycott, and the Cold War*. New York: Cambridge University Press, 2011.

———. "Moscow versus Los Angeles: The Nixon White House Wages Cold War in the Olympic Selection Process." *Cold War History* 9, no. 1 (2009): 135–57.

Senn, Alfred E. *Power, Politics, and the Olympic Games: A History of the Power Brokers, Events, and Controversies that Shaped the Games*. Champaign, IL: Human Kinetics, 1999.

Simpson, Christopher. *Science of Coercion: Communication Research and Psychological Warfare, 1945–1960*. New York: Oxford University Press, 1994.

Singer, Peter. *Marx*. Oxford: Oxford University Press, 1980.

Steinberg, David A. "The Workers' Sport Internationals, 1920–28." *Journal of Contemporary History* 13, no. 2 (1978): 233–51.

Stoner Saunders, Frances. *Who Paid the Piper? The CIA and the Cultural Cold War*. London: Granta Books, 1999.

Sunik, Alexander. "Russia in the Olympic Movement around 1900." *Journal of Olympic History* 10, no. 3 (2002): 46–60.

Taylor, Philip M. *Munitions of the Mind: A History of Propaganda from the Ancient World to the Present Day*. Manchester, U.K.: Manchester University Press, 2003.

———. "Through a Glass Darkly? The Psychological Climate and Psychological Warfare of the Cold War." In *Cold War Propaganda in the 1950's*, edited by Gary D. Rawnsley, 225–42. Houndsmills, U.K.: Macmillan, 1999.

Thomas, Damion. *Globetrotting: African American Athletes and Cold War Politics*. Urbana: University of Illinois Press, 2012.

Thomas, Evan. *The Very Best Men: Four Who Dared; The Early Years of the CIA*. New York: Simon and Schuster, 1995.

Thomson, Charles A., and Walter H. C. Laves. *Cultural Relations and U.S. Foreign Policy*. Bloomington: Indiana University Press, 1963.

Tikander, Vesa. "Helsinki." In *Encyclopedia of the Modern Olympic Movement*, edited by John E. Findling and Kimberly D. Pelle, 135–46. Westport, CT: Greenwood Press, 2004.

Trevelyan, G. M. *Clio, A Muse and Other Essays*. London: Longmans, Green, 1949.

Tudda, Chris. "'Reenacting the Story of Tantalus': Eisenhower, Dulles, and the Failed Rhetoric of Liberation." *Journal of Cold War Studies* 7, no. 4 (2005): 3–35.

Turrini, Joseph M. *The End of Amateurism in American Track and Field*. Urbana: University of Illinois Press, 2010.

———. "'It Was Communism versus the Free World:' The USA–USSR Dual Track Meet Series and the Development of Track and Field in the United States, 1958–1985." *Journal of Sport History* 28, no. 3 (2001): 427–71.

Vadney, T. E. *The World since 1945*. London: Penguin, 1992.

Vardy, Steven Bela. *The Hungarian-Americans*. Boston: Twayne, 1985.

Wagg, Stephen, and David L. Andrews. "Introduction: War minus the Shooting." In *East Plays West: Sport and the Cold War*, edited by Stephen Wagg and David L. Andrews, 1–10. New York: Routledge, 2007.

Watson, Robert P., and Larry Maloney. "The U.S. Olympic Committee." In *Encyclopedia of the Modern Olympic Movement*, edited by John E. Findling and Kimberly D. Pelle, 499–508. Westport, CT: Greenwood Press, 2004.

Watterson, John S. *The Games Presidents Play: Sports and the Presidency*. Baltimore: Johns Hopkins University Press, 2006.

Wenn, Stephen R. "A Suitable Policy of Neutrality? FDR and the Question of American Participation in the 1936 Olympics." *International Journal of the History of Sport* 8, no. 3 (1991): 319–35.

———. "A Tale of Two Diplomats: George S. Messersmith and Charles H. Sherrill on Proposed American Participation in the 1936 Olympics." *Journal of Sport History* 16, no. 1 (1989): 27–43.

Whitfield, Stephen J. *The Culture of the Cold War*. Baltimore: Johns Hopkins University Press, 1991.

Wiesen Cook, Blanche. *The Declassified Eisenhower: A Divided Legacy*. New York: Doubleday, 1981.

———. "First Comes the Lie: C. D. Jackson and Political Warfare." *Radical History Review* 31 (December 1984): 42–70.

Wilford, Hugh. *The Mighty Wurlitzer: How the CIA Played America*. Cambridge, MA: Harvard University Press, 2008.

Wilson, Harold E. Jr. "The Golden Opportunity: Romania's Political Manipulation of the 1984 Los Angles Olympic Games." *Olympika* 3 (1994): 83–97.

Windhausen, John D., and Irina V. Tsypkina. "National Identity and the Emergence of the Sports Movement in Late Imperial Russia." *International Journal of the History of Sport* 12, no. 2 (1995): 165–82.

Witherspoon, Kevin B. "'Fuzz Kids' and 'Musclemen': The U.S.–Soviet Basketball Rivalry, 1958–1975." In *Diplomatic Games: Sport, Statecraft, and International Relations since 1945*, edited by Heather L. Dichter and Andrew L. Johns, 297–326. Lexington: University Press of Kentucky, 2014.

———. "Going 'to the Fountainhead': Black American Athletes as Cultural Ambassadors in Africa, 1970–1971." *International Journal of the History of Sport* 30, no. 13 (2013): 1508–22.

Wong, John. "FDR and the New Deal on Sport and Recreation." *Sport History Review* 29 (1998): 173–91.

Yergin, Daniel. *Shattered Peace: The Origins of the Cold War and the National Security State*. Boston: Houghton Mifflin, 1977.

Young, David C. *The Modern Olympics: A Struggle for Revival*. Baltimore: Johns Hopkins University Press, 1996.

———. *The Olympic Myth of Greek Amateur Athletics*. Chicago: Ares, 1984.

Young, John W. *Cold War Europe, 1945–1991: A Political History*, 2nd ed. London: Arnold, 1996.

Yttergren, Leif. "J. Sigfrid Edström, Anti-Semitism, and the 1936 Berlin Olympics." *Olympika* 16 (2007): 77–91.

Zubok, Vladislav M. *A Failed Empire: The Soviet Union in the Cold War from Stalin to Gorbachev*. Chapel Hill: University of North Carolina Press, 2007.

Zubok, Vladislav M., and Constantine Pleshakov. *Inside the Kremlin's Cold War: From Stalin to Khrushchev*. Cambridge, MA: Harvard University Press, 1996.

Index

TOBY C. RIDER is an assistant professor of kinesiology at California State University, Fullerton.

Sport and Society